A VEGETARIAN SOURCEBOOK

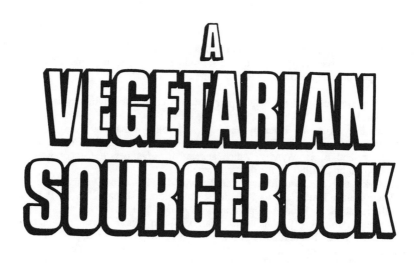

A VEGETARIAN SOURCEBOOK

KEITH AKERS

Vegetarian Press
P.O. Box 10238
Arlington, Virginia 22210

The author gratefully acknowledges permission from the following to use material in their control:
Academic Press, Inc., B. S. Reddy, and K. K. Carroll, for material from "Nutrition and Its Relation to Cancer," by B. S. Reddy, L. A. Cohen, G. D. McCoy, P. Hill, J. H. Weisburger, and E. L. Wynder, which appears in *Advances in Cancer Research* 31: 1980. Copyright © 1980 by Academic Press, Inc.
D. P. Burkitt and *The Lancet*, for material from "The Effect of Dietary Fibre on Stools and Their Transit-Times, and Its Role in the Causation of Disease," by D. P. Burkitt, A. R. Walker, and N. F. Painter. Copyright © 1972 by *The Lancet*.
Open Court Publishing Company, for material from *The Fragments of Empedocles*, translated by W. L. Leonard. Copyright © 1908 by W. L. Leonard.
Oxford University Press, for material from *The New English Bible*. Copyright © 1961, 1970 by The Delegates of the Oxford University Press and the Syndics of the Cambridge University Press.
St. Martin's Press, Inc., for material from *Beyond Cholesterol*, by Edward R. Gruberg and Stephen A. Raymond. Copyright © 1981 by Edward R. Gruberg and Stephen A. Raymond.
J. S. Steinhart and Duxbury Press, for material from *Energy: Sources, Use, and Role in Human Affairs*, by C. E. Steinhart and J. S. Steinhart. Copyright © 1982 by J. S. Steinhart.
The Unesco Press, for material from *Results of Research on Representative and Experimental Basins*, Volume 2, Proceedings of the Wellington Symposium, December 1970. Copyright © 1972 by Unesco; and for material from *World Water Balance and Water Resources of the Earth*. Copyright © 1978 by Unesco.
Westview Press, for material from the English language edition of *Water for a Starving World*, by Malin Falkenmark and Gunnar Lindh. Copyright © 1976 by Westview Press.
Dr. Robert Wissler and Williams and Wilkins Company, for material from "Atherosclerosis: The Role of Lipoproteins," by R. I. Levy and M. J. Stone, in *The Pathogenesis of Atherosclerosis*, R. W. Wissler, J. C. Greer, and M. Kaufman, editors. Copyright © 1971 by Dr. Robert Wissler.

Library of Congress Cataloging in Publication Data

Akers, Keith.
  A Vegetarian Sourcebook.
  Includes bibliographical references and index.
  1. Vegetarianism.   I. Title.
TX392.A425   1983   613.2'62   82-20407
ISBN 0-399-12802-6

The text of this book is set in Times Roman

PRINTED IN THE UNITED STATES OF AMERICA

Contents

List of Tables

List of Figures

Introduction

There are many books about vegetarianism, some good, many indifferent, and a few simply awful. Reading them, one cannot help wondering if vegetarians have anything at all in common except not eating meat. Some vegetarians are inspired by a wonderful compassion for all the living, suffering creatures on our planet; others think of little except how to keep themselves trim, fit, and alive a bit longer than they would otherwise expect to be. Some vegetarians support their views with detailed references to articles published in the most respected scientific journals; others appeal to exotic religious doctrines and untested pieces of folk wisdom. There is clearly no such thing as *the* vegetarian viewpoint on anything except diet.

Indeed, even diet is not something that vegetarians have in common. I have known vegetarians who lived mainly on white bread and jam, washed down with Coca-Cola; and I have known vegetarians who would rather die than let such items into their digestive tract (in fact, some of them thought they would die much sooner if they did). In other respects, my friends in the white bread and jam group were more particular than those vegetarians who would never touch refined flour or foods with cane sugar; for the former avoided using any animal products, while the latter walked around in leather shoes and wrapped themselves in furs when the weather grew cold. Both groups were being consistent with their reasons for being vegetarian; it is simply that these reasons were very different.

Despite all the books on vegetarianism, there is a need for a thoroughly reliable sourcebook covering all the main arguments for being a vegetarian of one sort or another. There cannot be a definitive book that will do this for all time, for new medical evidence keeps coming in, and the ecological situation and the treatment of farm animals are gradually changing. For the present, however, Keith Akers has done a remarkable job of assembling the evidence relating to vegetarianism from fields as diverse as nutrition, medicine, ecology, agriculture, literature, sociology, philosophy, history, and religion. His summaries of the material are always carefully documented, and while he has not attempted to conceal his support for vegetarianism, he has presented his evidence objectively and without that proselytizing tone that so often turns the uncommitted reader away from vegetarian tracts. Thanks to its comprehensiveness, its attention to detail and its consistently intelligent discussion, *A Vegetarian Sourcebook* is the most useful single volume I know covering all the arguments about vegetarianism.

I have been a vegetarian for more than ten years, and together with my wife have raised my children as vegetarians. My reasons for being a vegetarian are clearly summarized by Keith Akers in Section III of this book, so I need not repeat them here. I believe that the paramount argument for vegetarianism is the ethical argument based on what we do to animals when we treat them as objects that exist simply in order to please our palate. There are, however, many other arguments for vegetarianism, as the present book shows. I do not agree with all of them, but I can say that my wife and I enjoy our food and do not miss at all the large quantities of meat that we, like most Australians, have been brought up to eat. We live full and busy lives, and our children are thriving and not at all interested in the "yukky" meat they see on other people's plates. I know of many good reasons for a vegetarian way of life, and I know of no good objections to it. To those who are already vegetarians, I recommend this book as an invaluable source of references for those debates about vegetarianism that all vegetarians living in a nonvegetarian society get into from time to time. To those who are not vegetarians but are thinking about vegetarianism, I recommend this book as the best possible introduction to the subject; and I recommend even more strongly that you follow the argument where it leads and act accordingly.

Peter Singer
Melbourne, Australia
January 1982

Preface

"Why should I become a vegetarian?"

People will adopt a vegetarian diet for any number of reasons: because they want to get closer to God; because they want to lose weight; because they don't like the taste of meat; or because everyone else in their commune is a vegetarian. But in sorting out the good reasons for becoming a vegetarian, I have found that vegetarians generally fall back on three arguments, based on nutrition, ecology, or ethics. These arguments are:

- A vegetarian diet is healthier than a meat-oriented diet.
- A vegetarian diet is more efficient in its use of natural resources such as land, water, and energy.
- A vegetarian diet does not require the suffering and death of innocent animals.

All of these reasons for being a vegetarian contain important truths. All of them, however, require intelligent discussion and sometimes important qualification. This book aims to provide the information which such intelligent discussion requires.

What Is Vegetarianism?

A vegetarian is one who lives primarily on a plant food diet and who abstains from all meat, fish, or fowl; no vegetarian eats any food that *requires* the death of, or injury to, an animal. Some vegetarians, probably the vast majority in the United States, consume dairy products and eggs; others abstain from all animal food and rely entirely on plant foods.

The kinds of vegetarians usually distinguished are the "lacto-ovo-vegetarians," who eat dairy products and eggs in addition to plant foods; the "total vegetarians" (sometimes known as "pure vegetarians"), who eat plant foods but no animal foods; the "vegans," who abstain from animal food and animal products of any kind whatsoever (like leather, wool, etc.); and the "fruitarians," who live on fruit, nuts, and seeds. In the United States, the lacto-ovo-vegetarians are by far the largest vegetarian group, though the vegans seem to be the most articulate and outspoken. The exact number of fruitarians is not known, but it must be quite small. And there are endless distinctions within these categories. Some people are vegan except that they eat honey; others drink milk but don't eat eggs. In 1943 there were an estimated $2^1/2$–3 million vegetarians in the United States; more recently, this figure was estimated at about 7 million, roughly 3% of the population. Obviously, any discussion encompassing all the different types of vegetarians will be quite difficult. When dealing with the various issues, the author has presented the evidence as objectively as possible, allowing the chips to fall where they may respecting the advantages and disadvantages of various vegetarian diets. In doing so, the author has perhaps stepped on some vegetarian toes. So be it.

Existing discussions of vegetarianism vary considerably both in point of view and in quality of material. Impassioned but uninformed defenses of vegetarianism are counterbalanced by equally impassioned and equally uninformed attacks on vegetarian ideas. To complicate matters, there are some ambiguous concepts that do not clearly fall on either the vegetarian or the nonvegetarian side of the line.

Probably the most abused of these notions is the concept of "natural foods." There is a lot of talk about natural foods today; and many people feel that we would be better off if we returned to a diet that omits the many unnatural ingredients found in supermarket foods. But just what is a "natural food"? And what do natural foods and natural diets have to do with vegetarianism—if anything? Vegetarian thinkers since Plutarch have asserted, for a variety of reasons, that it is not natural to eat meat. Non-vegetarians often deny or belittle the importance of such contentions. We need to consider these issues in more detail.

The "Natural Foods" Controversy

For most people, natural foods are foods which occur in nature, as they occur in nature, without human intervention. Unfortunately, this way of thinking about "natural foods" is quite confused, and a quick trip to your local grocery or health food store will demonstrate that.

Products that contain animal fats or refined vegetable fats will be labeled "natural"; after all, fats of all kinds occur in nature. Products containing sugar will also be called natural; and it cannot be denied that sugars of all sorts also occur in nature. Livestock animals raised without being stuffed with antibiotics are described as organically grown. What sense can we make of this concept of what is "natural"?

This concept also ignores the other side of the coin: some foods that are artificially produced, processed, and manipulated by humans may be quite wholesome or appropriate to eat. Since the beginning of agriculture, humans have bred certain strains of wheat and other plants to create entirely new species, or new kinds of old species, which are more productive agriculturally. Must we reject these foods as "unnatural" because they would not occur in nature independent of human existence? And what about cooking? Must we abstain from eating potatoes and beans because they do not occur in cooked form in nature and would be inedible if they were not cooked? What about vitamin supplements? Not everyone likes to take them; but is taking such manufactured supplements necessarily bad?

The definition of a "natural food" as a food which occurs in nature ignores two things. First of all, humans are themselves part of nature and may actually manipulate nature in ways which are beneficial. Second, many poisons and unwholesome foods occur in nature without any human intervention. The deadly hemlock that Socrates drank, for example, would qualify as a "natural food," since the hemlock plant occurs in nature. Clearly, we need a new definition.

What are we talking about when we say natural foods? What we really mean are foods that are *appropriate* for humans to eat.

If we want to know what a natural food is, we must ask: Does it cause disease and death? Does it squander available resources? Does it increase the amount of suffering in the world? *These* are the questions we should be asking, and they are precisely the questions we are *not* asking. It is these questions which this book will examine.

The Ethical Basis of Vegetarianism

A diet that can lead to heart attacks, cancer, and numerous other diseases cannot be a natural diet. A diet that pillages our resources of land, water, forests, and energy cannot be a natural diet. A diet that causes the unnecessary suffering and death of billions of animals each year cannot be a natural diet.

The principles of ethics come from our own nature. The term "ethical vegetarian" usually means a vegetarian who does not eat animals out of compassion for them. But there is an ethical component in the nutritional and ecological reasons for becoming a vegetarian as well. Is not the impulse to preserve one's health an ethical impulse? Is not concern for the earth's resources an ethical concern?

The demands of ethics and the demands of nature are closely intertwined. It is natural to want to preserve health; it is natural to want to preserve the earth's resources; and it is natural to feel sympathy for animals. It is in these natural feelings that we find the ethical basis of vegetarian thought.

Becoming an Informed Vegetarian

I first started "flirting" with a vegetarian diet in 1974, when I was living in a small group house in Austin, Texas. My curiosity was aroused because about half of the people in the house were vegetarians. While this house was in many ways typical of the experiments in group living which grew out of the "counter-culture," it was probably unique in trying to accommodate both the vegetarians and the non-vegetarians. To a large degree, the house was successful. During much of this time I was a vegetarian by choice; sometimes, when the house budget was tight, the whole house became vegetarian out of necessity. Occasionally, though, I would eat meat.

In 1978 I read Peter Singer's book *Animal Liberation,* and my attitude toward all of this changed. Singer's book deals with the ethical problems of human treatment of animals in a very commonsense way. I had hardly read more than a couple of pages of the third chapter before I knew that I would be a vegetarian for the rest of my life. Singer's book strongly conveyed the fact that animals are real, that those neatly packaged and stamped parcels of meat in the supermarket were once living, breathing creatures which someone had to kill. Singer's book brought home the reality of animal existence.

By 1980 I had moved to the Washington, D.C., area, where I was pursuing a career in computers. There I met Robin Hur, who was also to have a great influence on my life. Mr. Hur was himself the author of a book which discussed the need for a pure vegetarian whole foods diet.* My first impression of this book was that it was bizarre and complicated. However, the opportunity for extended discussions with him gave me an excellent chance to pursue his ideas in greater detail. I discovered that there was a wealth of factual information about food issues of which the general public and even many specialists were entirely unaware.

Hur's insights contributed greatly to my disillusionment with many current vegetarian ideas. There were plenty of good arguments for vegetarianism, but critical issues were being largely ignored while relatively trivial problems received an extraordinary amount of attention. It was not unusual for a conversation about vegetarianism (or even a book about it) to dwell endlessly on topics such as protein complementarity, chemicals in food, and the health value of polyunsaturated fats. In the meantime, problems which threatened the peace, health, and security of everyone—like cancer and soil erosion—were being almost entirely ignored. Hur encouraged me to address them in this book, suggested countless ideas, and reviewed the manuscript at several different stages.

I am deeply indebted to both of these gentlemen. Without their contributions, this book would not have been written or published. Indeed, I might never have become a vegetarian at all.

---

* Entitled *Food Reform: Our Desperate Need* (Austin: Heidelberg Publishers, 1975).

Reading the Book

A Vegetarian Sourcebook is divided into three major sections, corresponding to each of the three basic arguments for vegetarianism: nutrition, ecology, ethics. Each of these three sections is self-contained, as are many of the chapters within each section. Thus, you need not start with Chapter 1 and proceed to the end, although you are certainly welcome to do so. Any method of reading which conveys the desired information certainly accomplishes the author's purpose.

The author is himself a vegetarian, and believes that practically any nutritionally adequate vegetarian diet is more healthful, more economical, and more ethical than the typical Western Diet, emphasizing meat, fish, and fowl. Meat consumption is destroying our health, our natural resources, and the lives of innocent animals. The contrast between this destructive diet and a vegetarian diet is the story which this book tells.

I
VEGETARIAN
NUTRITION

1
Issues in Vegetarian Nutrition

Nutrition of any sort has two basic elements: getting the good things and avoiding the bad things. This section on vegetarian nutrition demonstrates how a vegetarian diet gets the good things and how it avoids the bad things—bad things, in fact, which a meat-oriented diet must inevitably contain.

The consensus in the scientific community is that a vegetarian diet can be adequate—that vegetarians should have no trouble getting all nutrients required for health. There is nothing nutritionally unique about meat; all of the nutrients we need in our diets can be found abundantly in any number of plant foods. In fact, there is an emerging consensus that a vegetarian diet is actually *better* than a meat-oriented diet. The typical diet of many in the Western nations, which stresses heavy consumption of meat, is causing tremendous health problems. The high quantities of fat and protein and the total lack of fiber in meat are linked to a disturbing array of degenerative diseases such as cancer, atherosclerosis, diabetes, obesity, and many others.

Getting the Good Things

What are the issues concerning the adequacy of a vegetarian diet? Can a vegetarian get all the necessary nutrients? Is this complicated, involved, or tricky? We need to show the adequacy of a vegetarian diet by showing that it is not only possible to get the needed nutrients, but that it is not particularly difficult to do so either.

Protein is unquestionably the most important issue concerning the adequacy of a vegetarian diet. It is not particularly difficult to get protein on a vegetarian diet, but protein is an issue because our culture has made it an issue. It is hard for many of us to remember a time when protein was not considered the single most desirable and important nutrient on the nutritional scene. The rise of protein's importance in modern nutrition has been a gradual process in which both economics and culture have played significant roles.

The best reflections of this attitude, though in different ways, are the books of Adelle Davis (*Let's East Right to Keep Fit* and others) and *Diet for a Small Planet* by Frances Moore Lappé. *Diet for a Small Planet* is so accommodating and persuasive in its explanation of nonmeat proteins that many consider it the best argument for vegetarianism. Yet *Diet for a Small Planet* really accepts many of our culture's misconceptions about protein—that plant protein is harder to find than animal protein, and that if you rely on plant protein you should know what you're doing.

In fact, however, plant protein is just as good as animal protein, and the practice of protein complementarity—advocated by Lappé to overcome this supposed deficiency—is completely unnecessary for ordinary nutrition. In Chapter 2, "Protein," we will consider the nature of the protein requirement and of plant food protein.

The second most important issue in vegetarian nutrition is vitamin B-12. Most people have probably never heard of this little nutrient, but vitamin B-12 has a special status for vegetarians because it is not manufactured by plants. Vitamin B-12 is found in most animal foods (including meat, fish, eggs, and milk) and in a few plant foods where the vitamin-B-12-producing micro-organisms like to live (soy sauce, kelp, tempeh). There is some controversy over whether vitamin B-12 is a dietary requirement at all. These various issues will be considered in Chapter 3, "Vitamin B-12."

One hears very little about the other nutrients known to be essential for human health. Occasionally a total vegetarian will get a question like, "Where will you get calcium if you don't drink milk?" In general, plant foods—especially dark green leafy vegetables—are better sources of these other nutrients than are animal foods. These "other nutrients" will be considered in Chapter 4.

Avoiding the Bad Things

A vegetarian diet is not merely an adequate diet. A vegetarian diet avoids numerous health hazards brought on by the typical Western diet which emphasizes huge quantities of fat and protein, and which contains only negligible amounts of fiber. The developed nations of the world have been afflicted by a new set of diseases, diseases largely absent in the underdeveloped nations of the world whose populations consume little if any meat. Atherosclerosis and cancer are the best known of these "diseases of civilization," but obesity, diabetes, osteoporosis, gallstones, kidney stones, and gout are also diet-related.

Excessive consumption of fat and protein, and lack of fiber, are all factors in these degenerative diseases. Meat contains nothing but fat and protein, and totally lacks fiber. Meat consumption is not the *only* problem with the Western way of eating, of course; sugar, white bread, and "junk food" have combined to form a threat which is potentially just as great as that posed by meat consumption. But it is clear that meat consumption plays a major role, to say the least, in all of these problems.

Any of these dietary "bad things"—whether meat, sugar, or refined foods—can cause significant damage when consumed in excess year after year. Combined, their effects on health are even more dramatic. In Chapters 5 through 8—"Diet and Degenerative Disease," "Atherosclerosis," "Cancer," and "Various Other Degenerative Diseases"—we will examine how these diseases are related to the high-fat, high-protein, low-fiber diet we meat-eating Westerners follow.

2
Protein

"But how do you get enough protein?"

How many times have vegetarians had to face this question! Our culture seems to be obsessed with the importance of protein. People who haven't the faintest idea where to get calcium, iron, or vitamin C shrink in fear at the thought of giving up meat protein. They may know practically nothing about nutrition, but they *do* know that you need protein, and that meat has protein.

Ironically, protein is one of the easiest nutrients to get. If one is not starving from lack of food, it is almost impossible *not* to get enough protein. An entirely random selection of plant foods, containing enough calories to sustain life, will also provide more than enough protein virtually all of the time. Through a careless selection of foods, one might develop deficiencies of iron, vitamin A, or vitamin C; but it is almost impossible to develop a protein deficiency on a calorically adequate diet.

This contradicts not only popular opinion, but the opinion of many otherwise well-informed vegetarians. Many vegetarians have struggled to understand the theories of protein complementarity, to "make up" for the supposed deficiencies of plant protein; but the truth of the matter is, most plant foods have more than enough protein, and plant protein is nutritionally just as good as animal protein. There is nothing "inferior" about either the quality or the quantity of plant protein. To understand this, let us consider the relationship between protein requirements and caloric requirements.

Protein as a Percentage of Calories

The major constituents of most foods are carbohydrates, proteins, and fat. All three of these can be sources of food energy, or calories. They provide calories at approximately the following rate:

1 gram protein	= 4 calories
1 gram fat	= 9 calories
1 gram carbohydrate	= 4 calories[1]

If we know how much protein is in a food, and how many calories, we can calculate what percentage of the food's total calories is protein. Example: a 100-gram potato contains 76 calories and 2.1 grams of protein. What percentage of the total calories in this potato comes from protein?

Well, 2.1 grams of protein represent 8.4 calories (since each gram of protein contains 4 calories); and dividing 8.4 by 76, we discover that 11% of the calories in the potato are protein.

This is not only a basic concept in nutritional analysis, but the key to understanding the problem—or rather, the nonproblem—of protein in a vegetarian diet. We can analyze any number of foods in his manner. Using a table which lists the composition of foods and a little arithmetic, we can discover that corn has 15% of its calories in the form of protein, that broccoli has 45%, that carrots have 10%, and so on.

We can do this not only for individual foods but for the entire diet. We can take the protein requirement per day and the caloric requirement per day, and derive the total percentage of calories which should come from protein. When we do this, what do we discover?

According to the National Research Council[2] (hardly a bastion of nutritional radicalism), a 154-pound adult male requires 56 grams of protein and 2700 calories per day. What percentage of calories should this 154-pound male get in the form of protein?

$$\frac{56 \text{ grams of protein} \times 4 \text{ calories/gram of protein}}{2700 \text{ calories}} = \text{about } 8.3\% \text{ of calories}$$

The requirement for adult females weighing 120 pounds is 44 grams of protein and 2000 calories. This gives us

$$\frac{44 \text{ grams of protein} \times 4 \text{ calories/gram of protein}}{2000 \text{ calories}} = \text{about } 8.8\% \text{ of calories}$$

What do these statistics suggest? If corn, broccoli, potatoes, and carrots have 15%, 45%, 11%, and 10% of their calories as protein (respectively), then even if a vegetarian ate nothing but corn, potatoes, broccoli, and carrots, he should get plenty of protein, assuming that he fulfills the caloric requirement.

Yet corn, broccoli, potatoes, and carrots are by no means exceptional in terms of protein content. Table 1 lists more than 50 common plant foods and their caloric breakdown. As one can see, the vast majority of vegetables, legumes,

Table 1. Percentage of calories from protein, fat, and carbohydrate in some common plant foods.

Food	Calories per 100 grams	Percentage of Calories		
		Protein	Fat	Carbohydrate
Vegetables				
Beet	43	15	2	83
Broccoli	32	45	8	47
Cabbage (common)	24	22	7	71
Carrot	42	10	4	86
Cauliflower	27	40	7	53
Celery	17	21	5	74
Collards	45	43	16	41
Corn	96	15	9	76
Cucumber	15	24	6	70
Eggplant	25	19	7	74
Kale	53	45	14	41
Lettuce (iceberg)	13	28	7	65
Mushroom	28	39	10	51
Okra	36	27	7	66
Onion (green)	36	17	5	78
Onion (dry mature)	38	15	2	83
Potato	76	11	2	87
Pumpkin	26	15	3	82
Radish	17	24	5	71
Spinach	26	49	10	41
Squash (summer)	19	23	5	72
Sweet Potato	114	6	3	91
Tomato	22	20	8	72
Turnip	30	13	6	81
Turnip Greens	28	43	10	47
Watercress	19	46	14	60
Legumes				
Bean, lima	123	27	4	69
Bean, pinto	349	26	3	71
Chickpea	360	23	12	65
Lentil	340	29	3	68
Peanut	564	18	76	6
Pea	54	26	3	71
Soybean, fresh	134	33	34	33
Grains				
Barley (light)	348	11	3	86
Bulgur	359	10	4	86
Millet	327	12	8	80
Oatmeal (cooked)	55	15	16	69
Rice (brown)	360	8	5	87
Rye	334	14	5	81
Wheat (hard spring)	330	17	6	77
Nuts and Seeds				
Almond	598	12	81	7
Cashew	561	12	73	15

Table 1. *Continued*

Food	Calories per 100 grams	Percentage of Calories		
		Protein	Fat	Carbohydrate
Pecan	687	5	93	2
Sesame	563	13	78	9
Sunflower	560	17	76	7
Walnut (black)	628	13	85	2
Fruits				
Apple	56	1	10	89
Avocado	167	5	81	14
Banana	85	5	2	93
Blackberry	58	8	14	78
Blueberry	62	5	7	88
Cherry	70	7	4	89
Grape (American)	69	8	17	75
Lemon	27	11	7	82
Orange	49	8	4	88
Peach	38	6	2	92
Pear	61	5	6	89

SOURCES:
  (a) Ford Heritage, *Composition and Facts about Foods* (Mokelumne Hill, Cal.: Health Research, 1971).
  (b) U.S. Department of Agriculture, *Nutritive Value of American Foods,* Agriculture Handbook no. 456 (Washington, D.C.: Government Printing Office, 1975).
NOTE: All foods are assumed to be in their uncooked form except oatmeal. Calculations are based on these constants: 1 gram protein or carbohydrate = 4 calories, and 1 gram fat = 9 calories.

grains, nuts, and seeds get more than 10% of their calories from protein. Only fruits, as a rule, have less than this. So the real problem for the vegetarian is not "How do I get enough protein?" but rather "How do I get enough calories?"

Protein Quality

But what about the quality of plant protein? Is animal protein superior in quality to plant protein? Should a vegetarian compensate for the "inferior" quality of plant protein in some way—either by getting more total protein, or by some method of complementing different kinds of proteins? This idea, commonly held by vegetarians and non-vegetarians alike, deserves close examination.

In its most accommodating form, the idea of the "superior" nature of animal protein appears as the theory of protein complementarity. The body does not need just any kind of protein; it needs specific amino acids. Most of the 22 amino acids required for protein synthesis can be manufactured by the body.

Eight cannot; these eight "essential amino acids" must be supplied by the diet. If even one of these amino acids is absent, protein cannot be synthesized, and the other seven essential amino acids go to waste.

In her book *Diet for a Small Planet*, Frances Moore Lappé advances the idea of protein complementarity. In order to avoid protein malnutrition, she argues that the vegetarian should complement his proteins: combine a food weak in an amino acid with a food strong in that amino acid. Since each food has a unique amino acid pattern and is weak in some amino acids while being strong in others, this begins to get complicated. Indeed, too complicated for many a meat eater considering vegetarianism.

The problem with this theory is that it is simply irrelevant. You will still get enough protein and all of the amino acids whether or not you practice protein complementarity. As a practical method of getting protein, it is completely unnecessary.

Even if Lappé's analysis is entirely correct, and even if plant protein is inferior in quality to animal protein, it would still be quite easy to get enough protein without practicing protein complementarity—a fact which can be shown to be true from Lappé's own data. However, the evidence does not support the idea that plant protein is inferior in quality to animal protein. Some plant protein amino acid patterns, notably that of the potato, are superior to any meat proteins. Finally, considerations of protein quality are irrelevant. Numerous experiments have shown that plant foods can maintain subjects in good health even when they are the only source of protein; and plant foods provide more than enough of all of the essential amino acids.

Let's look at these points in more detail.

The "Worst Case" Scenario

Let us assume the worst. Let us assume that our hapless vegetarian never complements his proteins. He never eats beans and rice together—he eats rice for breakfast, beans for lunch and so on. Secondly, let us assume that Lappé's assumptions about plant protein are correct. According to Lappé's figures, only a portion of the protein in plant foods is usable—about 40% to 50% in legumes, nuts, and seeds, and about 60% in most vegetables and grains. A 154-pound male requires 43.1 grams of usable protein, 6.4% of his caloric intake. (This is less than the 8.3% figure cited earlier based on data from the National Research Council, but remember, Lappé is talking about usable protein, not total protein).

If we try to recalculate the percentage of calories which are usable protein from figures Lappé provides and the data in Table 1, what do we have? Lima beans, which has 27% of calories as protein, have 14% of calories as usable protein. Corn goes from 15% of calories as protein to 11% usable protein. Spinach goes from 49% to 25%; potatoes from 11% to 6.6%; mushrooms from

39% to 28%. But notice that all of these figures are still above the requirements for usable protein which Lappé herself cites (6.4% of calories).

In fact, of all the foods for which Lappé gives figures, and which appear in Table 1, only a few fall below our minimum level of 6.4% of calories as usable protein. Almost all the vegetables, grains, legumes, nuts, and seeds in Table 1 would still provide enough usable protein, even if they constituted the only item in the entire diet.

So even in the worst case, even after allowing for the "inferior quality" of plant protein, we must conclude that it is very easy to get enough protein on a plant food diet without practicing protein complementarity.

A Question of Balance

Scientists can determine whether a human being is getting enough protein by means of a nitrogen balance experiment. Nitrogen is one of the chief substances from which the body builds protein. Over 80% of the body's requirement for protein can be synthesized from nitrogen. In a nitrogen balance experiment, the body's intake of nitrogen (through food) is measured against its loss of nitrogen (through urine, feces, and sweat). If nitrogen intake equals or exceeds nitrogen loss, the subject is said to be in nitrogen balance and to be getting enough protein.

Nitrogen balance experiments have been done on humans using plant foods as the sole source of protein. These experiments have repeatedly shown that several well-known plant foods, not exceptionally high in protein content, are quite capable of maintaining humans in nitrogen balance, even when they are the only source of protein in the diet, without any benefit from the effects of protein complementarity. Both corn and wheat have been shown to be adequate sources of protein, maintaining subjects in nitrogen balance.[3] Another experiment showed that when rice was used as the sole source of protein, the rice protein alone maintained nitrogen balance, even when the rice provided only two thirds of the required daily calories.[4]

Especially striking are numerous studies done on potatoes, which have repeatedly shown that potato protein can maintain subjects in nitrogen balance when potatoes are the sole source of protein. The studies also showed that when the only source of protein is potatoes, the need for protein drops to a startlingly low 5% of calories—less than two thirds of the recommended dietary allowance.[5] Potato protein is just as good as egg protein (though its amino acid pattern is completely different), and in fact, it is *better* than beef protein or the protein of tuna fish.[6] It is amazing that the idea that plant protein is inferior to animal protein has lasted so long in the face of such contrary evidence.

Protein Complementarity—Forget It

Even those foods which have a "poor" pattern of essential amino acids usually have more than enough of them. Current estimated essential amino acid requirements reveal that the amino acid requirement for a 154-pound male is 6.37 grams per day—only about 11% of his total protein requirement of 56 grams. Most plant foods usually have at least 20% or more of their protein in the form of essential amino acids.

Consider rice: over 40% of the protein in rice is in the form of the essential amino acids. Fifty-six grams of rice protein would provide generous quantities of even the "limiting" amino acids, in which rice is weakest—"only" 266% of the requirement for isoleucine, and a mere 265% of the requirement for lysine. So, although rice does not have perfectly balanced protein, even the essential amino acids in which rice is most deficient are present in generous quantities. Rice provides even higher percentages of the requirements for the other essential amino acids. A similar analysis has been done of some of the other foods which one might suspect of being deficient in the amino acids, in Table 2.

How did the idea that vegetable protein is inferior to animal protein get started in the first place? Experiments on laboratory animals, especially rats, appear to have provided the basis for this idea. Rats did not grow as fast on certain vegetable proteins as on animal proteins, unless the vegetable proteins were supplemented with certain amino acids. Two scientists, T. B. Osborne and L. B. Mendel, are generally credited with this discovery, published in a paper in 1914.[7]

Believe it or not, almost all studies of protein value have been performed with rats. Yet obviously the protein requirements of humans are radically different from those of rats. Human milk can support the health and growth of human babies. Human milk, though, with 6% of its calories as protein, *cannot* support the growth of baby rats. Should we assume that if human milk cannot support baby rats it cannot support human babies either? Yet assumptions about the differences between animal and plant protein carried over from being a theory about rats to being a theory about humans.[8]

It is time for nutritional theory to grow up. We cannot continue to base our judgments of human protein requirements on the results of experiments on laboratory rats. Let us discard protein complementarity—however valid it might be for protein theory—as a guide to practical human nutrition.

Is Protein Deficiency Possible?

We frequently hear of malnourishment and hunger in the developing world. We see newspaper photos of shriveled bodies with bloated bellies and read that these desperate people are suffering from protein deficiencies. So surely it is possible to suffer from protein deficiencies, isn't it?

Table 2. Limiting amino acid content of selected "low-quality protein" plant foods.

Food	Limiting Amino Acid(s)	Mg's Amino Acid in 100 grams food*	% of RDA in 56 grams protein, for a 70-kg male
Barley	Isoleucine	421	292%
	Lysine	406	281%
Corn	Tryptophan	67	510%
	Isoleucine	350	667%
	Lysine	254	484%
Chickpea	Tryptophan	174	226%
	Sulfur-containing AA's	447	174%
Lentil	Tryptophan	231	249%
	Sulfur-containing AA's	415	134%
Rye	Tryptophan	87	192%
	Isoleucine	414	228%
	Lysine	401	221%
Rice (brown)	Isoleucine	300	267%
	Lysine	299	266%
Millet	Lysine	332	224%
Sunflower seed	Lysine	536	149%
Potato	Isoleucine	76	241%
	Sulfur-containing AA's	38	145%
Whole Wheat	Isoleucine	426	202%
	Lysine	374	178%
Carrot	Tryptophan	8	194%
	Sulfur-containing AA's	26	190%
Turnip	Sulfur-containing AA's	11	88%
	Lysine	17	113%
Sweet potato	Sulfur-containing AA's	36	169%
	Lysine	45	176%

* SOURCE: Food and Agriculture Organization of the United Nations, *Amino-Acid Content of Foods and Biological Data on Proteins* (Rome, 1970).

Of course these people are suffering from protein deficiencies. They are also suffering from deficiencies of calories, calcium, iron, and vitamins A through Z. In short, these people are starving to death. What they need is not so much protein as food in general.

A few years ago in India, it was estimated that there was about a 10% shortfall in the total calories provided by the average Indian diet, as compared to the minimum requirements. At the same time, there was about a 10% *surplus* in the amount of protein provided by the diet. And even in those cases where there was protein malnutrition, it was usually the consequence of a more general lack of food.[9]

What about protein deficiencies when one *does* get enough calories? This is a possibility, but a rather remote one. In order to develop a protein deficiency while still getting enough calories, one would have to consume a diet which contained foods which have a lot of calories, but little protein. What sorts of foods might this mean?

Fruits are one possibility. In most fruits, protein makes up on the order of 5% of the total calories. In apples, only 1% of the total calories is protein. Alone of the common plant foods, grapes are truly deficient in several of the essential amino acids: 56 grams of grape protein contain only 31% of the RDA of isoleucine. Bananas, oranges, and peaches all have adequate quantities of the amino acids, provided that one can somehow get enough total protein. Perhaps, then, if one relied heavily on fruit as a staple, and made an appropriately poor choice of fruits, one might be in danger of suffering from protein deficiency even after getting enough calories.

But fruit is generally a luxury item, not a staple. Anyone who can afford fruit can easily afford other foods (like corn, potatoes, or beans) to supply the missing protein. Even fruitarians—who advocate a diet that harms neither animals nor plants—do not live on a diet of fruit alone. Their diet includes nuts and seeds. It is quite possible to get enough protein on such a diet, because the nuts and seeds would make up for the relative lack of protein in fruit. The problem with a fruitarian diet, nutritionally speaking, is not protein but fat. Nuts and seeds have plenty of protein, all right, but they also have great quantities of fat, and too much fat can pose significant health problems.

More problematic is cassava. Related to the sweet potato, cassava is a root vegetable which gets about 1% or 2% of its calories from protein. In some areas of the world, such as West Africa, cassava is a staple. So a protein deficiency when cassava is the primary source of food is within the realm of possibility. Even minimal supplementation of cassava with other plant foods, though, can eliminate this problem. Experiments utilizing a diet of cassava, rice, and sorghum showed that young Nigerian men could be maintained in nitrogen balance when they received a scant 4% of calories as protein.[10] Ironically, cassava leaves themselves contain about 18% of calories as protein.

A final problem would be that category of foods commonly referred to as "junk." Sugar contains no protein. Soft drinks contain no protein. Jams and jellies get about 1% of their calories from protein. Alcoholic beverages contain only trace amounts of protein, with the exception of beer, which has a protein content of 3% of calories. The protein content of most cookies is at or below 4% of calories.

So the answer to the question "Is protein malnutrition possible on a calorically adequate diet?" is "Yes, but . . ." The kinds of diets which would be deficient in protein are ludicrous. One would really have to work at it to develop such a deficiency. One possibility is the diet of an alcoholic who supplements his drinking solely with junk food. Even if junk food made up 50% of one's calories, though, it would still be quite easy to get enough protein from the remaining 50%. A diet of beer and oatmeal, for example, while it would be a very, very bad diet, lacking such essential nutrients as vitamins A and C, would provide the recommended dietary allowance of protein.

Conclusions

It is almost impossible to avoid getting enough protein on almost any calorically adequate plant food diet. Virtually all vegetables, legumes, grains, nuts, and seeds contain more than enough protein to sustain the growth and maintenance needs of body tissues.

Protein complementarity, endlessly discussed by many vegetarians, is an unnecessary practice for ordinary human nutrition. While Lappe's *Diet for a Small Plant* has several important and progressive ideas about the waste, inefficiency, and social injustices created by the "Great American Stead Religion," as Lappé calls it, her advocacy of protein complementarity is ill-founded. (Lappé has now essentially reversed herself on this issue, saying that getting enough protein "is much easier than I thought.") Vegetarians and others interested in the nutritional aspects of plant foods should focus on problems more worthy of their attention.

3
Vitamin B-12

The general public has heard very little about this nutrient. Yet, right after protein, it is the most frequently discussed topic in vegetarian nutrition. That is because it is widely believed that vitamin B-12 can only be obtained from animal foods. This statement is frequently made by respected authorities who are in ignorance of the facts.

There is no question that lacto-ovo-vegetarians can easily obtain enough vitamin B-12; dairy products and eggs are generous suppliers of vitamin B-12. The controversy pertains only to those vegetarians who live on plant foods and do not eat any animal foods at all—the "total vegetarians" or "vegans." The controversy is fueled by reports which occur from time to time concerning total vegetarians who suffer from one or more of the symptoms of vitamin B-12 deficiency, most notably megaloblastic anemia. The evidence shows, however, that there are numerous sources of vitamin B-12 other than animal foods, and that vitamin B-12 is not a particularly difficult vitamin to get. In short, the Great Vitamin B-12 Controversy, like the protein controversy, is largely generated by lack of information concerning already available research data.

The Requirement for Vitamin B-12

Only incredibly small quantities of vitamin B-12 are thought to be needed in the diet. According to the National Research Council, 3 micrograms daily will meet the body's requirements. But Victor Herbert, a noted authority on the subject, puts the requirement at 0.1 micrograms, making even the National Research Council's microscopic figure 30 times in excess of the actual need.[1] Moreover, the consumption of lots of meat and milk, which is "normal" for those on a typical American diet, increases the need for vitamin B-12, so this figure is presumably even lower still for vegetarians.[2]

Vitamin B-12, along with folacin, is utilized for DNA synthesis. In its absence, megaloblastic anemia can develop, followed by damage to the central nervous system and eventually death. Pinpointing the exact cause of a vitamin B-12 "problem," however, is more complicated than initially appears, because vitamin B-12 interacts with numerous other nutrients and products manufactured by the body.

Most prominent among these is the "intrinsic factor" manufactured by the stomach. Without this intrinsic factor, the body will be unable to absorb vitamin B-12. Persons suffering from pernicious anemia do not have the ability to manufacture "intrinsic factor," and will eventually die if they do not receive injections of vitamin B-12; and persons who have the part of their stomach removed which produces the intrinsic factor will suffer a similar fate. But pernicious anemia has nothing to do with lack of vitamin B-12 in the diet, and in fact affects meat-eaters more than it affects vegetarians. It is due rather to the lack of intrinsic factor which makes it impossible for the body to absorb the vitamin B-12 into the bloodstream.

There are several other factors which interact with B-12 metabolism. Folacin deficiency can also produce megaloblastic anemia. In fact, folacin deficiency is the most common reason for megaloblastic anemia worldwide.[3] In addition, iron deficiency anemia (one of the commonest types of anemias) will also reduce the levels of vitamin B-12 in the bloodstream by inhibiting absorption. Vitamin B-6 deficiency will also reduce vitamin B-12 absorption.[4] Finally, oral contraceptives have been implicated in cases of megaloblastic anemia.[5]

Vitamin B-12, alone among the vitamins for which there is thought to be a dietary need, is not produced by plants. (Vitamin D is not produced by plants either, but the body can synthesize Vitamin D if it is exposed to sunlight.) Actually, it is not produced by animals either, but by microorganisms; these microorganisms live in the digestive tracts of certain animals (such as cows), producing all the vitamin B-12 they might need. These vitamin B-12-producing microorganisms are also widely distributed throughout the environment, soil, water, and the bodies of human beings. It is in this context that we should consider the evidence concerning total vegetarians and vitamin B-12.

Vitamin B-12 Deficiencies?

Medical literature provides numerous case histories of unfortunate vegetarians who apparently neglected to get their vitamin B-12: "Vitamin B-12 Deficiency Due to Defective Diet,"[6] "Megaloblastic Anemia in an Adult Vegan,"[7] and "A Syndrome of Methylmalonic Aciduria, Homocystinuria, Megaloblastic Anemia and Neurologic Abnormalities in a Vitamin B-12 Deficient Breast-fed Infant of a Strict Vegetarian,"[8] and so on. These case histories are intimidating even to those familiar with medical journals. They are frequently cited as proving that vitamin B-12 deficiency in vegetarians is a real problem.

However, on closer inspection the evidence is far less conclusive than initially appears. While all of the individuals described in these case histories obviously have a problem, it does not follow that the problem stems from lack of dietary vitamin B-12. Numerous other complicating factors, including lack of folacin, iron, Vitamin B-6, or the presence of pernicious anemia, or taking oral contraceptives, can produce the same symptoms. And indeed, these case histories frequently present persons who are clearly on grossly deficient diets in which these other complicating factors are present to a generous degree. Such a case history proves nothing; it could easily be the other deficiencies, rather than the lack of animal foods, which is the problem. In fact, not only do these case histories not rule out these other factors as the real cause of the megaloblastic anemia; they frequently document these other deficiencies, thus disproving the very point which they set out to support. Dr. Richard Bargen, an M.D. who compiled and reviewed a great number of these case histories, comments:

After careful review of all the literature, often quoted as demonstrating 'pure' vegetarians often suffer vitamin B-12 deficiency because of inadequate dietary intake, not one solitary case was found wherein a vegan, consuming an adequate, purely plant food diet suffered any ill health due to vitamin B-12 deficiency or any other deficiency. This finding contradicts the statements made in virtually every textbook of medicine and nutrition I've come across. These books' statements are then usually passed about among other writers of texts like a hereditary disease, but in this case are not confirmed by a review of the literature.[9]

Several studies have been done on "total" or "pure" vegetarians to see if any of the symptoms of vitamin B-12 deficiency would turn up.[10] Two groups of British vegans were studied, and one group of "third-world" total vegetarians in Iran as well. These studies are surprisingly uniform in their results. Even in the case of those on a total vegetarian diet for decades with no supplementary vitamin B-12, there were adequate vitamin B-12 levels and normal, indeed superior, health. One researcher commented on his study by saying, "The question seems to be, not why do some people on this form of diet develop vitamin B-12 deficiency, but why many do not . . . In this small group the notable feature of the histories lay in the paucity of the symptoms."[11]

Nonanimal Sources of Vitamin B-12

If these total vegetarians are not eating animal foods, then just where are they getting their vitamin B-12?

We must remember that only incredibly small quantities of this vitamin are thought to be necessary. At such microscopic levels, the environment is awash with vitamin B-12; it is found in the soil, in the water, and on many foods. One laboratory worker "found that it was necessary to acid-wash all pipettes, test tubes, and volumetric flasks and rinse them 15 times with tap water and 2 times with distilled water" in order to make her determinations for B-12 accurate. [12]

There are two sources of vitamin B-12 for total vegetarians: from vitamin B-12 producing bacteria in the body itself, and from plant foods and water which contain the vitamin B-12 producing microorganisms. Much vitamin B-12 is produced in the body itself. One of the sources of B-12 is bacterial growth in the mouth, around the teeth and gums, in the nasopharynx, around the tonsils and tonsillar crypts, in the folds at the base of the tongue, and in the upper bronchial tree. Up to 0.5 micrograms per day can be obtained in this way, and this is probably sufficient for the very small requirement that a total vegetarian has. [13] In addition, the presence of vitamin B-12 producing bacteria has been detected in the small intestine. [14]

Vitamin B-12 has also been found in rainwater [15] and in many plant foods. In small quantities, Vitamin B-12 has been found either in or on various foods such as the roots and stems of tomatoes, cabbage, celery, kale, broccoli, leeks, and the leaves of kohlrabi. An ounce of the roots of leeks, beets, and other vegetables will provide 0.1 to 0.3 micrograms of B-12, which is more than a day's supply. [16] There are other plant foods which provide "massive" quantities of vitamin B-12—"massive," that is, in relation to human requirements for the vitamin. These include nutritional yeast, tempeh, seaweed, algae, kelp, and fermented soy sauces. The human liver can store vitamin B-12 for years, so once it is ingested from one of these sources one can go for long periods of time without having to worry about a source of B-12.

The one source of vitamin B-12 which *cannot* be recommended is vitamin supplementation. This is because many vitamin supplements contain "break-down" products of vitamin B-12—substances which actually prevent vitamin B-12 from being absorbed into the bloodstream. Insidiously enough, these break-down products not only exert an anti-B-12 effect, they also cause a positive test in the standard measurements for the presence of vitamin B-12 in the bloodstream; thus simultaneously bringing about, and then masking, the very deficiency which they are supposed to prevent. [17]

Conclusions

The evidence purporting to prove that lack of animal foods will cause any of the dire conditions commonly alleged to be a consequence of lack of dietary intake of vitamin B-12 is totally lacking. A review of the evidence concerning alleged instances of megaloblastic anemia in total vegetarians indicates that these cases are due to factors other than lack of animal foods—generally, a diet lacking sufficient quantities of folacin, vitamin B-6, iron, and so forth. On the other hand, many total vegetarians have lived for years on diets which completely lack animal foods or any vitamin B-12 supplementation.

Total vegetarians can get vitamin B-12 from a variety of sources, including bacteria living in their mouths and small intestines, from foods containing large quantities of B-12 such as nutritional yeast, tempeh, fermented soy sauces, kelp, algae, and seaweed, and from rainwater. Indeed, due to the prevalence of vitamin B-12 in the environment, the question is not how one can obtain B-12 but rather how it could be avoided. The Great Vitamin B-12 Controversy, like the protein debates which went on for years and are still continuing today among journalists and scientists who have somehow still not gotten the word, is a controversy which exists almost entirely in the minds of those who are not aware of the evidence.

4
Other Nutrients

There are not as many controversies surrounding the many other nutrients necessary for human health. However, vegetarians should not take these nutrients for granted; they should familiarize themselves with enough elementary nutritional knowledge to get a good balanced diet—or at the very least, to avoid a grossly deficient one. Fortunately, this is not very difficult. In this chapter we will outline how this can be done and touch on some special areas of concern to vegetarians.

How to Evaluate Foods

Many foods are good sources of some nutrients, but poor sources of other nutrients. How can we evaluate these different foods in terms of the vitamins and minerals they contain?

The most obvious way is to consult a table which lists the nutrients contained in a given mass, weight, or volume of the food in question. This has been done in Table 3. For convenience, the quantities of all the various nutrients have been expressed as a percentage of the recommended dietary allowance (RDA) for that nutrient found in 100 grams (about 3¹/₂ ounces) of all the different foods. Thus, 100 grams of cabbage contain 4.17% of the RDA of vitamin B-2; 100 grams of cherries contain 16.66% of the RDA for vitamin C; and so on.

However, Table 3 must be used with care. The problem is that 100 grams of food can mean very different things, especially in terms of caloric content. Specifically, foods high in water and fiber and low in fat are going to be relatively understated in terms of nutrient content.

Foods which contain a lot of water are obviously going to have fewer calories, and fewer of everything else, per 100 grams; water contains no calories. Like-

Table 3. Percentage of the recommended dietary allowance (RDA) for adult women aged 23 to 50 provided by 100 grams (3½ ounces) of various plant foods.

Food	Calories	Protein	Calcium	Iron	Vit B-1	Vit B-2	Niacin	Vit A	Vit C
Vegetables									
Beet	2.15	3.64	2.00	3.89	3.00	4.17	3.07	0.40	16.67
Broccoli	1.60	8.18	12.88	6.11	10.00	19.17	6.92	50.00	188.33
Cabbage	1.20	2.95	6.13	2.22	5.00	4.17	2.31	2.60	78.33
Carrot	2.10	2.50	4.62	3.89	6.00	4.17	4.62	220.00	13.33
Cauliflower	1.35	6.14	3.13	6.11	11.00	8.33	5.38	1.20	130.00
Celery	0.85	2.05	4.88	1.67	3.00	2.50	2.31	4.80	15.00
Collards (leaves)	2.25	10.91	31.25	8.33	16.00	25.83	13.08	186.00	253.33
Corn	4.80	7.95	0.38	3.89	15.00	10.00	13.08	8.00	20.00
Cucumber	0.75	2.05	3.13	6.11	3.00	3.33	1.54	5.00	18.33
Eggplant	1.25	2.73	1.50	3.89	5.00	4.17	4.62	0.20	8.33
Kale (leaves)	2.65	13.64	31.13	15.00	16.00	21.67	16.15	200.00	310.00
Lettuce (iceberg)	0.65	2.05	2.50	2.77	6.00	5.00	2.30	6.60	10.00
Mushroom	1.40	6.14	0.75	4.44	10.00	38.33	32.30	0.00	5.00
Okra	1.80	5.46	11.50	3.33	17.00	17.50	7.69	10.40	51.67
Onion (dry mature)	1.90	3.41	3.38	2.78	3.00	3.33	1.54	0.80	16.67
Onion (green)	1.80	3.41	6.38	5.55	5.00	4.17	3.07	40.00	53.33
Potato	3.80	4.77	0.88	3.33	10.00	3.33	11.53	0.00	33.33
Pumpkin	1.30	2.27	2.63	4.44	5.00	9.17	4.62	32.00	15.00
Radish	0.85	2.27	3.75	5.55	3.00	2.50	2.31	0.20	43.33
Spinach	1.30	7.27	11.63	17.22	10.00	16.66	4.62	162.00	85.00
Squash (summer)	0.95	2.50	3.50	2.22	5.00	7.50	7.69	8.20	36.67
Sweet Potato	5.70	3.86	4.00	3.89	10.00	5.00	4.62	176.00	35.00
Tomato	1.10	2.50	1.63	2.78	6.00	3.33	5.38	18.00	38.33
Turnip	1.50	2.27	4.88	2.78	4.00	5.83	4.62	0.00	60.00
Turnip Green	1.40	6.82	30.75	10.00	21.00	32.50	6.15	152.00	231.67
Watercress	0.95	5.00	18.88	9.44	8.00	13.33	6.92	98.00	131.67
Legumes									
Bean, lima	5.53	17.27	5.86	13.83	18.06	8.26	10.00	5.59	28.27
Bean, pinto (dry)	17.43	52.01	16.85	35.49	83.92	17.44	16.94	0.00	0.00
Chickpea (dry)	18.00	46.59	18.75	38.33	31.00	12.50	15.38	1.00	0.00
Lentil	5.30	17.73	3.13	11.67	7.00	5.00	4.62	0.40	0.00
Pea, green	3.55	12.26	2.86	10.03	27.97	9.17	17.62	10.79	33.41
Peanut (dry, roasted)	29.09	59.50	9.03	12.35	31.94	11.00	131.41	0.00	0.00

Bulgur	8.41	14.14	2.50	7.40	5.19	2.47	18.23	0.00	0.00
Millet (dry)	16.35	22.50	2.50	37.78	73.00	31.67	17.69	0.00	0.00
Oatmeal	2.75	4.54	1.15	3.24	7.92	2.08	0.64	0.00	0.00
Rice (brown)	5.95	5.71	1.47	2.85	9.23	1.71	10.65	0.00	0.00
Rye (dry)	16.70	27.50	4.75	20.56	43.00	18.33	12.31	0.00	0.00
Wheat (hard spring)	2.24	4.08	0.87	2.72	6.12	1.70	4.71	0.00	0.00
Nuts and Seeds									
Almond	29.90	42.27	29.25	26.11	24.00	76.66	26.92	0.00	0.00
Cashew	28.05	39.09	4.75	21.11	43.00	20.83	13.85	2.00	0.00
Pecan	34.35	20.91	9.13	13.33	86.00	10.83	6.92	2.60	3.33
Sesame (whole)	28.15	42.27	145.00	58.33	98.00	20.00	41.54	0.60	0.00
Sunflower	28.00	54.55	15.00	39.44	196.00	19.17	41.54	1.00	0.00
Walnut (black)	31.40	46.59	0.00	33.33	22.00	9.17	5.38	6.00	0.00
Fruits									
Apple	2.80	0.45	0.87	1.67	3.00	1.67	0.77	1.80	11.67
Avocado	8.37	4.85	1.25	3.33	11.33	16.67	12.31	5.86	23.33
Banana	4.25	2.50	1.00	3.89	5.00	5.00	5.38	3.80	16.67
Blackberry	2.90	2.73	4.00	5.00	3.00	3.33	3.08	4.00	35.00
Blueberry	3.10	1.59	1.88	5.56	3.00	5.00	3.85	2.00	23.33
Cherry	3.50	2.95	2.75	2.22	5.00	5.00	3.08	2.20	16.66
Grape (American)	3.45	2.95	2.00	2.22	5.00	2.50	2.31	2.00	6.67
Lemon	1.35	2.50	3.25	3.33	4.00	1.67	0.77	0.40	88.33
Orange	2.45	2.27	5.13	2.22	10.00	3.33	3.08	4.00	83.33
Peach	1.90	1.36	1.13	2.78	2.00	4.17	7.69	26.60	11.67
Pear	3.05	1.59	1.00	1.67	2.00	3.33	0.77	0.40	6.67

SOURCE: Calculated on the basis of data in:
  (a) Ford Heritage, *Composition and Facts About Foods* (Mokelumne Hill, Cal.: Health Research, 1971).
  (b) U.S. Department of Agriculture, *Nutritive Value of American Foods*, Agriculture Handbook no. 456 (Washington, D.C.: Government Printing Office, 1975).

NOTES: Legumes and grains are assumed to have been cooked, unless otherwise specified. Other foods are assumed to be uncooked. Where data on a nutrient is unavailable, it has been assumed to be zero.

The recommended dietary allowances for these nutrients are as follows: 2000 calories, 44 grams protein, 800 mg calcium, 18 mg iron, 1.0 mg vitamin B-1, 1.2 mg vitamin B-2, 13 mg niacin, 5000 international units vitamin A, 60 mg vitamin C.

See National Research Council, *Recommended Dietary Allowances*, 9th ed. (Washington, D.C.: National Academy of Sciences, 1980). The requirement for vitamin A is now expressed in terms of "micrograms of retinol equivalents," rather than "international units." Because most data on foods list vitamin A content in terms of international units, the older unit has been utilized here. For a discussi n of these issues, see *Recommended Dietary Allowances*.

wise fiber—because fiber passes through the system undigested, it will obviously not help fulfill any of the nutritional requirements commonly listed. Yet the beneficial effects of fiber are now widely acknowledged, even though fiber does not show up on any nutritional charts. Finally, there is fat. Fat contains over twice as many calories per unit weight as either protein or carbohydrate. So fatty foods tend to have more calories per 100 grams.

For example, compare peanuts and pecans to the vegetables. At first glance, it looks as if peanuts and pecans are excellent sources of calcium and iron. They have far more calcium and iron than do cucumbers or cauliflower, when compared in 100-gram quantities. The fact is, though, that pecans and peanuts are relatively weak sources of calcium and iron, whereas cucumbers and cauliflower are *excellent* sources.

If you tried to fulfill your entire iron requirement by eating pecans, you'd have to eat 750 grams of them (over $1^1/_2$ pounds). This would give you, besides the needed 18 milligrams of iron, well over 5000 calories! If this didn't make you sick, it would certainly make you fat. To get your entire iron requirement from cucumbers, on the other hand, you would have to eat 1600-1700 grams of cucumbers—about 4 or 5 cucumbers per day. They would provide you with less than 250 calories.

Thus, nutrient comparisons on the basis of mass, weight, or volume can be misleading. Extraneous problems such as water or fat content can throw such comparisons completely out of kilter and render them meaningless. In Table 4 we have an evaluation of nutrient content and caloric content has been called the "nutrient density" of a food. This is defined as the percentage of the RDA of a nutrient in the food, divided by the percentage of the RDA of calories, times 100. (The value of 100 is an arbitrary constant adopted for reasons of convenience. It makes the resultant number the percentage of the RDA of that nutrient contained in 2000 calories of the food.)

So, if 100 calories of a food (5% of the RDA of calories for adult women aged 23-50) provide 10% of the RDA for iron, the food's nutrient density of iron is 10%/5% x 100 = 200. Thus, anything with a nutrient density of 100 or more has an adequate quantity of that nutrient; and if its nutrient density is 200, 300, or 500, then the food is an even better source of the nutrient. On the other hand, a value of less than 100 indicates that the food is a relatively poor source of the nutrient.

We can see from Tables 3 and 4 that getting all of these common vitamins and minerals is both possible and not terribly difficult. Of course, you wouldn't want to live entirely on celery—you'd have to eat celery all day. However, a large number of vegetables are excellent sources of vitamins and minerals, and if you consume a good selection of these foods, you will have little difficulty in getting enough of all the necessary vitamins and minerals.

The trick is to combine enough of the physically bulky but vitamin rich vegetables with the less bulky foods, such as potatoes, corn, grains, and leg-

Table 4. Nutrient densities of some common plant foods, relative to the recommended dietary allowance (RDA) for adult women aged 23 to 50.

Food	Protein	Calcium	Iron	Vit B-1	Vit B-2	Niacin	Vit A	Vit C
Vegetables								
Beet	169	93	181	140	194	143	19	775
Broccoli	511	805	382	625	1198	433	3125	11770
Cabbage	246	511	185	417	347	192	217	6527
Carrot	119	220	185	286	199	220	10476	635
Cauliflower	455	232	453	825	617	399	89	9629
Celery	241	574	196	353	294	272	565	1765
Collards	485	1389	370	711	1148	581	8267	11259
Corn	166	8	81	312	208	272	167	417
Cucumber	273	417	815	400	444	205	667	2444
Eggplant	218	120	311	400	334	370	16	666
Kale	515	1175	566	604	818	609	7547	11698
Lettuce (iceberg)	315	385	426	923	769	354	1015	1538
Mushroom	438	54	317	714	2738	2307	0	357
Okra	303	639	185	944	972	427	578	2871
Onion (dry mature)	179	178	146	158	175	81	42	877
Onion (green)	189	354	308	278	232	170	2222	2962
Potato	126	23	88	263	88	303	0	877
Pumpkin	175	202	342	385	705	355	2461	1154
Radish	267	441	653	353	294	272	24	5098
Spinach	559	895	1325	769	1282	355	12462	6538
Squash (summer)	263	368	234	526	789	809	863	3860
Sweet Potato	68	70	68	175	88	81	3088	614
Tomato	227	148	253	545	303	489	1636	3485
Turnip	151	325	185	267	389	308	0	4000
Turnip Greens	487	2196	714	1500	2321	239	10857	16548
Watercress	526	1987	994	842	1403	728	10316	13860
Legumes								
Bean, lima	312	106	250	327	149	181	101	511
Bean, pinto	298	97	204	481	100	97	0	0
Chickpea	259	104	213	172	69	85	6	0
Lentil	335	59	220	132	94	81	8	0
Pea, green fresh	345	81	283	788	258	496	304	941
Soybean, fresh	384	140	230	322	116	70	10	0
Peanut	205	31	42	110	38	452	0	0
Grains								
Barley	107	11	64	69				0

Table 4. (*continued*) Nutrient densities of some common plant foods, relative to the recommended dietary allowance (RDA) for adult women aged 23 to 50.

Food	Protein	Calcium	Iron	Vit B-1	Vit B-2	Niacin	Vit A	Vit C
Bulgur	168	30	88	62	29	217	0	0
Millet	138	15	231	446	194	108	0	0
Oatmeal	165	42	118	288	76	23	0	0
Rice (brown)	96	25	48	155	29	179	0	0
Rye	165	28	123	257	110	74	0	0
Wheat (hard spring)	182	39	121	273	76	210	0	0
Nuts and Seeds								
Almond	141	98	87	80	256	90	0	0
Cashew	139	17	75	153	74	49	7	0
Pecan	61	27	39	250	32	20	8	10
Sesame (whole)*	150	515	207	348	71	148	2	0
Sunflower	195	54	141	700	68	148	4	0
Walnut (black)	148	0	106	70	29	17	19	0
Fruits								
Apple	16	31	60	107	60	27	64	417
Avocado	58	15	40	135	199	147	70	279
Banana	59	24	92	118	118	127	89	392
Blackberry	94	138	172	103	115	106	138	1207
Blueberry	51	61	179	97	161	124	65	753
Cherry	84	79	63	143	143	88	63	476
Grape	86	58	64	145	72	67	58	193
Lemon	185	241	247	296	124	57	30	6543
Orange	93	209	91	408	136	126	163	3401
Peach	72	59	146	105	219	405	1400	614
Pear	52	33	55	66	109	25	13	219

SOURCE: Derived from Table 3.
NOTE: Nutrient density is calculated for each nutrient in each food as follows:

$$\text{Nutrient Density} = \frac{\text{Percentage of the RDA of the nutrient in 100 grams food}}{\text{Percentage of the RDA of calories in 100 grams food}} \times 100$$

… where the RDA is the recommended dietary allowance for adult women aged 23 to 50.

* The calcium, iron, and vitamin B-1 content of hulled sesame seeds is dramatically less than that of unhulled (whole) sesame seeds.

umes. So a good nutritional rule for vegetarians (or, for that matter, anyone else) is: get a variety of vegetables, especially fresh vegetables.

And some of the best, nutritionally speaking, are the dark green leafy vegetables. This groups includes kale, collards, broccoli, turnip greens, spinach, parsley, and watercress. Vegetarians who eat plenty of these and other dark green leafy vegetables, can practically forget everything else they know about nutrition. Calorie for calorie, dark green leafy vegetables provide:

- more calcium than milk,
- more iron than beef,
- about as much vitamin A as carrots,
- more vitamin C than oranges,
- generous quantities of vitamin B-1 (thiamine), vitamin B-2 (riboflavin), vitamin B-6 (pyridoxine), folacin, zinc, magnesium, pantothenic acid, niacin, and various other minor nutrients too numerous to mention.

Armed with Tables 3 and 4 the vegetarian should be able to plan his meals with whatever level of detail is required. Usually, any meal plan that includes sizable portions of fresh vegetables will be more than adequate. There are a few topics, however, that require some additional comment.

Special Needs of Mothers and Infants

Tables 3 and 4 only deal with the needs of adult women aged 23-50. What about the needs of other segments of the population? What about the needs of infants and nursing or pregnant women? Do they differ from those of the rest of the population?

Yes, but only in degree. There is probably more variation in the need for iron than for any other nutrient—a pregnant woman may require several times more iron than an adult male. Infants also have a considerably elevated requirement for iron. In Table 5 nutrient requirements of different segments of the population are compared. This table compares the required nutrient densities of all the various age groups with those of adult women aged 23-50.

Young children have a need for food which is digestible and which contains higher concentrations of vitamins and minerals. Fortunately, for infants such a food exists: breast milk. Infants up to six months old can and should be fed exclusively on mother's breast milk. Young children from the age of six months to two years can be fed partially on breast milk and partially on solid food. Sometimes the desired consistency of food can be obtained by mixing the child's food in a blender, and there are commercially available foods for young children as well, some of which are vegetarian.

Table 5. Nutrient density requirements of different age groups (as a percentage of those of adult women aged 23 to 50).

Age	Total Caloric Requirement	Protein	Calcium	Iron	Vit B-1	Vit B-2	Niacin	Vit A	Vit C
Children									
0–0.5	690	87	130	161	87	97	134	152	169
0.5–1.0	945	87	143	176	105	106	130	106	123
1–3	1300	80	154	128	107	103	106	77	115
4–6	1700	80	118	65	105	98	100	74	88
7–10	2400	64	83	46	100	97	102	73	62
Males									
11–14	2700	76	111	74	103	99	103	93	62
15–18	2800	91	107	71	100	102	99	89	71
19–22	2900	88	68	38	103	98	101	86	69
23–50	2700	94	74	41	103	99	103	93	74
51–75	2400	106	83	46	100	97	103	104	83
76+	2050	124	97	54	117	114	120	122	98
Females									
11–14	2200	95	136	90	100	98	105	91	76
15–18	2100	100	143	95	105	103	102	95	95
19–22	2100	95	95	95	105	103	102	95	95
23–50	2000	100	100	100	100	100	100	100	100
51–75	1800	111	111	62	111	111	111	111	111
76+	1600	125	125	70	125	125	125	125	125
Pregnant									
15–18	2400	144	104	222*	125	111	103	104	111
19–22	2400	140	104	222*	125	111	96	104	111
23–50	2300	146	130	231*	122	109	100	109	116
Lactating									
15–18	2600	115	115	205*	123	115	112	115	128
19–22	2600	112	115	205*	123	115	107	115	128
23–50	2500	116	120	213*	120	113	111	120	133

SOURCE: Calculated on the basis of data in *Recommended Dietary Allowances*, 9th ed., 1980.

NOTE: The values for adult women aged 23 to 50 are, be definition, 100 in this table; and all the other age groups are compared to this group. The "nutrient density requirement" is the recommended dietary allowance of the nutrient divided by the recommended dietary allowance of calories.

* In recent years the iron requirement for pregnant or lactating women has been revised sharply upwards. The National Research Council recommends a supplement of 30 mg–60 mg. The stated figure assumes a requirement of 48 mg. over twice the 1964 recommendation of 20 mg

Different people have different needs. Meeting these needs is a challenge for those on a vegetarian diet. However, none of them pose any fundamental problem for vegetarians.

Calcium

It is widely suspected that the adult RDA for calcium, set by the National Research Council at 800 mg, is too high. Indeed, the NRC admits that people have been able to maintain calcium balance on calcium intakes of as little as 200 to 400 mg/day. They recommend 800 mg/day because of the high protein diet of most Americans, presumably because a high protein diet increases the requirement for calcium.[1]

Many persons have been agitating to increase the calcium requirement beyond the present 800 mg. requirement. This is because of the prevalence of osteoporosis, a disease which especially affects older women, in which bone mass is progressively lost until bone fractures become much more likely or inevitable. While calcium is lost from the bones in osteoporosis, this is not the consequence of calcium deficiency; it is a consequence of excessive protein consumption. Eating lots of protein will increase the calcium requirement; and indeed, beyond a certain level of protein consumption, calcium will be lost from the bones no matter *how* much calcium is ingested. Excessive protein consumption is primarily a problem of meat-eaters, not vegetarians; and with reasonable and adequate protein consumption, the calcium requirement is almost certainly considerably less than the current 800 mg/day requirement. (See chapter 8 for further discussion of these problems with protein.)

For years it was thought that oxalic acid and phytic acid caused problems with calcium absorption. (Spinach and swiss chard are the two most common vegetables containing significant oxalic acid, and grains contain phytic acid.) However, these reactions are no longer thought to be important as long as liberal quantities of calcium are consumed.[2]

Dark green leafy vegetables have lots of calcium.

Iron

Some have estimated that as many as 50 million Americans suffer from iron deficiencies. Pregnant women, nursing women, and small children have the strongest need for iron. Women in their reproductive years need almost twice as much iron as men (18 mg as opposed to 10 mg per day). Much of the problem with iron lies in our bodies' inability to absorb the iron we have consumed. Much current research, therefore, is focusing on factors which increase the body's ability to absorb iron. The body's requirement for iron is only about 10% of the recommended dietary allowance of iron, but in most circumstances an absorption rate of 10% is about normal.

Two types of dietary iron are generally distinguished: heme iron and non-heme iron. The big difference between the two, as far as we are concerned, is that heme iron is found only in meat and animal products, and is apparently more easily absorbed by the body. When we consider these facts, it might seem at first glance that vegetarians (especially the total vegetarians who eat no animal products at all) would be at a significant disadvantage in getting the required iron.

However, the issue of heme and non-heme iron is not as critical as one might think. Only part of the iron in meat is of the heme variety anyway. Consequently, even for a meat eater, heme iron could not provide more than 5%-10% of the total dietary iron intake (perhaps one third of the total dietary requirement for iron, considering its increased capacity for absorption). Even for a meat eater, then, non-heme iron must provide the overwhelming preponderance of the total iron requirement.

As it turns out, there is a nutrient which increases the absorption of non-heme iron dramatically, a nutrient which vegetarians have no problem getting: vitamin C. The effect of vitamin C on absorption of non-heme iron is pronounced: adding 60 mg of vitamin C to a meal of rice more than tripled the absorption of iron, while adding an equivalent amount as papaya enhanced absorption of iron from corn fivefold.[3] Therefore, vegetarians should combine iron-rich foods with foods rich in vitamin C to enhance iron absorption. Dark green leafy vegetables are not only excellent iron sources, they are also rich sources of vitamin C.

Other factors affect iron absorption as well. Breast-fed infants, for some reason, have an unusually high rate of iron absorption (perhaps 50% of dietary iron). If the body's iron stores are relatively depleted, iron absorption increases, whereas if the body has plenty of stored iron, relatively less iron is absorbed. Finally, some foods appear to block iron absorption: dairy products and products containing tannins (such as tea).[4]

Vitamin D

Vitamin D is not found in plant foods at all, and in only a few animal foods (such as fish). Fortunately, vitamin D is not really a dietary requirement, for one can synthesize it from sunlight. It has been estimated that one's RDA for vitamin D can be absorbed from the sun with only a few minutes' exposure each day.[5] The body can store vitamin D for long periods of time, so exposure to the sun during the summer months enables the body to sustain itself through the winter indoors.

Many foods have had vitamin D added, especially milk and soymilk. One should be cautious about vitamin D supplementation as one *can* get too much. Some have estimated that the average American ingests six to seven times the maximal recommended daily allowance, and this could be quite toxic to the arterial system.[6] So while vitamin D supplementation is useful for people who don't get enough sunshine, it is potentially harmful to others.

Linoleic Acid

This essential fatty acid is worth mentioning because it is the only fat for which there is a known dietary requirement. Indeed, this dietary requirement was unknown until recently, when hospital patients fed fat-free diets intravenously developed deficiencies. Linoleic acid, an unsaturated fat, is found widely throughout the plant kingdom. The dietary requirement for linoleic acid has been estimated at 1% to 3% of calories.[7] A study of British vegans revealed that they were getting about 13% of their calories from linoleic acid.[8]

Minor Nutrients

In addition to the major nutrients listed in Table 4 or discussed in this chapter, there are many minor nutrients which are essential or very important to the body: vitamin E, vitamin K, folacin, biotin, pantothenic acid, phosphorus, magnesium, zinc, iodine, copper, manganese, fluoride, chromium, selenium, and molybdenum. In many cases it is almost impossible to devise a diet based on natural foods which lacks them, because they are so widely found in the plant kingdom. Anyone who gets a variety of plant foods and who gets plenty of the other nutrients will have no problem getting these minor nutrients as well.

Conclusions

None of these other nutrients are burning issues in vegetarian nutrition. In fact, it is widely recognized that plant foods are the best sources of many of these nutrients. Dark green leafy vegetables, particularly, are excellent sources of virtually all vitamins and minerals needed in the diet. There is no reason to suspect that any vegetarian diet that includes a reasonable variety of plant foods would lack any of these nutrients.

5
Diet and Degenerative Disease

Modern science has made great progress in the field of medicine. Many infectious diseases such as smallpox, malaria, or polio have been virtually eradicated in the West. However, the modern world has been afflicted with a host of diseases which are not infectious: heart disease, cancer, diabetes, stroke, obesity, arthritis, gout, and many others. These "diseases of civilization" are less prevalent in underdeveloped areas. They are all *degenerative* diseases.

These degenerative diseases develop differently from infectious diseases. Infectious diseases result from hostile micro-organisms, typically striking the very young. In ancient times, and more recently in the less developed countries, the young were decimated by infectious diseases. That is why the life expectancy in the ancient world was so low. Some have estimated that the life expectancy in ancient Rome was around 30 years; although if one managed to survive infancy, one actually had a very good chance of making it to old age.

Degenerative diseases, on the other hand, develop over a period of many years. Rarely afflicting the very young, these diseases usually claim their first victims at middle age. We become increasingly susceptible to degenerative disease with each passing year. These diseases are not caused by hostile invading organisms, rather by the deterioration of the body's own processes.

Some have claimed that degenerative diseases are just an inevitable consequence of aging, that the Western nations have a higher incidence of degenerative diseases for the simple reason that their populations are living longer. Curiously enough, though, the middle-aged and elderly in the underdeveloped areas of the world who cannot afford a meat-oriented diet suffer much less from most degenerative diseases. This has led many to believe that there is nothing inevitable about these degenerative diseases; that factors associated with our Western life style cause heart disease, cancer, obesity, diabetes, and the other diseases of civilization; and that the factor most responsible for the dramatic upsurge of these degenerative diseases in the more civilized world is our "civilized" diet.

Your Money or Your Life

Recent historical evidence implicates diet as a factor in degenerative disease. In Denmark, blockaded by the Allies as a result of World War I, the death rate fell to its lowest level in 20 years—by over 30%—when virtually the entire country was placed on a lacto-vegetarian diet.[1] During World War II, when restrictions on meat consumption were imposed on Norway because of the German occupation, death rates from both circulatory diseases and diabetes fell dramatically.[2] Autopsy studies on soldiers killed during the Korean War revealed extensive atherosclerosis ("hardening of the arteries," a condition responsible for most heart disease) in the arteries of the Americans. However, there was almost no atherosclerosis in the arteries of the Koreans.[3]

Countless explanations for the remarkable variations in the incidence of these diseases of civilization within and between populations have been put forward. It has been suggested, for example, that heart disease is caused by the stress of modern life; that cancer is a consequence of radiation, TV, or heredity; or that the whole thing is a statistical fluke, brought about by the better diagnostic procedures of the more advanced countries.

But it is obvious even from the above three examples that none of these explanations is adequate. The stress of modern life could hardly be greater than stress in times of war. Why, then, does heart disease *decrease* dramatically in wartime? With the exception of lung cancer, cancer rates have remained about the same in Western nations for the last 50 years, and this negates such explanations as radiation and TV. Most immigrants to a new country acquire the native's risk of developing heart disease or cancer, and this tends to negate the explanation that these problems are hereditary. Finally, better diagnostic procedures cannot account for the startling results of autopsy studies which cross international lines.

The evidence, which we will review in the remainder of this section, is very strong that diet is the single most important factor in many degenerative diseases. And of all the things wrong with the typical Western diet, meat consumption is the most critical.

In recent years, medical research has been making great progress against degenerative disease. We are advancing in the fight against cancer and heart disease. Does this mean that, perhaps, in a few years we will no longer have to worry about our bad dietary habits, that we will be able to eat meat without worrying about heart disease, cancer, and the rest?

This is quite doubtful. Although the rates of these diseases have been diminished, they are still monumentally high, much higher in the Western countries than in the underdeveloped nations. More fundamentally, though, this progress against degenerative disease is being achieved only at great economic cost. As the technology to fight heart disease and cancer becomes more effective, medical costs skyrocket. In 1981 hospital costs were up a record 19%, to $110 billion; and the total health care bill was up to $274 billion, also a record. There is every indication that medical costs will continue to shoot up in the future, far outstripping the rate of inflation.[4]

It becomes a question of your money or your life. We may eventually acquire, through sheer technological prowess, the ability to cure or at least to cope with these diseases, but we'll have to pay for it, and pay dearly. And it is all so unnecessary. For the most part, we know what causes heart disease; we know what causes cancer. Through dietary reform we could probably cut the incidence of these two killers *dramatically,* decreasing medical and emotional costs for everyone.

Indeed, if the incidence of these diseases in the less developed nations can be taken as a guide, truly radical dietary reform would probably cut the incidence of heart disease and cancer by 60%-80%. This dietary reform would have to be drastic, requiring the elimination of meat, most or all animal products, and most or all "junk food" and sugar. In short, reform would mean a total vegetarian whole foods diet. Many people might find this difficult, just as some people can't give up smoking although they know it causes lung cancer. But a total vegetarian whole foods diet would have two strong advantages over the current Western diet: it would be considerably more healthy and considerably less expensive.

Hazards of Animal Products

Meat in particular, and animal products in general, have three nutritional disadvantages: they contain too much fat, they contain too much protein, and they contain no fiber at all.

As we can see from Table 6, most of the calories in animal products are in the forms of protein or fat. Carbohydrates, which are the primary constituent of most whole plant foods, are almost entirely absent in most animal products. Indeed, of all the items listed, only milk has significant amounts of carbohydrate. And the carbohydrate of milk is in a form—lactose—which is unusable by much of the world's population, which cannot digest it after infancy. Lactose provides no fiber and is nutritionally equivalent to table sugar.

A diet which stresses consumption of meat cannot avoid high concentrations of both protein and fat. By consuming lean meats, one might avoid excess fat; by eating the fattier meats, one might avoid excess protein. But the only to avoid *both* is to avoid meat altogether. Since both high-fat diets and high-protein diets are hazardous, one cannot avoid degenerative diseases by shifting from one type of meat to another. One can only shift from one set of hazards to another.

Table 6. Protein, fat, and carbohydrate composition of 17 animal products, as a percentage of calories.

Animal Product	Protein	Percentage of calories Fat	Carbohydrate
Bacon	18	80	2
Beef (lean chuck)	21	79	0
Beef (ground)	51	49	0
Bologna	16	82	1
Cheese, cheddar	25	73	2
Cheese, American	25	73	2
Chicken, fryer	68	29	3
Cod (fillet)	71	29	0
Egg	32	65	2
Ham (lean with fat)	25	75	0
Ham (trimmed)	56	44	0
Lamb (leg)	37	63	0
Milk (3.5%)	22	49	30
Milk (skim)	40	3	57
Salami	21	77	1
Salmon	63	37	0
Turkey (light meat)	77	23	0

SOURCE: U.S. Department of Agriculture, *Nutritive Value of American Foods,* Agriculture Handbook no. 456 (Washington, D.C.: Government Printing Office, 1975).

The best publicized and most thoroughly documented of these hazards is fat. Fat is implicated in atherosclerosis, several forms of cancer, gallstones, diabetes, and probably many other diseases as well.

Meat and animal foods are loaded with fat. The leanest meats get about 20% or 30% of their calories from fat, but most meats have a higher percentage (from 50% to 80%) of calories as fat. Animal foods provide over half of the fat in the typical American diet, with refined vegetable fats making up most of the rest. Whole, unprocessed plant foods account for only a small fraction of the total. The average American gets over 40% of his calories from fat, and this is in great excess of any conceivable dietary need.

Protein is another problem with animal foods. Many people will ask, "But it doesn't hurt to get extra protein, does it?" In point of fact, the extra protein meat provides can only hurt. The body cannot store protein. The levels of protein consumption in the Western nations are not merely "higher than enough," they are far higher than are safe. The average American is probably getting from two to three times as much protein as he actually needs.[5] Some unfortunate individuals are undoubtedly getting even more than that.

One of the consequences of excess protein consumption is osteoporosis. As osteoporosis develops, the bones lose calcium, become softer, more porous, and more susceptible to fractures—a frequent development among the elderly. Protein's role in causing calcium losses is now widely recognized.[6] Excessive protein intake has also been linked to obesity, diabetes, and colon cancer. And finally, some researchers have suggested that excessive protein intake—rather than cholesterol or saturated fats—may actually be the chief villain in atherosclerosis. One cannot arbitrarily increase one's protein intake with impunity. Beyond a certain level, the body begins to sustain serious damage.

Finally, animal foods lack fiber—the indigestible part of food often referred to as "bulk." Animal foods contain virtually no fiber, but almost all plant foods contain fiber if they have not had it refined out of them. Fiber benefits the digestive system. Stools of individuals on a low-fiber diet are small and compact, leading to a certain amount of constipation, which over the years becomes viewed as "normal." This constipation enhances the chances of developing hemorrhoids and appendicitis, and later in life, diverticulosis. There are other, even more unpleasant complications: lack of fiber appears to assist the development of colon cancer.

These three items—too much fat, too much protein, and not enough fiber—are critical in any discussion of degenerative diseases today. Almost all these degenerative diseases are related to heavy consumption of meat and animal products in some way.

Hazards of Refined Foods and Sugar

Animal foods and meat are not the only problems in the Western diet, however. Processed and refined foods probably pose an equally great health hazard. In many cases, refined foods cause problems which compound and reinforce problems related to meat consumption.

The first and most obvious problem with refined and processed foods is that processing and refining remove many valuable vitamins and minerals. Most food companies have masked this problem by supplementing their sugar-coated, processed cereals (and other foods) with "added" nutrients. But they rarely put back all the vitamins and minerals they take out. They put back only the more "famous" vitamins and minerals like calcium, vitamin B-1, and niacin—more obscure but equally vital nutrients are likely to be neglected. Thus, those who depend on vitamin-supplemented, refined foods may very well be getting enough of the better-known nutrients, but suffering from deficiencies of the lesser-known ones.

Secondly, refined foods have generally had most, if not all, the fiber processed out of them. The problems resulting from the lack of fiber in meat are aggravated if even the plant foods one consumes have been rendered fiberless. The Western diet typically emphasizes both refined foods and animal products, and the net effect of these two tendencies is that many people in the West have subjected themselves to an almost fiber-free diet for a period of many years. There can only be a very heavy price to pay for such habits.

"The Natural Diet of Humanity"

Can one argue, on nutritional grounds, that a vegetarian diet is the natural diet of humanity—that is, the diet on which humans would be most healthy? When asked such a question, Nathan Pritikin replied, "Which vegetarian diet? As far as I know there are 200 different kinds of vegetarians. Identify yourself."[7]

Some vegetarians may be somewhat offended to find that dairy products and eggs are, in this and in other cases, part of the nutritional problem. Eggs, milk, cheese, meat, fish, and fowl all have about the same high quantities of fat and protein and about the same dearth of fiber. This does not mean that a lacto-ovo-vegetarian diet cannot be a healthy diet. Obviously, the elimination of meat cannot help but improve the diet with respect to the problems we are focusing on. A vegetarian who (for example) drinks skim milk and gets plenty of whole plant foods can hardly be faulted.

Objectively, we must say that meat is only part of the dietary problem confronting the Western world today. But we can say that the "natural diet of humanity" (taking this to mean the diet on which humans would be most healthy) is a vegetarian diet. Almost any vegetarian diet is an improvement over the typical Western diet, but the best diet of all would also eliminate refined and processed foods, as well as most (if not all) animal products—in short, a total vegetarian, whole foods diet.

This is a fairly radical claim, and one which should not be accepted uncritically. The evidence which implicates meat consumption as a major factor in many of these diseases also implicates a number of foods which may be theoretically acceptable to many vegetarians—foods such as eggs, sugar, and junk food in general. On the other hand, there can be little doubt that meat consumption is the single most important factor in most of these degenerative diseases. In the succeeding chapters, we will examine the evidence relating diet to degenerative diseases in more detail. But to see the consequences of our current eating habits, we need only look at the obituary column of a typical daily newspaper.

6
Atherosclerosis

Cardiovascular diseases—diseases affecting the circulatory system—are the leading cause of death in the United States today, and in many other Western nations as well. Hundreds of thousands die each year in the United States due to one or another of these diseases.

Thanks to the most advanced medical technology in history, more and more people are surviving heart attacks and strokes. But survival frequently means restricted activities, dependence on drugs, and constant anxiety for one's self, family, and friends. The monetary cost alone is staggering. The economic cost of cardiovascular diseases in the United States is in excess of $60 billion each year.[1] These expenses can only be expected to rise, far outstripping the rate of inflation. In monetary terms, cardiovascular diseases have the effect of a small war. In terms of the loss of human life, they have the effect of a large one.

The condition behind most cardiovascular disease is *atherosclerosis,* sometimes called (only a bit inaccurately) "hardening of the arteries." The evidence linking atherosclerosis to meat consumption is well known, widely publicized, and overwhelming. This is not to say that other factors are not also involved, but meat consumption is undoubtedly the most important factor.

As atherosclerosis progresses, lipids (fats, and fatlike substances such as cholesterol) collect at certain points in the arteries. These deposits occur only at points where the artery has been damaged or injured. When fatty deposits accumulate in this injury, or lesion, we call the area an atherosclerotic lesion. As the atherosclerotic lesion grows, the arterial passage becomes more and more restricted, increasingly blocking the flow of blood. Clotting may occur around the lesion, and such clots may become interwoven in the fabric of the artery wall. The lesion may literally harden as minerals such as calcium collect in it. At some point, the artery becomes so constricted that not enough blood can get through to feed vital tissues, and a "heart attack" or "stroke" occurs.

Virtually everyone in the Western nations has atherosclerosis; it is only a question of how advanced it is.

What Causes Atherosclerosis?

The evidence is strong that meat consumption is the chief cause of atherosclerosis. For some reason, vegetarians have a greatly reduced risk of suffering from the fatal complications of all of the various cardiovascular diseases. Populations and individuals eating meat, on the other hand, have a greatly increased risk, which increases as the degree of meat consumption increases. Thus atherosclerosis follows the same pattern as most of the other of the "diseases of civilization": it is relatively absent in poorer countries on more traditional plant food diets. Among the evidence supporting these conclusions is the following:

- Studies comparing vegetarians with nonvegetarians consistently show that vegetarians enjoy a large reduction in the risk of dying from heart disease. Researchers at Loma Linda University found that total vegetarian Seventh-Day Adventists had an expected mortality from coronary heart disease only 14% of that in the general public. Part of this reduction can be attributed to the fact that Seventh-Day Adventists do not smoke. But the mortality for meat-eating Adventists is 56% of the "normal" rate, exactly four times greater. And much of their reduction can be attributed to the fact that even meat-eating Adventists eat substantially less meat then the general public. In some categories, the reduction was even more dramatic for vegetarians: total vegetarian Adventist males aged 35-64, for example, had an expected mortality from heart disease only 12% of the "expected" rate, while Adventist meat-eaters had a coronary mortality over four times greater.[2] In another study of more than 10,000 vegetarians and meat-eaters, British researchers found that the more meat consumed, the greater the risk of suffering a heart attack.[3]
- Historical experience in times of war verifies these ideas. In Norway during the Second World War, meat consumption was sharply restricted due to wartime conditions; and the death rate from circulatory diseases of all types dropped sharply. After the war ended and meat consumption rose to prewar levels, the death rate from these diseases returned to its previous high level as well.[4] Similarly, in Austria in 1948 the chance of suffering a heart attack was eight times greater than it was in 1944, when meat consumption was much reduced due to the German occupation.[5]
- Finally, population studies have strongly suggested that as the degree of consumption of meat and other animal products rises, the likelihood of

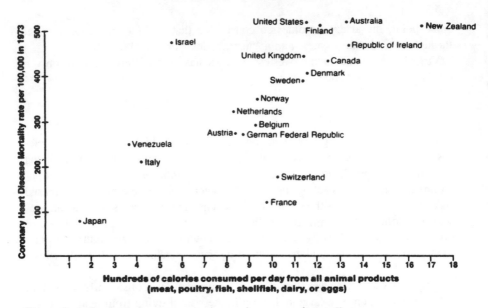

Figure 1. Animal product consumption and coronary heart disease.

Source: From data in J. Stamler, "Population Studies," in *Nutrition, Lipids, and Coronary Heart Disease* (New York: Raven Press, 1979) ed. R. I. Levy, B. M. Rifkind, B. H. Dennis and N. Ernst.

dying from coronary heart disease also rises—in proportion to the consumption of animal products (see figure 1).

Dietary Variables in Atherosclerosis

The debate over atherosclerosis is a complex one; and a bewildering variety of "risk factors" and theories have been proposed. We should examine a few of the more important dietary variables commonly associated with heart disease. But in doing so, we should beware of losing sight of the forest because of the trees. Among all these theories, two important conclusions suggest themselves: first, that dietary factors are more important than nondietary factors; and secondly, that meat consumption is the most critical of the dietary variables.

1. Cholesterol and fat are two commonly mentioned problems. Cholesterol is the most famous of all risk factors for heart disease. Actually, when people speak of "cholesterol," they may be talking of two different things—either of cholesterol in the diet, or cholesterol in the bloodstream ("serum cholesterol").

   Serum cholesterol does not travel around by itself in the bloodstream; rather, it is one of the ingredients of the *lipoproteins*. These lipoproteins

Table 7. The four major lipoproteins.

	Chylomicrons	*VLDL*	*LDL*	*HDL*
Density (g/me)	less than 0.95	0.95–1.006	1.006–1.019	1.063–1.21
Size (angstroms)	750–10,000	300–800	215–220	75–100
Protein: % of molecule	0.5–1.0	5–15	25	45–55
Lipids: % of molecule	99	95	75	55
% as Phospholipids	3–6	10–20	20–25	30
% as Triglyceride	less than 85	50–70	5–10	2
% as Cholesterol	2–5	10–20	40–45	18
Half-life	5–15 minutes	6–12 hours	3 days	4 days

SOURCE: R. I. Levy, and M. J. Stone "Atherosclerosis: Role of Lipoproteins," in *The Pathogenesis of Atherosclerosis*, ed. R. W. Wissler, J. C. Geer, and M. Kaufman (Baltimore: Williams and Wilkins Co., 1971).

are composed of different proportions of cholesterol, protein, and triglycerides (see Table 7). It is now believed by many that increased amounts of one of these lipoproteins—the "low density lipoproteins" (LDL)—is the problem in most heart disease. Persons who have an inherited disease called "familial hypercholesterolemia" suffer from very high concentrations of cholesterol in the bloodstream, and also develop heart disease over 20 times as frequently as "normal" members of the population, accounting for at least 5% of all heart attacks in persons under age 60.[6]

Cholesterol is also found in all animal foods, and there is a strong correlation between dietary cholesterol, serum cholesterol, and heart disease. As atherosclerotic lesions get worse and worse, they accumulate fats and cholesterol; and the worse they get, the higher the percentage of cholesterol in them. Autopsy studies offer strong evidence of a relationship between dietary cholesterol, serum cholesterol, and the degree and extent of atherosclerosis: basically, the greater the concentrations of serum cholesterol and the greater the quantity of cholesterol in the diet, the greater the extent of atherosclerosis.[7]

But is dietary cholesterol the real villain in causing high serum cholesterol levels? This issue is not as simple as it sounds and is being hotly debated today. The problem is that a lot of things may raise serum cholesterol besides dietary cholesterol. Some argue that saturated fats are the primary problem.[8] (Cholesterol is a fat-like substance but is not, technically speaking, a fat.) Others have taken the position that all fats, saturated and unsaturated, are a cause of heart disease.[9] A multitude of studies can be found to support of any of these positions.

Much has been made over the virtues of chicken and fish in comparison to red meats such as beef and pork. It has been said that eating chicken and fish will aid in the prevention of heart disease, because these meats are relatively lower in fat and contain more unsaturated than saturated fat, thus helping to lower the cholesterol levels. Unfortunately, these claims are not supported by the evidence. Studies in which human volunteers switched from diets including beef and eggs, to one including fish and chicken, showed that serum cholesterol levels were *not* appreciably lowered by switching to chicken and fish.[10] And an examination of the nutritional data suggests an explanation: while it is true that chicken and fish contain less fat than beef, it is also true that chicken and fish contain about *twice* as much cholesterol per calorie as does beef.[11] Indeed, some seafoods (such as crab, shrimp, and lobster) are exceptionally high in cholesterol content.

All of these diverse theories have roughly the same dietary implications. Meat is high in cholesterol, saturated fat, and total fat. Plant foods, by contrast, are usually low in saturated fat and total fat, and contain zero cholesterol. Vegetarians have lower levels of serum cholesterol than do meat-eaters, with total vegetarians having the lowest levels of all.[12]

2. Protein/Vitamin B-6. Some researchers have proposed that atherosclerosis may be caused by a combination of two dietary factors: too much protein and not enough vitamin B-6. One of the amino acids of protein is methionine, which breaks down into homocysteine after being ingested. To break down homocysteine further a specific coenzyme—vitamin B-6—is required. Thus, when an individual fails to get enough vitamin B-6, or gets too much protein (and thus too much methionine), homocysteine builds up in the bloodstream.

There is evidence that homocysteine is an important factor in heart disease. The evidence for this theory has been collected in an important book entitled *Beyond Cholesterol*.[13] Persons suffering from homocystinuria, a genetic disease in which the body is unable to break down homocysteine, typically develop severe atherosclerosis and die at a shockingly early age— frequently before their teens. Animals injected with homocysteine, or maintained on vitamin B-6 deficient diets, quickly develop severe atherosclerosis. Persons who have had coronaries typically have high levels of homocysteine and low levels of vitamin B-6 in their bloodstream. Furthermore, and most interestingly, both oral contraceptives and smoking—both of which tend to depress vitamin B-6 levels—have been found to be risk factors for atherosclerosis.

This theory is startling at first glance, because it appears to disregard the strong relationship between high-fat diets and heart disease. On closer examination, the practical implications of this theory are much the same as for the cholesterol/fat theories: it turns out that meat is not only high in cholesterol and fat, it is also high in methionine and relatively low in vitamin B-6. On the other hand, exactly the opposite is true for most plant foods. If one calculates the "H-values" (the vitamin B-6/methionine ratio) for various foods, with a high H-value implying the most healthy food and a low H-value representing the least, then one can see that plant foods dominate the higher H-value ranges (see Table 8).

3. High blood pressure is well correlated with heart disease. It is commonly believed that high blood pressure is largely a consequence of excessive salt intake. But the evidence is far more complicated than the public is being led to believe. In point of fact it is much more likely that meat—not salt—is the primary culprit in causing high blood pressure.

Studies of vegetarians have shown that vegetarians have lower blood pressure than the meat-eating population, and that this is unrelated to their salt consumption.[14] Several experimental studies confirm these observations. In one experiment, a group of subjects was placed on a lacto-vegetarian diet, while a second group was placed on a meat diet. The blood pressure of those on the vegetarian diet fell during a six-week period; but when placed on a meat diet, blood pressure remained unchanged.[15]

In another project, subjects were divided into three groups: a low-fat, a low-salt, and a "normal" group. Blood pressure in those on the low-fat diet fell; but the blood pressure of those on the low-salt and normal diets remained unchanged.[16] The evidence is strong, therefore, that meat consumption has more to do with high blood pressure than salt consumption does.

Table 8. H-values of some common foods.*

0–0.49	0.5–0.99	1–1.99	2–2.99	3–4.99	5–9.99	10+
white bread	bacon	kidney bean	barley	broccoli	kale	carrot
almond	ground beef	lima bean	snap bean	asparagus	apple	avocado
brazil nut	chicken	beef liver	beet green	cauliflower	turnip	banana
butter	ham	whole wheat	corn	filbert	parsley	cabbage
cheeses	ice cream	bread	pork cutlet	brussel	spinach	lettuce
cod	lamb	peanut	cucumber	sprouts	pumpkin	orange
egg	mushroom	soybean	walnut	brown rice	sweet potato	pepper
flounder	whole milk	beef kidney	calf liver	turnip greens		potato
nonfat milk	crab	brewer's		celery		radish
beef tongue	rye bread	yeast		lentil		tomato
	red bulgur	chicken		pea		
		liver				

SOURCE: *Beyond Cholesterol,* pages 133–141.
Note that this does *not* allow for the destruction of vitamin B-6 in cooking. Meat is almost always cooked, and the form of vitamin B-6 contained in meat is much more heat-sensitive than pyridoxine (the form found in plant foods). Thus, the true H-values of the meat products listed above would actually be even less than indicated by this table. Canning and freezing reduces vitamin B-6 content even further.

* The H-value is the ratio of vitamin B-6 to methionine found in the food, times 1000.

4. Obesity and diabetes are two other widely noted risk factors for coronary heart disease. It has been speculated that this has something to do with hyperinsulinism (too much insulin in the bloodstream), because this could in turn raise the level of fats in the bloodstream. Obesity, diabetes, and hyperinsulinism are all related to each other and to atherosclerosis.[17]

But these disorders are widely acknowledged to be diet-related. A diet high in meat and refined foods is the probable cause of much obesity and diabetes. Vegetarians suffer less from obesity; and both obesity and diabetes have been successfully treated by diets high in carbohydrates and low in fat.[18] The relationship of obesity and diabetes to heart disease lends further support to the theory that our Western diet, high in fat and low in fiber, is the factor most responsible for atherosclerosis.

5. It also appears to be true that high serum estrogen levels, in males, increase the risk of heart disease. In one early study, men who had suffered heart attacks were given estrogen with the hope of protecting them from heart disease. The rationale was that women suffered less from heart disease than men, and estrogen is a female hormone. But the experiment was ended prematurely and tragically when it was discovered that the subjects of this experiment were dying at a faster rate than expected. Years later, other investigators noticed that men who had increased serum estrogen derivatives were at increased risk for developing heart disease.[19]

But what are the implications of all this for diet? Vegetarian men have very low blood estrogen concentrations; they even excrete estrogens in their feces.[20] So this theory enhances, rather than displaces, the concept of the relationship of diet to atherosclerosis.

Nondietary Variables

There are three nondietary variables which are commonly said to have an influence on atherosclerosis: exercise, stress, and smoking. But what is the actual effect of these factors?

1. Exercise is closely identified with health in the popular mind; and exercise certainly makes one stronger. But does it help avert heart attacks? The answer is "yes," but the effects are much more limited than is commonly believed.

The beneficial effects of exercise are limited in several ways. In the first place, they do not last. When you stop exercising, the benefits of exercise stop also. A few years ago, a survey showed that professional athletes actually died earlier than the rest of the population: football players had a mean age at death of 57; baseball players, 64; and boxers, 61.[21] A second major complication is that too much exercise by someone who has advanced atherosclerosis may actually *trigger* a heart attack.[22]

But most importantly, the way in which exercise helps us is not by alleviating atherosclerosis, but rather by helping the body cope with atherosclerosis. A major immediate cause of heart attacks is fibrillation. This comes about when part of the heart is getting more oxygen than another part. Evenly oxygenated hearts—whether poorly or well oxygenated—do not, as a general rule, have the "oxygen differential" which can cause fibrillation and a heart attack. Exercise helps only by distributing oxygen more evenly throughout the heart, while not significantly altering the underlying atherosclerosis.[23]

So while exercise is beneficial to health under the proper conditions, its effect on atherosclerosis must be qualified significantly: the primary benefit is to postpone, rather than to prevent, the fatal complications of atherosclerosis.

2. Some have speculated that stress is a cause of heart disease. A whole theory of heart disease has evolved around the concept of a "type A" personality, meaning the kind of person who is busy, aggressive, and more susceptible to heart attacks than the "type B" personality, who is relaxed, sociable, and less susceptible to heart attacks.

This theory is counter-intuitive for several reasons. Why, for example, are the masses in poverty-ridden third world countries racked with war, social chaos, and famine somehow immune to the effects of stress? These countries have some of the lowest rates of heart disease and stroke.

But most importantly, it does not stack up with the evidence. Surely nothing is more stressful than to have your country torn by war and occupied by Nazis. Yet this is what happened to both Austria and Norway in the Second World War. In these countries, the death rate due to heart attacks and circulatory diseases actually decreased during wartime, when the "luxury" of meat consumption was greatly restricted. But when peace ensued, and the dietary habits of these persons returned to normal, the death rate for these diseases also returned to normal. The effects of stress, therefore, must be quite marginal in relation to factors such as diet.

3. Smoking is the one nondietary risk factor for atherosclerosis which is genuinely important. Persons who smoke have a greater risk of developing severe atherosclerosis than do nonsmokers.[24]

However, some sense of perspective must be maintained when evaluating the relative importance of smoking in comparison with dietary factors. The Adventist health study cited above showed that nonsmoking meat-eaters, while at less of a risk for heart disease than the rest of the population, still had an expected mortality from coronary heart disease four times greater than that of nonsmoking total vegetarians. Thus, meat would seem to be more significant in heart disease than smoking.

Conclusions

Diet is the factor most responsible for atherosclerosis; and meat consumption is the most critical dietary variable. Nondietary factors such as lack of exercise, stress, and smoking may have some influence; but except for smoking, their impact is at best quite marginal in relation to the effect of diet.

A wide variety of "risk factors" and theories about them have been suggested. Debate is continuing over the precise mechanisms involved in the development of this disease. But regardless of interpretation, vegetarians have less of *all* of these risk factors. Vegetarians have lower intake of cholesterol; lower intake of saturated fat; lower serum cholesterol levels; lower blood pressure; for males, lower estrogen levels; lower intake of methionine and higher of vitamin B-6; and lower incidence of obesity.

And finally, vegetarians themselves have a greatly reduced chance of dying from the results of atherosclerosis. A vegetarian diet would therefore greatly reduce, prevent, or even reverse the progress of atherosclerosis.

7
Cancer

Cancer is rivaled only by heart disease as a cause of death in the Western countries. What causes cancer? Countless hours of research and untold millions of dollars have been thrown into the search for answers to this question. But dietary factors are by far the most important of all the different factors associated with the many different forms of cancer. One recent authoritative review states: "At present, we have overwhelming evidence of remarkable variations in the overall cancer incidence and of the incidence of specific types between countries and within countries. None of the risk factors for cancer is probably more significant than diet and nutrition."[1]

A scientific committee of the National Research Council recently echoed these scientific discoveries, urging drastic changes in the national diet. "The evidence reviewed by the committee," they conclude, "suggests that cancers of most major sites are influenced by dietary patterns." They go on to call for a reduction in the consumption of fatty foods, and corresponding increases in the consumption of vegetables, whole grains, and fruits.[2]

Diet is not the only factor responsible for cancer, of course. Everyone is familiar with the evidence that smoking is a major cause of lung cancer. But diets high in fat and protein and low in fiber have been linked to the commonest cancers in the Western world: colon cancer, breast cancer, prostate cancer, and many others. Since meat contains virtually nothing but fat and protein and has no fiber, the implications for diet are obvious.

The Nature of Cancer

The term "cancer" refers to a malignant tumor. A tumor is a group of cells which grows haphazardly, out of the control of the rest of the body. A benign tumor remains in its place of origin and does not invade other tissues. A malignant tumor—i.e., a cancer—has the capacity to invade other tissues. Some of the cells of a malignant tumor may become detached from the main tumor mass and be carried off to a distant part of the body, there starting a new colony of cancer cells. This is called a *metastasis*. If a malignant tumor has metastasized before it is detected and treated, further treatment or a cure is considered much more difficult, if not impossible. Fortunately, most tumors are not cancerous—some have referred to benign tumors as a "normal" disease.

Cancer originates in a breakdown in the cell-regulation process. There is a means by which cells are informed when they need to grow and reproduce, and when they should not grow. In cancer cells, though, a cell mutation arises which causes the cell-regulation mechanism to break down. The body can't "communicate" with cancer cells. They multiply indiscriminately, without regard to the needs of the surrounding tissues.

Many different substances have been isolated as possible or actual carcinogens—tumor-initiating agents. Carcinogens appear to operate by attacking the DNA molecule. The cancer process is initiated through inadequate repair, misrepair, or damage to DNA. However, there is a difference between the appearance of a tumor, even a malignant tumor, and a cancer in the clinical sense. Carcinogens are sometimes referred to as cancer-causing agents, and this is roughly correct in the sense that carcinogens can initiate tumors. But tumor-*promoting* agents may actually be more significant, in the final analysis, in causing the appearance of diagnosable cancer.

In the absence of tumor-promoting agents, some cancers disappear spontaneously or never get started at all. So the question "What causes cancer?" implies at least two other questions as well: "What initiates cancer?" and "What promotes cancer?" For in many cases, if not most, without tumor promotion there may be no cancer in the diagnosable sense at all.

As with atherosclerosis, our knowledge of the exact mechanisms by which cancer operates is imperfect. There is disagreement over precisely which factors are the most important. There is little doubt, on the other hand, about the ultimate causes of most of the cancers which are so common in the Western world. These causes are dietary; specifically, diets high in fat and protein and low in fiber—meat-oriented diets.

Causes of Cancer

Cancer is not a monolithic phenomenon; proven risk factors for one kind of cancer may be entirely irrelevant to another. Different types of cancer are generally classified according to the organ, or cell type, in which the cancer originated. Though the causes of cancer vary, it is not primarily an inherited disease or a random fact of life. It has been estimated that from 80% to 90% of all cancers are environmental in origin[3]—whether these factors are chemicals such as asbestos, or "bad habits" such as smoking, alcohol consumption, and meat consumption.

This may surprise many who are under the impression that the causes of cancer are very mysterious, or that "everything causes cancer." The environmental causes of cancer are surprisingly well defined, even when we lack the precise knowledge of how these causes operate. The evidence for this is the wide variation in rates of cancer throughout the world.

Stomach cancer, for example, is becoming quite rate in the United States, though it was once much more common. On the other hand, colon cancer, breast cancer, and prostate cancer are much more prevalent in the United States and other Western countries where high levels of meat consumption are common.

Heredity can be largely ruled out as a cause of cancer. When a person migrates from one area of the world to another, that person takes on the risk of getting whatever form of cancer is associated with the new area. Japanese who move to the United States have roughly the same risk of getting colon cancer as everyone else in the United States—not the lower risk that Japanese living in Japan have. The same has been found to be true for the other common kinds of cancer.[4] Thus, it is extremely unlikely that cancer is due to heredity or some other random, uncontrollable fact of life. These migration studies, as they have been called, have been critical in our understanding of cancer.

Dietary factors are not the only environmental problems that increase the incidence of cancer. Tobacco smoking is strongly related to lung cancer, for example. But dietary factors appear to be by far the most important—affecting even the smoker's chances of getting lung cancer. Cancers related to diet fall into two broad groups: those cancers related to dietary deficiencies, and those cancers related to dietary excesses. The "deficiency" cancers include cancer of the stomach and cancer of the liver, both of which are relatively rare in the United States. Epidemiological studies have suggested that these cancers are linked to a lack of fresh fruit and vegetables in the diet. The "excess" cancers include many of the cancers common in the Western world—cancer of the colon, breast, prostate, ovary, testis, pancreas, uterine corpus, and probably many others besides. These are, in effect, the "cancers of civilization."

There is a lot of talk about cancer being caused by such things as environmental pollution, chemicals or additives in food, radioactive fallout, automobiles, or television. Aren't these things also part of the Western way of life? But the evidence does not support the idea that any of these are involved in cancer in any major way. With the exception of lung cancer, most cancers have been relatively stable in the United States for the past 30 to 50 years, but the use of pesticides, additives, automobiles, television, etc., has gone up dramatically since World War II. If these things cause cancer, then we should be seeing equally dramatic rises in cancer rates—but we haven't.[5] Moreover, specific studies have failed to link increased use of pesticides or additives to increased cancer rates in the Western world.[6] This doesn't mean that we should be complacent or careless about pesticides or additives. It does mean that there is no demonstrated massive effect of such chemicals on cancer incidence, and that any such effect must be quite trivial when compared to the effects of diet on cancer.

Alone of all the major cancers, lung cancer *has* risen sharply since World War II. But this is clearly related to the rise of cigarette smoking. The cancer-causing potential of pollution, TV, automobiles, and the rest, therefore, seems quite doubtful.

Generalized Effects of Nutrition on Cancer

One of the first to investigate the connection between diet and cancer was Dr. Max Gerson.[7] As far back as the 1920s and 1930s, Gerson advocated an "anti-cancer" diet for the treatment of cancer. This diet prohibited meat, fish, eggs, butter, fatty foods, protein foods, alcohol, and tobacco. He treated his patients with fruit and vegetable juices, and a soup made from various vegetables. He also advocated a series of injections from liver extracts.

If this sounds a bit peculiar to us today, it *certainly* sounded peculiar to Gerson's contemporaries. Many regarded him as quack, or little better than one. But Gerson seemed to be on to something, because in many cases his treatment worked. He told a Senate subcommittee that "beginning cancers are easy to treat"[8] and estimated that even of the most hopeless cancer cases, he could save perhaps 30%. Gerson believed that the root cause of the cancer problem was the Western diet. He compiled extensive documentation on fifty of his patients, the authenticity of which has not been challenged.

Gerson was not the only early cancer researcher to suggest a general relationship between nutrition and all kinds of cancers. They were all ignored by established medical scientists until fairly recently. They were not always right, but as a consequence of their concerns, substantial evidence has accumulated that nutrition has several generalized effects on cancer:

- Increasing caloric intake in laboratory animals makes them more susceptible to tumors; and likewise restriction of caloric intake inhibits the incidence of tumors.[9]
- Obese mice suffer from many more tumors than mice of normal weight.[10] Likewise, obese humans have a much greater chance of getting or dying from cancer than nonobese humans.[11]
- While the results of experiments on laboratory animals placed on high protein diets vary, such diets do seem to increase the likelihood of certain kinds of tumors,[12] and to increase the likelihood that a developing tumor will be malignant.[13]

- Laboratory animals on high-fat diet have a greater risk of developing several different kinds of cancers.[14]
- A bad diet may have a tumor-promoting effect on lung cancer. While smoking is generally acknowledged to be an almost essential ingredient for lung cancer, smokers with high serum cholesterol levels suffer lung cancer seven times more frequently than smokers with low serum cholesterol levels.[15] Other studies suggest that smokers who eat greater amounts of plant foods, especially dark green leafy vegetables, carrots, and other plant foods high in vitamin A, have a lower incidence of lung cancer than smokers who eat less of these foods.[16]

This data indicates a prima facie case for the role of diet in cancer. A diet high in total calories, high in fat, high in protein, which produces obesity, and which is low in plant foods containing vitamin A, seems to increase one's chances of developing cancer. Diets low in fat and protein, which do not promote obesity, which are not excessively high in calories, and which are high in dark green leafy vegetables, carrots, or other foods containing vitamin A, seem to offer some sort of protection against cancer.

There is even more impressive evidence linking diet to certain specific types of cancer. The involvement of nutrition in the more common types of cancer is now being actively investigated. The less common types of cancer will undoubtedly receive their share of attention as time goes on. In most of these "cancers of civilization," one or more of three factors has a prominent role: too much fat in the diet, too much protein, and not enough fiber.

Colon Cancer

Strong correlations between colon cancer mortality and the consumption of both fat and animal protein exist. There is also much evidence that lack of fiber is an important factor. Colon cancer is the most common cancer in the United States today. Evidence points to meat consumption as its chief cause.

Fat's role in producing colon tumors in laboratory animals has been thoroughly investigated. Fat promotes, rather than initiates, colon tumors in these animals, with devastating effect.[17]

High-fat diets also produce an increased secretion of bile acids, and bile acids—by themselves—have the same tumor-promoting effect on laboratory animals that fat does.[18] Experiments on humans have also shown that high-fat diets increase bile-acid secretion.[19] So the role of fat in colon cancer appears to be fairly well established.

Protein intake is also highly correlated with colon cancer. Extracts from the charred surface of fish and beef contain mutagens—substances which increase the probability of cell mutation.[20] Certain studies on laboratory animals following high-protein diets strongly suggest that protein has a tumor-promoting effect

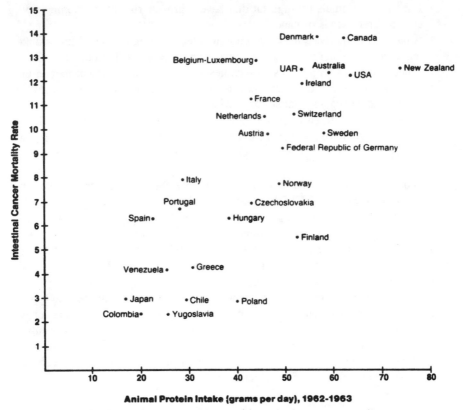

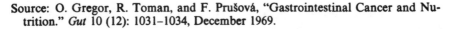

Figure 2. Animal protein consumption and intestinal cancer mortality.

Source: O. Gregor, R. Toman, and F. Prušová, "Gastrointestinal Cancer and Nutrition." *Gut* 10 (12): 1031–1034, December 1969.

on colon cancer.[21] These animals developed larger and more numerous tumors and high concentrations of fecal ammonia. Studies on human volunteers also show that large quantities of meat protein greatly increase fecal ammonia concentrations, though what this might have to do with colon cancer has never been resolved.[22]

Yet another critical factor in the development of colon cancer is lack of fiber. Several experiments on laboratory animals have shown that fiber has a preventative effect on colon cancer.[23] This is probably because the fiber protects the colon from carcinogens or tumor-promoting substances in the digestive system.

There are unresolved issues here. But the epidemiological evidence and the evidence relating to laboratory animals seem to indicate that high levels of meat consumption are a major cause of colon cancer.

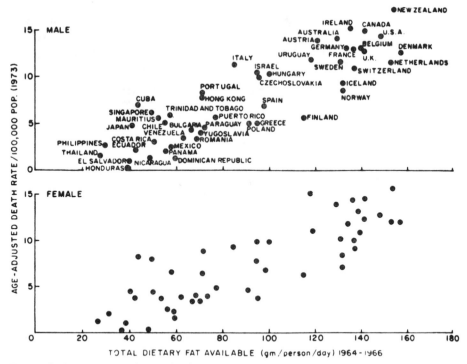

Figure 3. Fat consumption and colon cancer mortality.

Source: K. K. Carroll and H. T. Khor, *Progress in Biochemical Pharmacology* 10: 308, 1975. Cited in B. S. Reddy, et al.: "Nutrition and Its Relationship to Cancer," *Advances in Cancer Research* 32: 237, 1980.

Breast Cancer

Breast cancer, the most common form of fatal cancer in women in the United States and many other Western countries, has received special attention from researchers. Like colon cancer, it is highly correlated with dietary variables, most notably fat. The leading theory is that fat stimulates the release of prolactin, an enzyme which regulates lipid metabolism and lactation in women.

Prolactin's role in mammary cancer in laboratory animals is well established. Laboratory animals on high-fat diets have higher prolactin levels and more mammary tumors. Interestingly enough, when a high-fat diet is combined with an antiprolactin drug (to negate the diet's effect on prolactin secretion), the incidence of mammary tumors returns to its normal level.[24]

There is more doubt about prolactin's role in humans. Some researchers have reported little or no difference between prolactin levels in women in high-risk countries and low-risk countries, or in women with breast cancer and in healthy women.[25] Others report elevated levels of prolactin in metastatic breast tumor

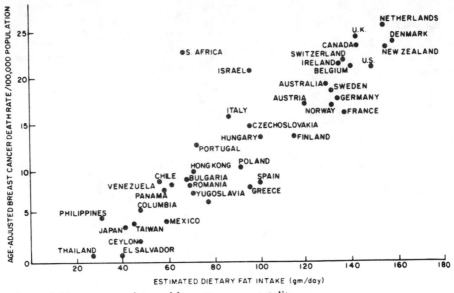

Figure 4. Fat consumption and breast cancer mortality.

Source: K. K. Carroll and H. T. Khor, *Progress in Biochemical Pharmacology* 10: 308, 1975. Cited in B. S. Reddy, et al.: "Nutrition and Its Relationship to Cancer," *Advances in Cancer Research* 32: 237, 1980.

patients and in those with a family history of breast cancer, and a greater pituitary reserve of prolactin in advanced breast cancer patients. Chronic users of reserpine, an antihypertensive which stimulates prolactin secretion, are in a two- to six-fold increased risk group.[26]

This evidence is suggestive but hardly conclusive. Part of the problem with these contradictory reports may be that prolactin secretion varies widely depending on the time of day it is measured. It is possible, for example, that much prolactin secretion takes place in the middle of the night during sleep, when it's not likely to be measured.

In one experiment, four volunteers were put on a control diet and then switched to a vegetarian diet. The vegetarian diet had 33% of calories as fat, as opposed to 40% on the control diet. This might seem like a small difference, but the results were highly significant. Prolactin release began to decline an hour earlier on the vegetarian diet, and was only half of what it was on the control diet at 5 A.M. (see Figure 5). Peak levels of prolactin secretion occurred at about 4 or 5 in the morning.[27]

Meat consumption is almost certainly a significant factor in breast cancer, because of the high-fat content of any diet which emphasizes meat or animal products.

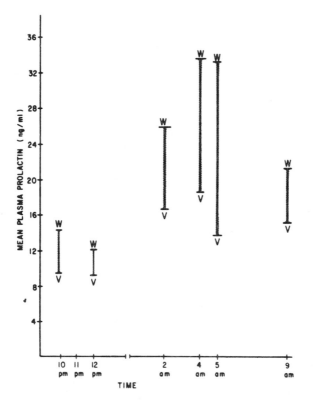

Figure 5. Prolactin secretion on a Western and a vegetarian diet. Bars represent the difference between the mean plasma prolactin concentrations in four healthy premenopausal women after two months on a Western diet (W) and after two months on a vegetarian diet (V).

Source: B. S. Reddy, et al.: "Nutrition and Its Relationship to Cancer," *Advances in Cancer Research* 32: 237, 1980.

Other Cancers

Other cancers in which diet and nutrition may play an important role have been investigated to a lesser degree.

Prostate cancer is the third most common form of fatal cancer in men in the United States. Like breast cancer and colon cancer, it is highly correlated with total fat consumption. Autopsy studies have shown that the incidence of prostate cancer is high in those areas where fat consumption and breast cancer are also high. Prostate cancer affects up to one fourth of all men in Western countries by the time they reach old age.[28]

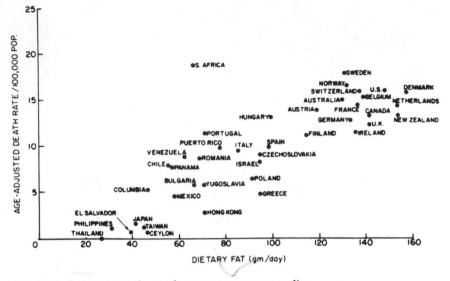

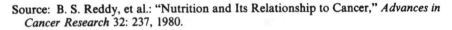

Figure 6. Fat consumption and prostate cancer mortality.

Source: B. S. Reddy, et al.: "Nutrition and Its Relationship to Cancer," *Advances in Cancer Research* 32: 237, 1980.

Some cancers appear to be related to nutritional deficiencies. Stomach cancer, increasingly rare in the United States as already noted, appears to be related to a lack of fresh fruits and vegetables. Cancer of the esophagus is related to alcohol and tobacco in Western Europe, but is related to lack of fruit and raw vegetables in Central Asia, where there are frequently deficiencies of vitamin A and riboflavin. Cancer of the liver also appears to be associated with nutritional deficiencies.[29]

Such variables as fat, animal protein, and sugar consumption have been correlated with such cancers as cancer of the pancreas, ovarian cancer, Hodgkin's disease, leukemia, and lymphosarcoma.[30] Bladder cancer is most strongly associated with animal protein consumption in incidence, and with coffee consumption in mortality.[31] Smokers who have high serum cholesterol levels or low intakes of plant foods which contain vitamin A greatly increase their chances of getting lung cancer.

Conclusions

The effect of diet on cancer deserves more attention than most people have been giving it. The most prevalent cancers in the United States are closely related to a diet having lots of fat, lots of protein, and very little fiber. Meat consists exclusively of fat and protein, and contains no fiber. These facts speak for themselves.

8
Various Other Degenerative Diseases

While atherosclerosis and cancer are the leading causes of death among the degenerative diseases today, they are by no means the only troubles brought on by a Western diet. In fact, a whole family of such diseases can be linked to meat consumption. In this chapter we will glance at a few of the more common ones.

Obesity

There is probably no affliction which people in Western countries are more concerned about than obesity—commonly referred to as "being fat." Books on dieting are almost guaranteed best sellers. Unfortunately, this barrage of commentary has made only a marginal dent in the actual occurrence of obesity.

What causes obesity? Obviously, given the laws of conservation of energy, the obese must be taking in more calories than they use, they are overeating. But what causes overeating? This is the critical question.

We don't know exactly why, but low-fiber foods make it easy to overeat, while high-fiber foods make weight control easier. Subjects in one experiment who ate refined foods consumed substantially more than subjects who ate a high-fiber unrefined diet. On the unrefined diet, persons actually lost weight and reduced their energy intake by 22%; but they were not aware of their lower energy intake and did not complain of being hungry.[1]

Several reasons have been suggested as to why low fiber, high fat, high protein foods might cause overeating. To begin with, high fat foods have a greater density of calories per unit weight of food; fats are over twice as "dense" in calories as are carbohydrates or proteins. Secondly, foods which are low in fiber require less chewing. Chewing may in itself contribute to a subjective feeling of being satiated. Fiber rich foods which require more chewing have been shown to leave subjects feeling less hungry than low-fiber foods containing the same number of calories.[2]

The third possibility is that low-fiber foods overstimulate insulin output, thus causing "hyperinsulinism." Persons who are obese typically suffer from hyperinsulinism.[3] Normally, insulin is secreted by the pancreas to metabolize glucose as energy for body tissues. But insulin has other far-reaching metabolic effects as well, including stimulating the production of fats by the liver and the creation of fatty tissue.[4]

Too much insulin in the bloodstream could lead to rapid metabolization of glucose and thus low blood sugar. Low blood sugar, in turn, might cause a tired, hungry feeling which would encourage overeating—and at the same time stimulate the bodily processes which turn this extra food into fat. Sugar and protein, especially in combination, are known to stimulate insulin output.[5] Fats block insulin action,[6] requiring the pancreas to secrete more insulin to achieve a given effect. So the relationship of diet to hyperinsulinism is very important.

Low-fiber foods may contribute to obesity for any number of reasons. But regardless of the explanation, meat consumption can only aggravate the problem of weight control.

We should expect, then, that weight loss for those suffering from obesity would be easier on a vegetarian diet. This is borne out by the evidence. The Pritikin diet, in fact, is nothing more than a diet which reduces consumption of meat, animal foods, refined foods, and sugar, and emphasizes whole plant foods. The Pritikin diet has been quite successful in enabling many people to lose weight.[7] Nathan Pritikin has stated that his diet, without the animal protein, would be the healthiest diet of all.[8] But if you take animal protein out of the Pritikin diet, then what do you have except a total vegetarian whole foods diet?

Pritikin is not alone in endorsing whole foods vegetarianism for weight loss. Dr. Jean Mayer, a former Harvard nutritionist, has warmly endorsed a vegetarian diet for weight loss, saying, "In becoming a vegetarian, you will eat a greater percentage of your calories from cereal grains, dried beans and peas, potatoes and pasta—the very foods most dieters avoid with zeal. And you will lose weight."[9]

Studies on vegetarians have repeatedly shown that vegetarians suffer less from obesity than the rest of the (non-vegetarian) population. One study found a sample of total vegetarians to weigh an average of 10 pounds less than the rest of the population.[10] Another study suggested that they weighed 30 pounds less.[11] Yet a third study found that a group of total vegetarians had 30% less body fat than the non-vegetarian population.[12] The Kempner rice diet, widely experimented with in the 40s and 50s and which consisted entirely of plant foods (namely, rice, with a vitamin and mineral supplement), has been repeatedly shown to result in substantial weight loss.[13]

We have excellent reasons to believe, then, that a vegetarian diet would further both the prevention of and the cure for obesity.

Diabetes

Diabetes is one of the leading causes of death in the United States. Some have claimed that if one counted all diabetes and diabetes-related deaths, this disease would surface as the third leading cause of death in America today.[14]

Diabetes is strongly linked to obesity. In fact, it has been suggested that the two disorders are merely different manifestations of a single metabolic problem. In diabetes, there is a relative *lack* of insulin, and therefore higher than normal levels of blood glucose. Sometimes this appears to be because the pancreas just isn't secreting enough insulin, but some diabetics actually have higher than normal insulin levels. Because of insulin resistance their insulin is unable to metabolize the glucose. Whatever the reason, this lack of *effective* insulin action leads to high blood sugar levels, the most characteristic symptom of diabetes.

Obesity, linked to oversupply of insulin, might appear to be the opposite of diabetes, linked to undersupply of insulin. But maturity-onset diabetes (the most common form of diabetes) only develops over many years. Chronic oversupply of insulin appears to lead to both insulin resistance and insulin exhaustion. Eventually the pancreas loses its ability to put out all that insulin year after year.[15] This theory is supported by the fact that after many years, the chronically obese typically develop diabetes or a semi-diabetic condition not quite serious enough to be labeled diabetes.[16] One researcher concludes, "It appears that a majority of grossly obese persons develop diabetes if obesity persists for more than thirty years."[17]

Would a vegetarian diet help treat, or help prevent, diabetes? Interestingly enough, much research on diabetes is now focusing on this very question. Diets high both in carbohydrates and fiber have had startling results in the treatment of diabetes: insulin resistance decreases, and dependence upon insulin therapy decreases or ceases altogether. Obviously, a high-carbohydrate, high-fiber diet will either be vegetarian or near vegetarian. In one remarkable study, 20 lean diabetics—all of whom were on insulin therapy—were put on a diet which had 70% of the calories as carbohydrates, and was high in fiber. After only 16 days, of the 10 patients who were getting less than 20 units of insulin per day, 9 were able to discontinue the use of insulin therapy altogether![18] Other studies have yielded the same remarkable results.[19]

Problems With Excessive Protein or Excessive Fat Consumption

There are more problems which are associated with excessive protein consumption, excessive fat consumption, or both. These include osteoporosis, kidney stones, glomerulonephritis, gallstones, gout, and rheumatoid arthritis.

Osteoporosis is a degenerative disease in which calcium is lost from the bones. The bones become more porous and brittle, and can thus break more easily. This is an especially difficult problem with older women. Several studies have shown that the body loses calcium on high protein diets, no matter how much calcium is consumed.[20] In one such study, subjects were given 36 grams of nitrogen per day—enough to synthesize many times the amount of protein needed daily. The result was a loss of bone tissue equivalent to about 4% of skeletal mass per year. Of course, most people, even meat eaters, do not get this much protein; but a loss of even 1% of skeletal mass per year would produce severe osteoporosis by age 60. "Osteoporosis," the study concludes, "would seem to be an inevitable outcomes of a high-protein diet." High-protein diets are damaging because they cause the body to "borrow" calcium from the bones as a buffering agent. Vegetarians have lower levels of calcium in their bloodstream; vegetarians also have a larger bone mass than do nonvegetarians.[21]

This does not mean, however, that all of the calcium taken from the bones necessarily leaves the body. A study of released hospital patients in Great Britain showed a marked correspondence between kidney stones and consumption of animal protein, but showed no such correspondence between kidney stones and dietary calcium, phosphorus, or refined carbohydrates.[22] This suggests the rather grim possibility that a high-protein diet might not only contribute to a loss of calcium from the bones, but also to the formation of calcium stones in the kidneys.

This is unfortunately not the end of the problems caused by excessive protein consumption. Over a period of years, excessive protein leads to progressive deterioration of kidney function. This can take the form of glomerulonephritis, which if it continues can destroy kidney function entirely. If this happens, the only alternatives will be a kidney transplant or a dialysis machine. Neither of these are particularly pleasant. Low-protein diets have been quite effective in treating persons with kidney damage.[23]

Gallstones are a problem related to a high-fat diet. Gallstones are composed mostly of cholesterol and sometimes calcium. The pattern of gallstone incidence generally follows that of the other degenerative diseases linked to high-fat diets: obese people and those with high serum triglycerides or diabetes are all more likely to develop gallstones than are healthy members of the population.[24]

Ironically, unsaturated fats appear to be a major cause of cholesterol gallstones. While polyunsaturated fats have the favorable effect of lowering blood cholesterol levels, that cholesterol has to go somewhere, and the body gets rid of cholesterol in the bile secreted by the liver. So increased consumption of polyunsaturated fatty acids—a by-product of the "anticholesterol campaign"—is associated with an increase in the incidence of gallstones.[25] To make matters worse, cholesterol gallstones are one of the major risks factors for biliary tract cancer.[26]

Gout (gouty arthritis) is a notorious disease of the rich, a function of their "rich" diet. The biggest risk factor for developing gout is high levels of serum uric acid. This, in turn, is associated with high levels of serum triglycerides and serum cholesterol—the familiar components of a high-fat diet.[27] The Framingham study disclosed a very close correlation between serum uric acid, serum cholesterol levels, serum triglyceride levels, and gout.[28] So the relationship between a high-fat diet and gout is clear. Gout is also strongly related to a diet high in protein and high in purines. Most foods which are high in protein are also high in purines as well.

Rheumatoid arthritis may also be related to a high-fat diet. This type of arthritis is quite common in Western societies. But in a rural black South African community, which lacked the "privilege" of a Western meat-oriented diet, a study failed to disclose a single case of active rheumatoid arthritis in the entire population of 801 persons.[29] A second study in South Africa comparing a rural black community with an urban black community showed that rheumatoid arthritis afflicted 0.87% in the rural area and 3.30% in the urban area. This suggests that as populations come closer to a Western style of living, the incidence of rheumatoid arthritis increases.

Problems Associated with Lack of Fiber

Several degenerative diseases are connected with lack of fiber in the diet. Diverticulosis, hemorrhoids, and appendicitis are all worth mentioning in this regard.

Diverticulosis of the colon is almost certainly connected with lack of fiber in the diet. This condition comes about when little pouches or sacs—diverticula—protrude from the wall of the colon. If these diverticula become inflamed, diverticulosis becomes diverticulitis, which can be quite painful. Diverticulosis is quite common in most Western communities: 10% of those over the age of 40 and one third of those over the age of 70 have evidence of this disease. Diverticulosis has only become a major problem in the last 70 years or so, paralleling the rise of fiber-free foods in the food economy.[31] Repeated and chronic constipation is the probable cause of this condition. If one is chronically constipated,

Table 9. Mean weight of stools and transit time in different populations.

Subject	Country	Race	Type of Diet	Mean Transit Time (hours)	Mean Weight of Stools (grams)
Naval enlisted men and wives	U. K.	White	Refined	83.4	104
Students	South Africa	White	Refined	48.0	173
Nurses	South Africa	Indian	Mixed	44.0	155
Urban School-children	South Africa	African	Mixed	45.2	165
Vegetarians	U. K.	White	Mixed	42.4	225
Rural School-children	South Africa	African	Unrefined	33.5	275
Rural villagers	Uganda	African	Unrefined	35.7	470

SOURCE: D. P. Burkitt, et al, *The Lancet* 2:1408, 1972.

the colon must work very hard to propel the hard stools through the colon. At some point, dealing with an abnormally hard stool, part of the mucous membrane is forced through the muscular coating of the colon, creating a pouch—the diverticulum.

Dr. Denis Burkitt, in his studies of the relationship between fiber and disease, attempted to correlate stool size with diet. He came up with some interesting, if predictable, results (see Table 9). In general, the more "civilized" the diet, the smaller the size of the stools and the longer their transit time.

A high-fiber diet is quite effective in treating the painful symptoms of diverticulitis. In one study, 70 patients with diverticulitis were advised to eat high-fiber foods such as whole wheat and bran. Before the high-fiber diet, these 70 patients had manifested a total of 171 different symptoms. After the high-fiber diet, 88% of these symptoms were either relieved or eliminated (36% relieved, 52% eliminated). The number of patients taking laxatives was reduced from 49 to 7. Lack of fiber is undoubtedly a major problem in the development of diverticulosis.[32]

Hemorrhoids, painful swellings of blood vessels in the region of the anus, are in all likelihood brought about by years of constipation. Since lack of fiber can cause constipation, it is quite likely that lack of fiber is responsible for many, if not most, cases of hemorrhoids. Live diverticulosis, hemorrhoids are found predominantly among people who follow Western diets. Hemorrhoids are frequently found in South African whites, but rarely found in South African blacks.[33]

In most cases, appendicitis is caused by a fecalith which obstructs the appendix. A fecalith is a small concretion of feces. A diet which produces small, compact feces encourages fecalith formation. Appendicitis is still very rare in rural Africa, but is becoming less rare in those areas most affected by Western customs as time passes. In the Sudan, appendectomy comprised less than 1% of all major surgical operations during 1928-1931; but during 1958-1961, this had risen to 13.4%. In the United States and England, appendectomies are the most frequent emergency operations.[34]

Conclusions

Actually, none of these is a "minor" disease. All are widespread and cause a lot of physical suffering. Broken bones, arthritis, kidney stones, gallstones—many accept these things as inevitable parts of getting old. They need not do so. These afflictions are all largely brought about by a diet too high in fat and protein, and too low in fiber. A vegetarian diet—especially a total vegetarian whole foods diet—is low in fat and protein, and high in fiber, and would greatly reduce the incidence of all of these diseases.

II
VEGETARIAN
ECOLOGY

9
Environment and Food

Hardly a single environmental problem in the world today is unrelated to meat consumption. Water pollution, soil erosion, energy shortages, the destruction of forests—all of these problems and others are part of the environmental costs of meat in our diet. Our urbanized, literate society, which picks up food in neat little packages in supermarkets, has been shielded from the grim realities of how food reaches the table. All we have been exposed to is the price tag.

Meat consumption on the American scale can never be the diet of more than a small minority of the world's people. The reasons for this are not economic, technical, or social—they are ecological; the world simply does not have the resources to sustain an American-style diet on a global level.

Livestock agriculture requires a vastly greater investment of natural resources than plant food agriculture—for the same nutritional return, or less. Land, energy, and water requirements for livestock agriculture range anywhere from 10 to 1000 times greater than those necessary to produce an equivalent amount of plant foods. And livestock agriculture does not merely *use* these resources, it *depletes* them. This is a matter of historical record. Most of the world's soil erosion, groundwater depletion, and deforestation—factors now threatening the very basis of our food system—are the result of this particularly destructive form of food production.

The United States and a few other "privileged" countries can enjoy a diet high in meat year after year only because of extraordinarily abundant natural resources and the most advanced agricultural technology in the world. Yet such is the pressure which livestock agriculture places on natural resources that even the United States will not be able to continue its diet indefinitely. Already the agricultural system is beginning to crack under the strain. The question is not whether the rest of the world can be brought up to the United States' destructive standard of living; rather, will the stress caused by an agriculture which provides even a fraction of the world with meat three times a day eventually prove the undoing of our society, our culture, and our way of life?

Consequences of Livestock Agriculture

Livestock agriculture dwarfs all other land uses in the United States. Over 90% of all agricultural land—and more than half the *total* land area of the United States—is devoted to the production of animal products. Well over two thirds of the 444 million acres of cropland now being used for any purposes are being used for livestock agriculture. To that we can add the 950 million acres or so now being used for grazing of livestock animals. (See Chapter 10, "Land Use.")

In spite of the shocking amount of abuse to which the land has been subjected, there will probably be no land shortage in the United States in the next ten to twenty years. There is still a substantial cropland reserve—unused land which could be converted for use as cropland if the need arose. This 111-million-acre reserve constitutes a formidable cushion against agricultural uncertainties.

But this does not mean land use in agriculture will not be an issue in the United States during the next ten to twenty years. Several alarming trends are combining to cut into our cropland reserve. Among these are:

- Soil erosion. More than 5 billion tons of topsoil are eroded each year in the United States, almost all of it the result of livestock agriculture. (See below, Chapter 14, "Soil Erosion.") It is difficult to quantify exactly how many acres of land are lost due to soil erosion, because land which is considerably eroded can sometimes still be used. It would appear, though, that the equivalent of about 4 inches of topsoil from 4 million acres of cropland are being eroded each year—not counting the additional erosion from grazing land. This is bound to affect either the productivity of the land, or the number of acres of land available for agriculture, sooner or later.
- Demands for wood. The demand for wood products is increasing in the United States, as is the United States' dependence on foreign imports for wood supplies. Amazingly enough, millions of acres of forest land are being converted to grazing land each year. Meanwhile, the very countries from which the United States imports wood are experiencing drastic deforestation.
- Decreasing energy supplies. American agriculture is tremendously energy-intensive, using more fossil fuel energy than it produces in food energy. The energy input to the food system has dramatically increased in the last 50 years, and now accounts for an estimated 16.5% of the total energy budget. (See Chapter 13, "Energy.") Plant food agriculture, of course, is far less energy-intensive than livestock agriculture.

- Urbanization. Cities tend to spring up on or near fertile agricultural land, and urbanization is today making serious inroads into agricultural land in the United States. An estimated 3 millions acres of land, most of it cropland or potential cropland, are converted for urban uses each year. And for each acre lost directly to urban uses, another acre is lost indirectly, as a consequence of "buckshot urbanization"—agricultural land which has been surrounded by nonagricultural land and taken out of production long before it is physically converted for a nonagricultural use.[1]
- Disappearance of water resources. Much U.S. cropland, including some of the most productive, depends on irrigation. The threat of groundwater depletion becomes more real each day in many parts of the United States. Falling water tables have been a fact of life for years in the American West. Already, the increasing energy costs of pumping water out of the ground have forced many farmers to curtail irrigation. This can only seriously affect the amount of land eligible for agricultural use in the future.

Each of these problems is serious enough in itself, but when the effects of soil erosion, groundwater depletion, urbanization, etc., are all added together, we see that on the order of 5 million acres of cropland are being lost each year. Even a relatively simple analysis of land use conversion in the United States (see Table 10) shows that the problem is very serious. Already, some are predicting that we could utterly deplete our cropland reserve by the year 2000.[2] Some of the economic effects of this will be felt long before then; rising wood and energy costs are being felt already.

The Larger Perspective

The situation in the rest of the world is even more grim. Many developing nations are struggling to imitate the model of American agriculture, although in most cases these are the very nations which can least afford to do so. Soil

Table 10. Land use conversion in the United States, 1967–1975, on nonfederal land.

| | Net Gain from, or loss to ... (millions of acres) | | | | | |
	Pastureland and Rangeland	Urban and Water Build-up	Cropland	Forest Land	Other	TOTAL
Pastureland and Rangeland	——	−4	+21	+48	− 1	+64
Urban and Water Build-up	+ 4	——	+ 5	+ 7	+ 7	+23
Cropland	−21	−5	——	+ 3	− 7	−30
Forest Land	−48	−7	− 3	——	−12	−70
Other	+ 1	−7	+ 7	+12	——	+13

SOURCE: United States Department of Agriculture: *1980 Appraisal,* Part I, page 50.

erosion is worse in the developing world than in the United States. Urbanization is proceeding at an extremely rapid pace in the developing world—much faster than in the West.[3] Deforestation in the developing nations—where most of the world's remaining forests are—is such that at the present rate forests will be entirely cut by the year 2020. (See Chapter 11, "Forests.") Clearly, the world is on a collision course with reality, the end result of which cannot be postponed for more than a generation or two.

The United States did not invent livestock agriculture. Early Roman, Arab, African, Greek, and Indian civilizations all put a heavy emphasis on livestock at certain periods, and the social and ecological consequences of their actions are a matter of history. Many of the so-called cradles of civilization, so fertile in ancient times, are deserts today due to the destructive environmental effects of livestock agriculture. The only real difference between the land degradation taking place today and that which took place in ancient times is that now, because of increases in human population, it is much more difficult for humans to flee from the environmental consequences of their actions.

Ecology is the study of living organisms' relationships to each other and to their environment. The inefficiency and wastefulness of livestock agriculture is clearly an important ecological issue. The environmental effects of our meat-oriented food economy have a broad range of economic, social, and political consequences, all of which merit our close attention.

10
Land Use

Livestock agriculture is much less efficient in its use of land resources than plant food agriculture.

This is one of the oldest arguments in favor of vegetarianism. It plays a role in Plato's *Republic*. Percy Bysshe Shelley invoked the argument in his discussions of "natural diet." Mikkel Hindhede used the argument to help persuade Denmark to adopt a lacto-vegetarian diet when Denmark was blockaded by the Allies as a result of World War I. "If Central Europe had adopted a similar diet," he said, alluding to the disastrous German agricultural policies which emphasized meat production, "I doubt that anyone would have starved."[1]

This argument is not only ancient, but widely accepted—even by proponents of livestock agriculture. Some unenlightened souls question its relevance, but none deny its truth. To see why this is so, we need to examine the concept of a food chain.

Food Chains

Food relationships between organisms are referred to as a *food chain*. Each organism depends on plants or animals which it eats for its food supply, but it also depends on the organisms which its food depends on. For example lions eat zebras which eat grass. So lions depend not only on the supply of zebras, but (indirectly) on the supply of grass which nurtures the zebras. Ecologists call grass a primary producer of organic matter, since grass makes food directly from inorganic matter—soil, light, water, and air. Plants are at the bottom of all food chains. Next we have the primary consumers of organic matter (plant-eating creatures), secondary consumers (creatures eating plant-eating creatures), and so on. Organisms which are the same number of steps away from the bottom of the food chain are at the same *trophic level.*

In the real world things are frequently more complicated than the "lions/zebras/grass" food chain. Human beings, for example, eat plants, plant-eating animals (e.g. cows), and even animal-eating animals (e.g. fish)—thus existing at three different trophic levels.

However, there is an important point to be made here. Energy is lost with each successively higher trophic level. The energy the lion derives from eating zebras is only a fraction of that which the zebras derive from eating grass. The higher one goes on the food chain, the more available energy is lost. This is a consequence of the second law of thermodynamics—the law of entropy, whereby energy always flows from a more ordered, or useful, form, to a more random and therefore less useful form. This law is well exemplified by the actual distribution of organisms throughout our ecosystem. The higher on a food chain a species exists, the lower its total numbers or total biomass will be, because those animals eating higher on the food chain have a much smaller food supply than those eating lower on the food chain. There are a lot of plant-eating animals, but "big fierce animals"—like tigers and lions—are relatively rare.[2]

It is clear that humans have a larger potential supply of food energy (expressed in calories) in the plant kingdom than in the animal world, but can this be said of the various other nutrients humans require? Not surprisingly, the inefficiency of eating animals for food does not stop at energy. It is equally inefficient—and frequently even more inefficient—in terms of obtaining the other important nutrients. Any comparison of the nutritional returns of plant food agriculture and livestock agriculture supports this.

Per-acre comparisons concerning calories, protein, calcium, iron, vitamins A, B-1, B-2, and niacin can be found in Tables 11 and 12. These tables reveal such interesting facts as that an acre of land growing broccoli will produce 10 times the calories, protein, or niacin that beef production on the same land will produce. The land growing broccoli will also produce 24 times the iron, 80 times the vitamins B-1 and B-2, 650 times the calcium, and 9500 times the vitamin A.

The Issues

Given such statistics, there can be little doubt that livestock agriculture is vastly inefficient compared to plant food agriculture. No one disputes this. However, two lines of attack are commonly made on such comparisons: (1) They are irrelevant; for much land is not of suitable quality for plant food agriculture, while it can support livestock agriculture. (2) They are unimportant, for in fact there is no shortage of available land in the world today at all.

About the first argument. There are two ways of feeding animals: you can either grow crops on the land and feed them to animals, or you can graze the

Table 11. Per-acre nutritional returns from several plant and animal foods.

Nutritional Item	Oats	Broccoli	Pork	Milk	Poultry	Beef	(Units)
			One acre used as feed for . . .				
Calories	2760	1220	470	410	330	110	Thousand Kcal
Protein	110	137	29	22	54	14	Kilograms
Calcium	400	3900	13	750	20	6	grams
Iron	29000	42000	3760	246	2343	1760	milligrams
Vitamin A	0	9500	0	920	100	10	Thousand IU's
Thiamine	3700	3780	658	205	99	44	milligrams
Riboflavin	1300	8736	282	1066	429	110	milligrams
Niacin	20000	34440	5781	656	22000	3014	milligrams

SOURCES:

   (a) U.S. Department of Agriculture, *Agricultural Statistics 1979* (Washington, D.C.: U.S. Government Printing Office, 1979).
   (b) U.S. Department of Agriculture, *Nutritive Value of American Foods* (Washington, D.C.: U.S. Government Printing Office, 1975). USDA Handbook No. 456.
   (c) C. W. Cook, "Use of Rangelands for Future Meat Production," *Journal of Animal Science* 45 (6): 1476, December 1977.

NOTE: This assumes that an acre used as feed for animals yields 2.8 million Kcal.

animals on a patch of land, letting them forage for themselves. Per-acre comparisons are relevant if you feed crops grown on productive cropland to animals, but irrelevant in a grazing system. The big advantage of a grazing system is that it can utilize land which might be too rocky, steep, or infertile to be good cropland. Ruminant animals—cows, sheep, goats, and other animals which can digest grasses which would be totally useless to humans as food—are the animals usually used for grazing purposes.

About the second argument. In the United States, the government actually pays farmers *not* to grow crops. In spite of this, our bountiful harvests are driving prices so low that many farmers are going out of business. It has been estimated that less than half of the potential cropland in the world is actually

Table 12. Per-acre nutritional returns from several plant and animal foods, expressed as multiples of the returns from beef.

Nutritional Item	Oats	Broccoli	Pork	Milk	Poultry	Beef
Calories	25.4	11.0	4.3	3.7	3.0	1.0
Protein	7.9	9.8	2.0	1.6	3.9	1.0
Calcium	66.7	650.0	2.2	125.0	3.3	1.0
Iron	16.5	23.9	2.1	0.1	1.3	1.0
Vitamin A	0.0	9500.0	0.0	92.0	10.0	1.0
Thiamine	84.0	85.9	15.0	4.7	2.3	1.0
Riboflavin	11.8	79.4	2.6	9.7	3.9	1.0
Niacin	6.6	11.4	1.9	0.2	7.3	1.0

SOURCE: Table 11.

being farmed. So (it is argued), why shouldn't this extra land be utilized to give people the meat which they obviously want in their diet?

Both of these lines of attack—concerning the suitability of land and the availability of land—are very strong arguments in favor of livestock agriculture. Therefore, we should examine them very closely.

The Suitability of Land

Is some land suitable for grazing but not for crops? And does this mean that such land should be used for meat production? This argument has been repeated so often by the supporters of livestock agriculture—and by others who should know better—that it deserves a very close examination. It is open to four basic criticisms:

1. Using grasslands for livestock agriculture creates great environmental problems, which (at best) greatly limit its usefulness. Grazing systems require *much* more land than feedlot agriculture,* in which animals are simply given feed grown on cropland. Grazing systems have to be extensive in order to avoid the catastrophic consequences of severe overgrazing—which generally renders a piece of land unsuitable for *any* purpose.

   Overgrazing and the consequent soil erosion are extremely serious problems worldwide. By the most conservative estimates, 60% of all U.S. rangelands are overgrazed, with billions of tons of soil lost each year. Overgrazing has also been the greatest cause of man-made deserts. So serious are these problems that they will be considered in greater detail in Chapters 14 and 15.

2. Grazing cattle on land competes with numerous nonfood land uses, most significantly forests. In fact, the demand for grazing land is the single greatest cause of deforestation historically. The land suitability argument does not apply to forest land—almost any land suitable for grazing is suitable for growing trees. This may not have an immediate economic payoff, but it is ecologically desirable, as forests favorably affect climate, water resources, and soil resources. The ecological importance of forests is very great, and we will consider the problems which livestock agriculture has created for forest resources in greater detail in Chapter 11.

---

* On the order of 10 times more. The most productive rangelands produce about 14 pounds of cattle per acre;[3] about half of this, or 10,000 KCal, will wind up on the dinner table.

3. In addition to the environmental problems caused by grazing systems, there are economic problems as well. More and more farmers are turning to feedlot agriculture and "factory farms," where animals are fattened on feed grown on cropland. At present prices, grains are less expensive than forage resources. Cattle raised entirely or partially in feedlots yield a fattier and more palatable type of meat. Feedlot cattle can be brought to market faster than cattle which are only grazed.[4] Recent years have seen a dramatic rise in the number of cattle being raised in feedlots. In 1962, about 27,000 acres of land were being used as feedlots in the United States; by 1983, this is projected to have more than doubled, to 64,000—a pace which far exceeds either the increase in population or the demand for meat.[5]

4. Even if we grant grazing a role in a resource-efficient, ecologically stable agriculture, milk should be the end result, not beef. Milk provides over 50% of the protein and practically four times the calories of beef, per unit of forage resources from grazing. "When only forage is available, then egg, broiler and pork production are eliminated and only milk, beef, and lamb production are viable systems," state David and Marcia Pimentel, scientists and authors of *Food, Energy and Society.* "Of these three, milk production is the most efficient."[6]

An ecologically stable, resource-efficient system of grazing animals for human food could not be anything faintly resembling today's livestock agriculture. It would be a smaller, decentralized, less intensive system of animal husbandry devoted to milk production.

The Availability of Land

The second tack frequently taken by supporters of livestock agriculture is to argue that the inefficiency of livestock agriculture is unimportant because there is in fact no shortage of land—either in the West or throughout the rest of the world. "Shortages" relative to what kind of diet? If the Western diet is the standard of the necessary level of food consumption, the world was hopelessly short of land long ago.

The American way of life requires about 2 acres of cropland and 4.4 acres of grazing land per capita. (See Table 13. About 0.5 acres of cropland per capita can be attributed to exports, but the U.S. imports a lot of beef from Central and South America, too.) What if we tried to "raise" the entire world to our standard of living?

Our present world population of 4 billion implies a land requirement of 8 billion acres of cropland and 17.5 billion acres of grazing land. Only 3.7 billion acres of cropland and 7.5 billion acres of grassland pasture presently exist in the world, less than half the land needed.[7]

At first glance this total may not seem entirely out of reach. A widely cited United Nations Food and Agriculture Organization (FAO) report of a few years ago stated that only 45% of the potential arable land in Asia, Africa, and South America is currently cultivated.[8] This might be cause for some hope; it might

Table 13. Agricultural land use in the United States in 1977.
A. Selected crops and their use (in millions of acres)

Crop	Total acres planted	Total acres for feed	Total acres for export
Wheat	75.1	6.7	42.8
Rye	2.6	1.0	——
Corn	83.6	50.2	25.9
Oats	16.4	15.0	——
Barley	10.6	4.7	1.6
Sorghum	16.5	11.2	5.1
Soybeans	58.7	34.6	24.1
Hay	60.6	60.6	——
Vegetables	3.2	——	——
Fruits and Nuts	3.4	——	——
Cotton	13.3	——	——
Tobacco	1.0	——	——
Peanuts	1.5	——	——
Other crops	14.5	——	——
Total Cropland used for crops	360.0	185.9	99.5

B. Classification of agricultural land use (in millions of acres)

Type of Land Use	Total acreage	For livestock agriculture	For all other agriculture
Cropland for domestic crops	260.5	185.9	74.6
Cropland for export crops*	99.5	49.7	49.8
Cropland used only for pasture	83.0	83.0	0.0
CROPLAND TOTAL	444.0	318.6	124.4
Grassland Pasture	718.0	718.0	0.0
Forest Land Grazed†	246.0	246.0	0.0
GRAND TOTAL	1408.0	1282.6	124.4

SOURCE: U.S. Department of Agriculture, *Agricultural Statistics 1979* (Washington, D.C.: Government Printing Office, 1979). When in doubt, land use has been allocated to domestic use rather than exports, and to plant food agriculture rather than livestock agriculture.
* Assumes that 50% of all export acreage is for livestock feed. This is probably a conservative assumption.
† H. W. Anderson, M. D. Hoover, and K. G. Reinhart, *Forests and Water*, USDA Forest Service General Technical Report PSW-18/1976.

appear that the present cropland base of the world could someday be expanded to support a worldwide diet at least resembling that consumed in North America. But when we read the FAO's report more carefully, we find that its conclusions are qualified. Most of the land considered potentially arable in South America has low-quality soils and is very difficult to get to—factors making it "unavailable or not sufficiently attractive for development in the near future."[9] Moreover, any such expansion would almost certainly be at the expense of the already rapidly depleting forest areas.

The same is true of Africa, where nonforested areas are already experiencing severe competition between grazing and cultivation. In Asia, the Far East, the Near East, and northern Africa, most of the potentially arable land already is under cultivation. So we see that bringing additional land under cultivation is terribly difficult.

The fact is, most of the easily available land has already been cultivated, and much of the uncultivated remainder could only be brought into cultivation by clearing forest areas, which should be protected. The best land is already taken; why would people cultivate the worst land first? Since a lot of current cropland is being irrigated or treated with fertilizers and pesticides in order to coax higher yields out of it—or to coax anything at all out of it—common sense would suggest that the remaining land would only be cultivated with similar or greater difficulties.

And quantity of land is only the beginning of the problem. We have not taken into consideration the very great differences in yields. Wheat and corn yields are much higher in the United States and other Western countries than in the Soviet Union, Asia, and Africa.[10] The "Green Revolution," high-yielding crop varieties, and advanced agricultural techniques require a great deal of supporting technology and natural resources which only an industrialized society can provide, or even afford: tractors, irrigation, fertilizers, and so on.

But let us suppose that all these difficulties were overcome. Let us suppose that all this additional land were brought into production, and all the technology and fertilizers were provided to bring crop yields up to Western standards. Even granting these highly unlikely assumptions, such an agricultural system could hardly survive more than a few years. Energy consumption would skyrocket, more than tripling in the less developed countries.

In fact, energy increases would be even more dramatic than this. Because much of the potentially arable land is of relatively low quality, it would require more energy-intensive fertilizers and more energy-intensive irrigation systems than the relatively fertile American soils. Irrigated land presently comprises only 15% of the world's total cropland; but of the new land at least 50% would have to be irrigated.[11] So the demand for water supplies, already overwhelming in much of the world, would increase dramatically.

Nor can fish provide any help here. There are signs that the fishing industry (which is quite energy-intensive) has already overfished the oceans in several areas. And fish could never play a major role in the world's diet anyway: the entire global fish catch of the world, if divided among all the world's inhabitants, would amount to only a few *ounces* of fish per person per *week*.[12]

In short, the idea of providing the entire world with a Western diet is quite silly. But, someone might ask, is the amount of available land at least sufficient to satisfy today's demands for meat—which provides only a fraction of the population with a Western-style diet? A few simple statistics can show how futile even this would be.

If the population triples in the next 100 years, that would mean that meat production would have to triple as well. Instead of 3.7 billion acres of cropland and 7.5 billion acres of grazing land, we would require 11.1 billion acres of cropland and 22.5 billion acres of grazing land.

But this is slightly more than the total land area of the six inhabited continents! One could, of course, fall back on radical measures: aggressive clearing of forests; rapid expansion of irrigated lands; rapid implementation of energy-intensive technology and high-yielding crop varieties. By such means one *might* acquire the land needed to maintain current levels of meat consumption for another twenty or thirty years.

One can see that this is an absurd exercise, though, because other equally scarce natural resources would soon become limiting factors. We are desperately short of forests, water, and energy already. Even modest increases in the world population during the next generation would make it impossible to maintain current levels of meat consumption. On a vegetarian diet, by contrast, the world could easily support a population several times its current size.

Conclusions

There is no question as to whether the world's population can ever be sustained on a Western-type diet. The demands of livestock on agricultural land make such a supposition completely absurd. In point of fact, land resources will not even be sufficient to sustain current levels of meat consumption for more than a generation or so, even if there are no further problems with our resources of wood, water, and energy.

The real situation, as we will see in the ensuing chapters, is even more grim than this. Livestock agriculture makes exhaustive demands on many resources, not just land resources. If present trends continue, we could easily have a real crisis in food production. The resources necessary to sustain livestock agriculture will evaporate, and we will be faced with sustaining an increasingly large and impoverished population on even fewer resources than we have today.

11
Forests

Forests are a critical natural resource. In the developing world, over 80% of the people rely on wood for energy, and the use of wood as fuel is increasing steadily. In the industrialized nations, increasing demands for paper and timber are making an economy without wood unthinkable.

And yet, forests are being eliminated at an alarming rate. The demand for cattle grazing land remains the primary enemy of forest land in many parts of the world today, especially in North and South America. The problem is compounded by other demands on forest land. Forests are being reduced not only by agriculture, but by greed, carelessness, and economic necessity.

What Forests Provide

Forests provide human beings with wood for fuel, paper, and construction purposes. They also provide passive benefits to their environments; they favorably affect the water resources of the region, improve the soil and climate, and provide recreational and wilderness areas.

The most obvious use of forests is for wood supplies. As we can see from Table 14, the demand for wood is expected to skyrocket, far exceeding the relative increases in population. As intense as the pressure now is on forest land worldwide, this pressure can only be expected to increase dramatically.

Today, much wood is used for fuel—nearly 50% of all wood use in 1974. But this tremendous wood consumption accounts for only 7% of the total energy budget of the world.[1] This opens up a tantalizing possibility: could some new (or old) source of energy be substituted for wood fuel in the nations where it is heavily used, thereby saving a great number of forests from destruction?

Table 14. Trends in world consumption of wood.

Type of Wood	Consumption in million cubic meters 1974	2000	Percentage Increase
Fuel wood	1170	1950	33%
Poles, sawn wood, panel products	1078	3010	179%
Wood pulp products	263	910	246%
TOTAL	2511	5870	134%

SOURCE: Norman Myers, *Conversion of Tropical Moist Forests* (Washington, D.C.: National Academy of Sciences, 1980).

Given the extent and speed of the destruction of the forests in the less developed nations, it would seem that coal, or even nuclear power, might be a better idea ecologically. While such a substitution probably makes more sense than what is going on now, it is not likely to happen very soon. The poor in the developing world, who are the primary users of wood as fuel, can forage for wood, but not for coal. In fact, when populations become wealthier, a shift away from wood fuel toward coal or other fossil fuels does occur.[2] But such a shift away from wood and toward other fuels—while it would make sense on a worldwide basis—is not likely to occur in the next decade or so. Thus, the average consumption of one ton of wood per person per year in the developing world is likely to continue for some time.

The expected increases in consumption of wood as fuel, while nothing to be sneezed at, are dwarfed by the expected increases in consumption for other purposes. Between 1974 and 2000, the need for solid wood for construction and other purposes will have increased by 179%. Wood for paper uses will leap by 246%. Even if wood fuel consumption ended completely in the near future, forests would still have a vital role in the economic future of mankind.

Forests also passively benefit human beings. They greatly influence the water resources of their environments. Forests absorb water and transmit it downward into groundwater supplies. The infiltration capacity of undisturbed forest land is so high that runoff from forest areas following heavy rainfall is minimal.[3] Thus, forested areas help prevent floods. Deforestation, on the other hand, has left many regions open to floods. Disastrous floods in the upper reaches of China's Yangtze River, which drowned hundreds and left over a million homeless, were recently publicly blamed on the ecological disruption resulting from indiscriminate tree-felling.[4]

Forests favorably affect climate in a number of ways. Several observations suggest that forests are a factor in increasing precipitation. Rainfall on a forested area in Tennessee was significantly greater than that on a nearby area which had been denuded of vegetation by smelter fumes, even after the effect of wind variability had been taken into account.[5] This suggests that forests have a significant effect on local climates. Soviet geographers similarly report that each 10%

increase in forest cover results in a 2.5% increase in precipitation, once again after correcting for the influence of wind variability.[6]

Forests also influence the amount of carbon dioxide found in the air. There is widespread agreement that the amount of carbon dioxide in the atmosphere is changing the earth's climate. If present trends continue, the global temperature could rise by 5° to 7° Fahrenheit in the temperate zones by the middle of the next century. Besides making the summers hotter, this would partially melt the polar icecaps, raise the level of the sea, and flood most of Florida and other low-lying coastal areas. Trees incorporate 10-20 times as much carbon per unit area as crops or pasture. The amount of carbon released into the atmosphere annually has been calculated at between 1.8 and 4.7 gigatons—with 80% of this due to deforestation.[7]

Forests greatly benefit the soil resources of a region. Due to the absence of runoff from rainfall, soil erosion from forest land is practically nonexistent.[8] This, plus the dead leaves enriching the soil, allows for a build-up of topsoil in forested areas.

Finally, many people enjoy forests for recreational purposes. In the United States, the number of visitors to national parks has increased from 4.5 million to 240 million per year, a demand which is not expected to moderate in coming years.[9]

What Causes Forest Land to Be Lost

Loss of forest land in the United States is a serious problem, rapidly getting worse. In 1900, there were about 509 million acres of nonfederal forest land in the United States, but by 1950 this had declined to 420 million acres, and in 1975 it had declined further to 376 million acres.[10] Analysis of use conversion between 1967 and 1975 reveals that most conversions of forest land were to *grazing land*. We lost 70 million acres of forest land during this time, over two thirds of it to grazing land.[11]

This has had a critical impact on the wood economy in the United States. Before 1970, the United States was a net exporter of wood; but since then, it has become a net importer, with the trade deficit in wood reaching several billion dollars per year by the late 1970s.[12] Considering our growing needs and diminishing forest lands, we must face the question, "How much longer can our forest land last?"

In the United States, then, the single greatest enemy of forest land is the demand for cattle grazing land. But deforestation is hardly limited to the United States. The "Global 2000 Report" estimated that by the year 2020—if deforestation continues at its present rate—virtually all of the physically accessible forests in the less developed countries will have been cut.[13]

Estimates vary as to the exact extent and rate of destruction of tropical moist forests (which are the dominant types of forest remaining today). Some have put the rate of conversion of forests to nonforest areas at 13.8 million acres per year; others estimate this conversion at 27.2 million acres or even 51.9 million acres—a rate of almost 100 acres per *minute*. [14]

Since such estimates are generally advanced tentatively, and since they vary considerably, it is hard to come to solid conclusions. We can conclude, however, that these trends cannot continue forever, and that theoretically, all the forests in the world could be cut in the next generation or two—even if we assume *no* increase in the demand for forest products. Since demands for wood are expected to more than double in the last quarter of the twentieth century, the world may well face a major crisis in the demand for wood by the year 2010 or so.

What is causing this deforestation? In Latin America, the demand for cattle grazing land is probably the dominant factor, and it is expected to become even more important in the years to come. Between 1950 and 1975 the area of man-established pasture in Central America more than doubled, almost entirely at the expense of tropical forests. [15]

One of the major causes of modern deforestation is shifting cultivation, whereby an area is cleared and farmed for a few years and then abandoned for a new area. Shifting cultivation is not necessarily ecologically destructive. In fact, in parts of the world it has been practiced for thousands of years with no ill effects. It is destructive if these "forest farmers" have to reuse their abandoned areas before forests have had a chance to grow back. Unfortunately, such reuse is happening in many parts of the world, resulting in tremendous soil erosion and often permanent degradation of the land. [16]

There would almost certainly be plenty of land in countries suffering from such problems, and consequently no need for the destructive overuse of forests by shifting cultivators, were it not for the tremendous demands livestock agriculture makes on the land. A social system which promotes a land-intensive agriculture is a social system which makes land expensive and hard to find. In a poor country, this translates into increasing numbers of people who cannot find good land at all, and who consequently are forced to overuse the land that they do have access to.

The major causes of deforestation both in the United States and elsewhere in the world are inextricably linked to the production of animal foods, especially meat, and the grazing land requirements for cattle. Present trends indicate that the world will experience a crisis in the need for forest products in another generation or two.

The History of Deforestation

Deforestation is not unique to the twentieth century. It has occurred throughout recorded history, and even prior to recorded history. Reforestation has also been taking place throughout history, so the total quantity of forest land has probably fluctuated somewhat, but some general conclusions can be reached.

Through the process of ecological succession, most grasslands, if left alone, revert to some kind of woody vegetation or forest over a number of years. Pasture used for grazing animals is, in its natural setting, a passing stage in the evolution toward forest land. Almost all of the great grasslands of the world were created by man and maintained in their grassy state through the use of fire and grazing animals. [17]

Deforestation began with the discovery of fire, one of the first tools used by humans to manipulate the environment to their advantage. Preagricultural hunter-gatherers used fire to create grasslands in which the animals they hunted would be more prevalent. [18] Deforestation continued after the development of agriculture and, it seems, picked up steam. Ancient, and even not-so-ancient, history is full of accounts of now barren land which was once forested. In many cases this land has been not merely converted to grassland, but reduced to the status of a barren wasteland.

Early explorers from ancient Carthage tell of seeing countless fires set by humans to clear forest areas as they explored the coasts of Africa. [19] Alexander the Great marched through virgin forest land in India, which is today desert. [20] The renowned Cedars of Lebanon covered much land which is today covered with scrub vegetation or even bare rock. [21] By the thirteenth century, wood was a strategic material in the Eastern Mediterranean; and it was often necessary to tear down old buildings in Damascus to find material for new ones. [22] The destruction of English forests and the requirements for wood by a then flourishing iron industry created fuel shortages in the seventeenth century. Iron production in England declined as the iron industry moved to Scandinavia and North America—a trend which was reversed only by the introduction of coal as the primary source of heat energy. [23]

Deforestation continues worldwide. Between 1882 and 1952, land classified as "inaccessible forest" declined from 43.9% to 21.1% of the total land area of the world. [24] Deforestation will continue to create major problems during the next fifty years or so.

Where Can Forests Exist?

Where can forests exist? Just about anywhere. Almost any grasslands which can support cattle can grow trees. There are many better uses for the land which livestock agriculture is so prolific in gobbling up. Forests represent a particularly critical alternative.

Many times afforestation has proven successful on land not even considered good enough for grazing cattle. For example:

- A 1913 USDA Forest Service bulletin describes a successful program of afforestation on overgrazed rangeland which was considered to be "unfitted for agriculture." [25]

- A 1916 Pennsylvania Department of Forestry bulletin recommends planting forest trees on land which would be worthless even for grazing.[26]
- A Soviet publication describes the establishment of a forested "shelter belt" between Kamyshin and Stalingrad during 1948-1956, accomplished despite an extremely arid climate and as few as 2-4 months of frost-free weather.[27]
- An Indian publication recommends species and techniques for planting trees on ravine soils, shifting sand dunes, cold desert, lateritic soils, skeletal soils, waterlogged areas, and saline alkaline soils.[28]
- Pines have been reported to grow rather well on some almost pure quartz sands in the southeastern United States.[29]

Afforestation techniques have proven successful on extremely inhospitable land. So it is almost always true that land which can be used by cattle could also support forests.

Conclusions

The demand for wood is accelerating much faster than the growth of the population. "Wood famines" are by no means a new phenomenon historically. The forests of Iran, Iraq, northern Africa, Greece, India, and China today are mere remnants of what they used to be, having been decimated by governments and peoples long since gone by.

Conversion of forest land to grazing land is a major factor in this decline. Virtually all land in the world suitable for grazing, and some which is not, is also suitable for forest land. Once again, the demands of livestock agriculture on our natural resources is a major stumbling block to humanity's struggle for a livable environmental balance with nature.

12
Water

Water may well be the most vulnerable resource affected by modern agriculture. Long before all of our fossil fuels have been burned up, and long before all our arable land has eroded away, many parts of the world will be faced with critical water shortages. In some areas, the water supply has already given out, and the inhabitants have left for other parts of the world.

The problem with water is not so much that there isn't enough of it, but that there isn't enough of the right kind, in the right places, at the right time. The Amazon River basin gets more precipitation than human beings there can possibly use, but this is of little help to arid lands thousands of miles away. There are virtually unlimited quantities of seawater, but this is useless for most human water needs. Given an unlimited, free source of energy, we could desalinate ocean water and pump it inland to irrigate the Sahara Desert; but unlimited and free sources of energy do not appear to be on the horizon.

Why Water Is Critical

Most of the world's agricultural land gets its water directly from rain. Only irrigated land makes major demands on our surface or groundwater supplies. This raises the question: how important are surface and groundwater supplies for our agricultural system?

At first glance, the dependence of agriculture on such water supplies would not seem to be that great. Only about 10% of the cropland in the United States and 15% of all cropland worldwide is irrigated.[1] Since (by some estimates) less than half of the world's arable land is currently cultivated, water supplies would not seem to play a very critical role in agriculture. Even if there were water shortages in one region or another, why couldn't we just move on from these irrigated areas to other areas not requiring irrigation?

There are several reasons why this is not a practical idea, and why water shortages will spell real trouble for an area's agricultural system, despite the relatively small percentage of land which is irrigated:

- Irrigated land is some of the most productive land in the world, producing a disproportionate amount of the world food supply. Irrigated land produces 25% of the total value of crops in the United States, and 50% of the total value of crops worldwide.[2]
- Most of the world's land which can be easily cultivated is already under cultivation. The remainder could only be brought under cultivation at great expense.[3]
- Finally, much of the remaining uncultivated arable land in the world will itself require irrigation. Projections for increasing the world's cultivated land also call for greatly increasing the percentage of land which is irrigated.[4]

Thus, irrigated land plays a critical role in the world's food supply already, and it would be virtually impossible to replace such land with nonirrigated land.

Where does this great thirst for water come from? In the United States, virtually all of the agricultural water demand can be attributed to livestock agriculture. If the United States were to adopt a vegetarian economy, irrigated agriculture would become completely unnecessary, thus solving one of the great problems of the American West. It has been estimated that 80% of the total water requirements for the average daily food intake in the United States goes for animal products (meat, milk, etc.), with 11% going for fats and oils, and only 9% for plant food products. A pound of wheat contains more calories than a pound of beef; but the beef requires from 40 to 50 times more water.[5]

Extent, Nature, and Use of Water Resources

There are basically two sources of fresh water for human use: streamflow and groundwater. Streamflow is the total runoff from rainwater, which makes its way to rivers, streams, and lakes. In addition to this water, there is also water which can be extracted from the ground—groundwater.

Water continually cycles in and out of our environment. As it flows down to the oceans, it evaporates from the oceans and returns to us in the form of rainwater, forming the *hydrological cycle*. The total volume of water present at any given time is less important than the *rate* at which water passes through the environment.

Many areas of the world, not blessed with generous quantities of rainfall, must rely on groundwater for some or even most of their water supply. When

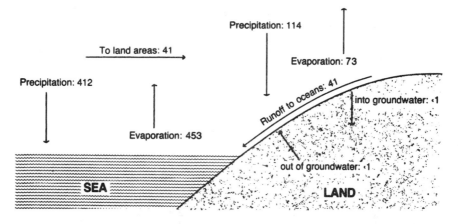

Figure 7. The hydrological cycle. (Numbers represent flow units; each flow unit = 1000 cubic kilometers per year.)

Source: Based on M. Falkenmark and G. Lindh, *Water for a Starving World* (Boulder, Colorado: Westview Press, 1976).

water enters the ground, it trickles downward until it reaches a point where the soil is saturated with water—a point called the water table. If conditions permit, wells can be dug deep enough to get water out of the ground, from below the water table.

How are water resources used? An important distinction must be made between *consumptive* water uses and *nonconsumptive* water uses. In nonconsumptive use, the water is returned to the stream from which it came (or to the ground). It may be polluted, but that is a different problem—the water is still available for further use downstream and has not been consumed.

In consumptive use, the water is evaporated and is thus lost entirely to the remainder of the hydrological cycle. Those counting on using the same water are out of luck. While the nonconsumptive use of water might exceed 100% of the total water supplies (the water could be purified and then reused any number of times), the consumptive use can never exceed 100% of the total flow of water in the long run.*

Only 10% of the water that industry uses is evaporated, as opposed to 60% of the water used by agriculture. As one can tell from Table 15, agriculture and industry use roughly the same amount of total water in the United States—but over 80% of all the *consumptive* use is agricultural. Surprisingly, personal water use plays an almost negligible role, accounting for less than 8% of all water use in the United States.

---

* Actually, there is a remote possibility it could exceed 100%—if water which was evaporated was re-precipitated as rainfall, in the same basin. But even then, only one third of precipitation makes it into the water supply before being evaporated.

Table 15. United States water resources and water use.

A. Water use by source (in km³/year)

	Total Use	Consumption
Streamflow Used	354.0	118.2
Groundwater Used	113.7	28.7
Saline Used	82.4	—
TOTAL WATER USED	550.1	147.1
(Total available streamflow)	(2000.3)	

B. Water use by category of use (in km³/year)

	Total Use	Consumption
Domestic and Commercial		
Central (municipal)	29.3	6.9
Noncentral (rural)	2.9	1.8
Commercial	7.6	1.5
Manufacturing	70.7	8.3
Agriculture		
Irrigation	219.2	119.4
Water for Livestock	2.6	2.6
Steam Electric	122.8	1.9
Minerals	9.8	3.0
Other (fish hatcheries, public lands, etc.)	2.6	1.7
Total Freshwater	467.7	147.1
Saline	82.4	—
TOTALS	550.1	147.1

SOURCE: U.S. Department of Agriculture, *1980 Appraisal,* Part I.

Total water use is skyrocketing (see Figure 8). It is theoretically possible that, sometime in the next hundred years or so, demand for water could exceed total available runoff in the world. Long before this apocalyptic scenario is realized, however, there are two more immediate problems that humans will have to cope with: groundwater depletion and water pollution.

While groundwater use in the United States is relatively small—only 20% of total water use—this is a very critical 20%. Much of this use is for irrigated agriculture; and thus much of this groundwater is being consumed (evaporated), and not merely recycled back into the ground. True, groundwater supplies are constantly being recharged, but at a slow rate. If groundwater is extracted from the ground at a faster rate than the rate at which it is being replaced, ground-water mining is said to be taking place. In many areas of the United States and the world, groundwater mining *is* taking place, and this constitutes a serious threat to our water supplies.

Water pollution is a second threat to the water supplies of the world. Wastes from livestock agriculture are a major cause of pollution to rivers, lakes, and streams. Indeed, some Soviet scientists are of the opinion that problems from

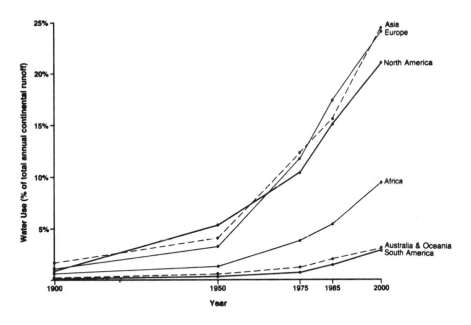

Figure 8. World water use, by continent, as a percentage of total annual continental runoff.

Sources: (a) G. P. Kalinin and I. A. Shiklomanov, "Exploitation of the Earth's Water Resources," in USSR Committee for the International Hydrological Decade: *World Water Balance and Water Resources of the Earth* (Paris: UNESCO Press, 1978).

(b) M. I. L'vovich, *World Water Resources and Their Future* (Washington, D.C.: American Geophysical Union, 1979). English translation by R. L. Nace.

water pollution are much more serious than problems from groundwater mining, and that a worldwide water pollution crisis will be upon us within the next 30 or 40 years.

We need to examine these problems in greater detail.

Groundwater Depletion

The problem with groundwater is that, at the rate it is being used in the United States, sooner or later we are going to run out of it.

At first, world groundwater resources would appear to be plentiful. The total amount of groundwater is many times that of the total streamflow of water each year throughout the entire world. But several practical limitations considerably reduce the total amount of groundwater available for irrigation or other uses.

It is not always practical to extract water from the ground. Because of the high surface tension of water, it tends to cling to small grainy particles. Only if the pore spaces into which groundwater has seeped are relatively large, is groundwater extraction practical. An underground area in which this is the case is known as an *aquifer*.

About two thirds of all groundwater supplies lie more than 750 meters below the surface; thus extraction is difficult, expensive, and energy consuming.[6] Finally, much groundwater—especially groundwater deep below the surface—is saline and therefore no more useful than ocean water.[7] The total usable groundwater in the world is only a fraction of the total groundwater.

The tremendous demands of irrigated agriculture are rapidly depleting our available groundwater supplies. The result is that water tables in many parts of the world are falling, year after year. Indeed, the land itself is falling—as the empty spaces formerly occupied by groundwater are crushed by the earth above it. Many of our aquifers are well on their way to being completely drained.

The Ogallala Aquifer, which covers an underground area spanning several states from western Texas to Nebraska, is especially vulnerable. By 1961, it had already been 20% depleted.[8] It is estimated that most of the remainder will be gone in another 40 years.[9] This does not mean that we will have to wait 40 years to feel the effect of groundwater depletion. As water tables continue to fall as a consequence of this groundwater depletion, the energy costs of pumping the water out of the ground rise correspondingly. These costs are already forcing many farmers in Texas to curtail their irrigation.[10] Gerald Higgins, an economist with the Texas Department of Water Resources, predicts that "corn will disappear from the Texas High Plains within the next few years."[11]

Another consequence of falling water tables is land subsidence. As more and more water is withdrawn from the ground, more and more pore spaces will empty and collapse, and the land will actually fall.

Numerous documented cases can be cited. The land underneath Mexico City has been severely affected by land subsidence. Between 1880 and 1940, the land in this area subsided about 1 1/2 inches per year; after 1940, the rate of land subsidence picked up dramatically, increasing to as much as 20 inches in the year 1953. This adversely affected the city's buildings, and broke their sewer and water pipes. Drains which formerly carried storm water away down slopes now required pumps to force storm water up and out of the lower part of the city.[12]

In California's San Joaquin Valley, land is subsiding at a rate of about one meter every three years.[13] In Texas's Houston-Galveston region, which is also affected by oil pumping, five feet of land subsidence occurred between 1943 and 1964—with the water table falling by as much as 200 feet in some places![14] And in Florida, recent well-publicized cases of "sinkholes" can be attributed in no small degree to land subsidence due to falling water tables.

A final consequence of groundwater depletion is the increasing mineralization of groundwater. Fresh water is virtually mineral free, but groundwater contains a small amount of minerals—mostly salt. When groundwater is used for irrigation, about 60% of the water evaporates back into the atmosphere, so the water left behind is slightly saltier. As it filters back down through the ground, one of two things happens: the salt is left behind in the soil, or the saltier water filters down into the groundwater supplies. Neither of these is particularly good; either the soil becomes more saline or the groundwater becomes more saline. After a certain point, further irrigation or further farming becomes impossible.

We know that salinization of soils has occurred in history; it is thought to have been one of the major reasons behind the collapse of ancient Mesopotamian civilizations.[15] Salinization of the soil can be averted if fresh water (not groundwater) from rivers or streams is used to flush, or leach, the salt out of the soil.

For the problem of salinization of groundwater, though, there is no real solution. Artificial recharge of aquifers with fresh surface water has been tried, with little success.[16] Mineralization of groundwater supplies is now the chief pollution problem in many areas where irrigation is being used.[17] It is also a serious problem in many coastal areas, where falling groundwater levels have led to seawater intrusion into ground where fresh water once existed but was extracted for irrigation.[18]

The groundwater depletion made necessary by livestock agriculture, therefore, has created numerous, growing, and intractable water problems.

Water Pollution from the Livestock Industry

Water pollution caused by agriculture is a very great problem. "Agriculture is the most widespread cause of nonpoint source pollution," according to the United States Department of Agriculture.[19] Many of the areas experiencing widespread water problems in the United States today are located near agricultural areas—the Texas Panhandle, Oklahoma, Kansas, Illinois, and the Ohio River Valley (see Figure 9).

Livestock agriculture can pollute water supplies in two ways: through livestock wastes, and through the wastes produced by slaughterhouses. By far the greater cause of water pollution is livestock wastes. Slaughterhouses can be a significant local problem, but in the aggregate they produce only about 1% of the water pollution that livestock wastes do.[20]

We can get an idea of the severity of the problem by considering the *biological oxygen demand* which livestock wastes make. The biological oxygen demand (or BOD) is the oxygen demand of aerobic bacteria which decompose waste products. If there is not enough oxygen dissolved in the water to sustain the bacteria, the water is depleted of oxygen and anaerobic processes set in, leaving the water a stinking unhygienic mess totally unsuitable for any human purposes. A nasty side effect of such oxygen depletion is that all other oxygen-dependent

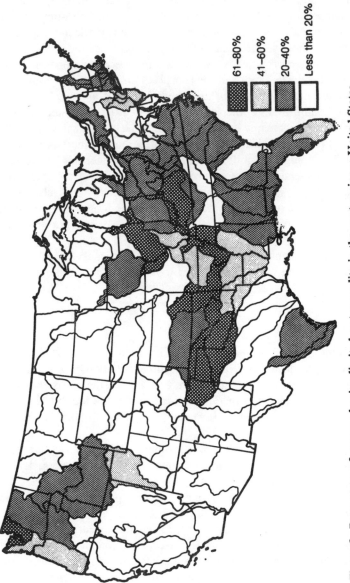

Figure 9. Percentage of streams having limited water quality in the conterminous United States.

Source: U.S. Department of Agriculture, *1980 Appraisal.* Part I.

61–80%

41–60%

20–40%

Less than 20%

life, such as fish, also die. Thus, one of the primary symptoms of polluted water is dead fish floating on the surface.

In 1960, the total BOD of all livestock wastes was 34.9 billion kilograms of oxygen, over five times the BOD of all human wastes (about 6.6 billion kilograms).[21] How close does this come to totally exhausting the oxygen supply of U.S. water resources? Actually, assuming that there is 20 mg of oxygen in each liter of water, then the total oxygen in the total streamflow in the U.S. is slightly *less* than the BOD of livestock and human wastes combined! However, there are several mitigating factors which account for the fact that the water supply didn't totally disappear in 1960:

- Oxygen is constantly being reintroduced into the water system. Even if at one point all the oxygen is entirely depleted by wastes, oxygen reintroduced into the water downstream could be used to handle further wastes.
- Standard treatment of wastes can reduce the BOD of wastes by 90%-95%.
- Not all livestock wastes are dumped into the water; much is spread onto the land. (It makes sense to use livestock wastes as fertilizer, but at present prices, it is cheaper to buy commercial fertilizer.)[22]

Notwithstanding these mitigating factors, during the sixties there were a disturbing number of fish kills which dramatized the pollution potential of livestock wastes. In 1964 and 1965, several large fish kills were reported in Kansas, in which over 1 1/2 million fish died—almost all of this attributed to livestock wastes.[23] Fish kills occurred again in 1967; and in Kansas City, St. Joseph, and Jefferson City, the oxygen content of the Missouri River dropped perilously close to zero for several weeks.[24]

Because of these problems with fish kills, the preferred method of disposal of livestock wastes is application of manure to soil (hopefully after some treatment and conditioning to minimize odors and water pollution).[25] But even when land is available for this purpose, nitrates or nitrogen from the wastes often seep down into the groundwater supplies, thus contaminating groundwater. The effects of such groundwater pollution appears to be significant in some places.[26]

The problem of water pollution from livestock wastes is thus serious. Livestock wastes create problems no matter what is done with them; it is only a question of finding the place where they will do the least damage.

Interaction Between Agricultural and Industrial Pollution

Worldwide, water use and water pollution are increasing dramatically. Industrial water use is increasing even faster than agricultural water use.

It has been estimated that industrial waste water, even after treatment, requires a dilution with unpolluted water of 1 to 5 or 1 to 10, if not more.[27] The dramatic increase in industrial water use worldwide, on top of the increasing agricultural demand, has created a very serious problem. Soviet hydrologist M. I. L'vovich states:

> Even a larger degree of errors in these forecasts does not essentially affect the fundamental conclusion to the effect that in a short time, a period on the order of between two and four decades, the volume of effluents could increase to such an extent that even if all this dirty water is treated and the treatment is of considerably better quality than it is now, an enormous volume of clean river water will be consumed for natural decontamination of sewage. Approximate computations demonstrate that all world runoff resources would have to be spent for this purpose.[28]

Of course, before such a scenario is realized, we will probably have encountered serious economic problems due to water scarcity. One Eastern European scientist has estimated that when water use exceeds 20% of total streamflow, problems of water availability become the dominant factor in the economy (see Table 17). As one can see from Table 15, water use already exceeds 20% of streamflow in the United States, and it will probably exceed 20% in Europe, North America, and Asia by the year 2000.

Technology and groundwater mining can temporarily alleviate these economic problems. Israel is said to utilize 95% of all streamflow in some way.[29] In some parts of the southwestern United States, it is probably true that total water use exceeds 100% of total streamflow already. But these areas are only being kept "afloat" economically by groundwater mining and highly sophisticated water technology. By such methods one can postpone, but not evade, serious economic problems due to water scarcity.

Conclusions

Water availability will be a major constraint on expansion of agriculture in the future. Irrigated land is playing a greater and greater role in world crop produc-

Table 16. World water use and consumption by category, in km³/year.

User	1970 Use	1970 Consumption	2000 Use	2000 Consumption
Public Utilities	150	25	440	65
Industry	630	25	1900	70
Agriculture	2100	1600	3400	2600
Water-storage basins	110	110	240	240
TOTALS	2990	1760	5980	2975

SOURCE:
   G. P. Kalinin and I. A. Shiklomanov, "Exploitation of the Earth's Water Resources," in USSR Committee for the International Hydrological Decade: *World Water Balance and Water Resources of the Earth* (Paris: UNESCO Press, 1978).

Table 17. Economic implications of water use.

Category	Total Water Withdrawals (as a percentage of total streamflow)	Water Availability
A	less than 5%	Possibilities for covering water needs are favorable. Interference for increasing natural water resources is required only at places with particularly concentrated requirements.
B	5%–10%	Possibilities of water supply are in general acceptable. The number of districts with temporary water shortage is increasing. The preparation of regional water plans may become necessary.
C	10%–20%	Water resources are inadequate. Comprehensive planning and considerable investments are required for solving water problems.
D	greater than 20%	Water is a limiting factor of the economic development.

SOURCE:

K. Szesztay, "The Hydrosphere and the Human Environment," in *Results of Research on Representative and Experimental Basins* (Paris: UNESCO, 1972), Volume 2. Studies and Reports in Hydrology No. 12.

tion. As water tables continue to fall and energy costs of pumping irrigation water rise, water problems will become increasingly prominent. At the same time, pollution from livestock wastes, mineralization of groundwater supplies from overirrigation, and increases in industrial water pollution make water quality as crucial an issue as water availability.

Livestock agriculture is responsible for virtually all of the water availability problems in the United States. It is responsible, as well, for a hefty percentage of the water pollution problems. The same general situation is undoubtedly true for much of the rest of the world. *An agricultural economy stressing meat is going to be vastly less efficient with water supplies than a vegetarian economy.*

Meat consumption is thus creating difficult problems with water use in the world today. At best, we can expect water to become an increasingly scarce and critical factor in the world food economy in the next twenty to thirty years. At worst, we can expect water to put an upper limit on economic development, in both the less developed countries and the industrialized world.

13
Energy

Energy is the natural resource of which Americans are most aware. The energy crisis, as it has been called, is indeed quite serious. Its relative importance has been somewhat exaggerated, though, due to the fact that the United States and numerous other Western nations have to import so much of their oil. If we had to import water from South America, or import topsoil from Saudi Arabia, then these resources might get the same close attention.

Momentarily, at least, the energy crisis appears to be under control. But energy is a critical factor in food production, and an energy-intensive agricultural system can only exacerbate energy shortages in the Western world.

Why Energy Is Critical to Agriculture

One way of looking at the relation of energy to agriculture is to compare the fossil fuel energy invested in agriculture to the food energy which agriculture returns.

Almost all agriculture in ancient times, and much agriculture throughout the world today, produces more food energy than it requires in fuel and labor energy. Indeed, this was true even of the United States before about the year 1910. Since 1910, however, the fuel energy invested in the American agricultural system has grown rapidly and far exceeds the food energy which it produces (see Figure 10).

In fact, this increasing energy subsidy for American agriculture has been precisely the key to its success. There is a steady increase in the use of tractors, mechanization of all sorts, fertilizers, and irrigation—all of which are heavily energy dependent. Corresponding to this tremendous increase in the energy subsidy for agriculture, there came a payoff: great economics in labor require-

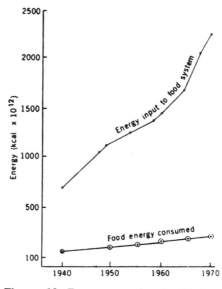

Figure 10. Energy use in the United States food system, 1940–1970.

Source: J. S. Steinhart and C. E. Steinhart, "Energy Use in the U.S. Food System," in P. H. Abelson, ed., *Food: Politics, Economics, Nutrition, and Research* (Washington, D.C.: American Association for the Advancement of Science, 1975).

ments. One farmer fed 10 people in 1930, but 48 people in 1971.[1] While there were unpleasant side effects to this process (soil erosion, the Dust Bowl, etc.), in terms of agricultural output, the last seventy years or so of American agriculture have been quite successful.

In short, the energy subsidy has not really mattered until recently. Energy was cheap and plentiful. But now that energy costs are increasing by leaps and bounds, the question of the use of energy by agriculture is a critical issue. Energy availability directly and immediately affects the ability of the United States, and much more of the rest of the world, to produce food.

Why Meat Production Is a Problem

Animal food production is tremendously inefficient in terms of energy requirements. It is responsible for almost all of the energy problems in Western agriculture. The production and harvesting of animal foods, including meat, fish, and fowl, gobble up almost all the energy in the United States food system.

Table 18. Food calories produced, per calorie of fossil fuel energy input, in several plant and animal foods.

Food	Food calories produced per calorie of fossil fuel energy input
Corn (Mexico)	83.33
Sorghum (Sudan)	38.46
Rice (Philippines)	9.50
Wheat (India)	9.06
Oats (U.S.)	2.47
Potatoes (U.S.)	2.18
Corn (U.S.)	1.80
Wheat (U.S.)	1.71
Soybeans (U.S.)	1.45
Rice (U.S.)	1.25
Beef (rangeland, U.S.)	0.28
Eggs (U.S.)	0.25
Lamb (rangeland, U.S.)	0.16
Milk (U.S.)	0.14
Broilers (U.S.)	0.07
Catfish (U.S.)	0.04
Beef (feedlot, U.S.)	0.03

SOURCES:
  (a) D. Pimentel and M. Pimentel, *Food, Energy and Society* (New York: John Wiley and Sons, 1979), pp. 56 and 59.
  (b) Table 1 and Table 6.
  (c) U.S. Department of Agriculture, *Nutritive Value of American Foods*, Agriculture Handbbok No. 456 (Washington, D.C.: U.S. Government Printing Office, 1975).

In Table 18, we can see why. Even under the conditions of mechanization and intensive cultivation now prevalent in American agriculture, plant foods produce more food energy than they require in terms of fossil fuel energy for their production. In other words, in terms of *economic* energy resources (such as food, coal, and wood) plant foods are net *producers* of energy. On the other hand, animal foods are net consumers of economic energy—it requires more calories of fossil fuel to produce them than they yield in food energy. This is true not only of land agriculture, but of fishing as well. Both coastal and deep-sea fishing are truly inefficient in terms of economic energy requirements.[2]

There is no doubt that plant foods are more energy-efficient than animal foods in their production of calories, protein, calcium, vitamin C, or any other nutrients. We are talking about consumption of energy by animal foods which is 10, 100, or even 1000 times greater than the energy requirements for production of an equivalent amount of plant foods.

Why the Problem is Going to Get Worse

Energy use in the U.S. food system has been variously estimated at 12%, 16.5%, or 20% of total energy use.[3] These estimates vary primarily according to the level of detail they provide, and what they count as being part of the food system—whether they include such items as transportation, refrigeration, cooking, and so on.

Much has been made of the great productivity of American agriculture, and our technical "genius" is being eagerly imported in other parts of the world. Unfortunately, much of the success of American agriculture is due to the tremendous quantity of energy put into the system. The reduced productivity of third-world agriculture is due in no small part to the fact that the third world has much less access to the fossil fuel so readily available in the West. The United States invests more than twice the energy in agriculture (on a per capita basis) than the less developed countries of the world expend on energy for *all* purposes.[4]

In the last few decades, much has been made of the Green Revolution and attempts to bring increased productivity to the less developed nations of the globe. The Green Revolution is highly dependent on energy inputs and other resources not readily available throughout the world, as one might expect. The expansion of the Green Revolution would mean more and more pressure on energy supplies throughout the world. Given this relationship between productivity and energy, we can anticipate that agriculture—both in the United States and elsewhere—will place an increasing strain on energy resources in the future.

Further complications render the whole situation even more problematic. Irrigated agriculture is expected to play an increasing role in food production in coming years. Whereas only 15% of the world's land is irrigated today, as much as 50% of the new land being brought into production will have to be irrigated in the future.[5] Much irrigated agriculture depends on energy to pump groundwater to the surface. Indeed, as water tables continue to fall, the energy expenses involved even in already irrigated land can only become greater and greater.

Most of the people in the developing nations depend on wood for energy. As more and more forests are cleared for grazing land, wood energy will grow more and more scarce.[6]

Energy and agriculture will be in increasing competition for water. Much has been made of the possibilities of synthetic fuels and the extraction of oil from shale. In point of fact, critical water shortages in the West will limit production of oil shale to a few percent of U.S. petroleum production.[7] Water is also required for cooling in electric power plants. If all new electric power plants (including nuclear) use once-through freshwater cooling, then by the year 2000 they could require 40% to 60% of the yearly runoff in the United States. Most of this water would be reusable, but much would be evaporated, because evaporation plagues water cooling systems.[8]

Soil erosion will put increasing pressure on energy supplies. Soil erosion is a serious problem in the United States and in many other countries. In the U.S., the use of energy-intensive fertilizers has more or less offset the loss of productivity due to soil erosion. However, decreasing yields on cropland will necessitate the use of more fertilizers. Fossil fuels will be required to produce all this fertilizer.[9]

Conclusions

While the energy crisis was not produced by agriculture, agriculture's energy demands add to the problem. Livestock agriculture is much less efficient in its use of fossil fuels, or any other fuels, than plant food agriculture. Indeed, all forms of Western livestock agriculture, as well as fishing, consume more calories of fossil fuel energy than they produce in calories of food energy.

Food production is already heavily dependent on energy supplies, and every rise in energy prices will inevitably affect the price of food. This can only serve to underline the importance of the difference between the energy-intensive forms of animal food agriculture now practiced in the United States, and a vegetarian agriculture which would be dramatically more energy-efficient.

14
Soil Erosion

Agriculture's effects on soil have been quite significant. The land totally ruined by agriculture, throughout human history, has been estimated at about 20 million square kilometers—more than the total cultivated land area in the world today (14-15 million km²).[1] Serious soil erosion comes about through overgrazing, bad cropping practices, or both. Most soil erosion in the world—and almost all soil erosion in the United States—is a consequence of livestock agriculture.

A certain small amount of soil erosion is normal and inevitable. However, it is usually balanced by the continual process of soil formation. The key problem, therefore, is the *rate* of soil erosion.

Weathering

Basically, soil is decomposed rock. Different layers of earth can be distinguished as one penetrates further and further beneath the surface. The outermost layer is generally called "topsoil," the layer which is most relied on by agriculture.

The process of soil erosion and the process of soil formation are both parts of a single, more general phenomenon referred to by geologists as "weathering." The same general processes which cause the erosion of topsoil from the surface cause soil formation below the surface. In nature, these two processes are roughly in balance. In fact, in many areas (e.g. temperate forest zones) more topsoil is being formed than is being eroded away.

But how fast does this process of soil formation operate? Soil scientists are notoriously reluctant to answer this question. This is because rates of soil formation may vary widely—by factors of 5 to 100—depending on local conditions such as the nature of the parent mineral, rainfall, and so on. However, no one pretends that it is a rapid process. It may take 100 to 1000 years to form a single inch of topsoil. H.H. Bennet, the first head of the Soil Conservation Service of the U.S. Department of Agriculture, put the figure at one inch of topsoil every 300 years.[2] Land cultivation tends to speed up the process of soil formation considerably, however. Under ideal agricultural conditions, soil formation may take place at the rate of 1 inch every 30 years, though under normal agricultural conditions 1 inch every 100 years would be more likely.[3]

The usual way of calculating soil formation and soil loss is in tons per acre per year. Since one inch of topsoil covering one acre of land weighs about 150 tons or so, this means that soil formation is approximately $1/2$ ton/acre/year. Under normal agricultural conditions, it is more like $1 1/2$ tons/acre/year, while under ideal agricultural conditions, it might be 5 tons/acre/year.[4] For some reason, this last figure—the most optimistic—is accepted as the official soil erosion tolerance of cropland. For grazing land (which is not cultivated), the tolerance should be put at about $1/2$ ton/acre/year.

Seriousness of Soil Erosion in the United States

There is little question that soil erosion on cropland in the United States is a serious problem. Several estimates have been made to the effect that the average annual loss of soil on U.S. cropland is about 12 tons/acre/year.[5] Even assuming that 5 tons/acre are being formed each year, the overall picture is not good. A net total of 2.5 billion tons of topsoil is lost from cropland each year—the equivalent of losing over 4 million acres of cropland which had topsoil 4 inches deep.

Of course, not all such erosion is taking place on the same land; but even if it is spread out over much land, it will have to be reckoned with sooner or later. Loss of topsoil adversely affects yields long before the land is totally lost. We can only assume that cropland is being lost to erosion at the rate of about 1% per year. This is bound to have serious economic implications sooner or later.

The grazing land situation is also quite serious. According to the USDA, the losses on 400 million acres of rangeland come to about 5.2 tons/acre/year.[6] Given a soil tolerance of $1/2$ton/acre/year, we can add another 2 billion tons of soil to the total lost each year. And this does not take into consideration the erosion on grazed forest land, or other grassland not included in the above sample. Even if these areas have a rate of erosion one half the other rangeland, we can add another billion tons or so to the grand total of soil lost to erosion each year. And almost all of this lost topsoil—upwards of 5 billion tons each year—can be attributed to livestock agriculture.

There are ways of dealing with soil loss on cropland, of course. "No-till" and minimum-tillage techniques have reduced soil erosion to 3 or 4 tons per acre—a considerable reduction over the national average.[7] Unfortunately, such systems have economic disadvantages. They increase the incidence of pests. There is no economic incentive to adopt such techniques, and this is the primary reason they have not caught on. Small farmers need immediate income and cannot be swayed by consideration of how productive their land will be in thirty or fifty years. Large farmers, especially when the farm operators are large corporations which may have highly diversified interests, have no economic interest in maintaining long-term soil quality.[8]

The only meaningful way to reduce soil erosion due to overgrazing is to reduce the intensity of grazing. The big obstacle here is also economic: there is an immediate payoff for overgrazing, in terms of the increased productivity of grazing land, and there is an immediate penalty for not overgrazing.

Grazing and Its Effects

Historically, overgrazing has been a far more serious environmental problem than misuse of cropland. Frequently, grazing has led to the creation of deserts—and overgrazing is widely admitted to be the primary cause of desertification.

At first glance, grazing does not seem to produce that much more soil erosion than does misuse of cropland. If we can take the results for the United States as typical, then perhaps 4-5 tons/acre/year of topsoil are lost due to the net effects of erosion from grazing, while about 7 tons/acre/year of net topsoil erosion occurs on cropland. We must remember, however, that the output per acre of grazing land is much less than that of cropland—even when the crops are simply used as feed for livestock animals. An acre of cropland growing oats produces 2700 MCal* of food; when the oats are fed to cattle, this drops to 110 MCal. But an acre of grazing land produces only about 10 MCal of beef.

A more meaningful assessment of grazing, then, would be net pounds of topsoil lost through erosion per megacalorie. Once we do this, the true effects of grazing become more obvious: while oats have a net erosion of 5.2 pounds/ megacalorie, feedlot beef results in 127 pounds/MCal, and rangeland beef 800 pounds/MCal. No clearer picture of the relative ecological effects of livestock agriculture and plant food agriculture could be imagined.

Grazing affects the land both by pulverizing the soil through the trampling of cattle back and forth through the fields, and by actually removing vegetation when the cattle eat the plants. Trampling can be severe, and is in fact a much greater problem than plant-eating. Trampling compacts and grinds the soil into tiny particles. Once the soil becomes more granular, it grows more susceptible to both wind and water erosion. Water can't infiltrate the soil; thus rainfall runs off the surface. The soil underneath dries out and flooding becomes more likely.[9]

---

* MCal = megacalorie, a million of the physicists' calories, or a thousand food calories.

These effects, however, are only the beginning. Once vegetation is removed from the soil in significant quantities, soil erosion increases rapidly. While all grazing causes some erosion, there is a certain critical point in grazing intensities beyond which the erosive effects of introducing additional cattle are dramatically and exponentially increased. This critical point is the point at which the protective vegetative covering begins to disappear.[10]

The most important cause of soil erosion is splash erosion[11]—the erosion caused by the physical impact of rain on the soil. Vegetation breaks the fall of rain and greatly reduces the kinetic energy with which it strikes the ground. As long as some vegetation remains on the land, the soil can temporarily sustain a great deal of abuse. But once vegetation is gone, it is possible for land to be permanently reduced to wasteland in a matter of hours.

There is ample evidence of the effects of such "super-erosion" in the American Southwest. Toward the end of the nineteenth century, the cattle industry appeared in the Southwest in force, encouraged by the expansion of railroads. By 1880 the entire range was incredibly overstocked, laying the entire region open to tremendous erosion. Numerous accounts exist of now-barren areas in the Southwest which once supported dense groves of cottonwood and other vegetation. In the San Pedro valley there was luxuriant vegetation in 1870; but by 1900, due to overgrazing, it was almost entirely gone. There is no way of estimating how many millions of acres of land were turned to desert during these few years.[12]

Overgrazing is the rule, not the exception. Even John Block (President Reagan's Secretary of Agriculture), who is hardly an environmental radical, has stated that there is a crisis of soil erosion on U.S. agricultural land, and that 60% of all rangelands are overgrazed.[13] While it is commonly said that overgrazing is merely the result of carelessness or poor management on rangelands, every social system in history which has utilized grazing on a large scale has suffered tremendous losses of soil. The temptation to overgraze is practically built into the system. The more cattle you put on a parcel of land, the more "productive" that land becomes . . . while it's still there.

But some net soil erosion would seem to be an intrinsic part of grazing cattle, regardless of any management techniques. How does one determine the level of grazing that could be tolerated without net soil deterioration? Since the process of soil formation is fairly slow, this safe level of grazing is probably quite low. It could be argued that animals instinctively avoid overgrazing in their natural environment, through such mechanisms as territoriality. (Any animals which did not avoid overgrazing would be weeded out by the process of natural selection.) If this is true, then any grazing system in which animals are raised in densities greater than those found in the wild is overgrazing, and the only ecologically acceptable form of livestock agriculture would be hunting. For all practical purposes, this would mean that there is no safe level of grazing.

Conclusions

Soil erosion is a very serious problem both in the United States and elsewhere in the world. While we lack accurate statistics on soil erosion in many other countries, some have estimated that the soil erosion in the developing world is even worse than it is in the United States.[14] The equivalent of millions of acres of land each year are lost to soil erosion, both in the United States and in many other countries.

The erosive effects of livestock agriculture are far, far greater than the erosive effects of plant food agriculture. In the United States almost all soil erosion can be attributed to livestock agriculture. *A total vegetarian economy, even in the complete absence of other reforms, would eliminate 90% of such erosion.*

15
Agriculture and History

In the popular mind, environmental destruction is a phenomenon of the recent past, evoking images of industrial pollution, oil spills, nuclear power, chain-saws, and chemicals. In fact, environmental alteration and degradation by humans is older than history. Human interaction with the environment has rendered many plant and animal species extinct. We have literally altered the face of the earth.

The total land area rendered barren by human activity is about 20 million km², more than the total land area under cultivation in the world today.[1] This process has been going on, at different speeds, for thousands of years. While many factors contributed to this result, most scientists agree that livestock agriculture has been the single greatest cause of environmental destruction in history.[2] In many cases we are able to reconstruct, through archeological or historical records, what the vegetation of an area must have been like before the advent of this particularly destructive food system.

The chief difference between today's environmental problems and those which occurred in history is that today it is becoming harder and harder to leave behind the effects of our own destructiveness. There is nowhere else to go. The whole planet must face the consequences.

Environment in Prehistory

Large-scale alteration of the environment by humans not only predates recorded history, it predates the rise of agriculture. This is the first big surprise for anyone examining the historical relationship between humans and nature. Massive alterations of plant communities occurred through man's use of fire.

Massive alterations of animal communities occurred through man's early hunting activities, resulting in the extinction of numerous species.

Was prehistoric man a vegetarian? Sometimes he was; sometimes he wasn't. Before the development of agriculture, humans hunted animals and gathered plants for food. In some groups of humans, hunting was probably very common; in others, less common or nonexistent. Hunting goes back over two million years[3] and is responsible for most preagricultural alterations of the environment.

In nature, grasslands tend to revert to forest. Humans, however, were able to create large grasslands by means of repeated applications of fire. Grasses return to an area almost immediately after a fire, but large trees return only years later. The so-called natural grassland is not a true form of climax vegetation, but rather a subclimax maintained in its condition by the use of fire.[4] Fires occur naturally, but in the last couple of hundred thousand years or so, humans have been the primary causes of fire.[5]

Primitive human communities preferred grasslands to forests for several reasons. Brush and woody vegetation help conceal both human and animal enemies. Burning vegetation may improve certain kinds of vegetation desirable to humans by improving the sprouting; the Iroquois and Powhatan peoples, for example, burned forests in early North America in order to improve the berry harvest. But most importantly of all, burning forests created pastureland on which the species which humans hunted for food could thrive. The grasslands of North America owe their existence to the use of fire by American Indians, and that is the source of the great herds of bison which were found there. The savannas of Africa are also undoubtedly products of primitive man's application of fire.[6]

Besides fire, the other major instrument of man's domination of the earth in preagricultural days was hunting. Humans, in fact, completely wiped out many species of animals during this period of time. A major spate of extinction occurred about 50,000 years ago, with over 75 species being eliminated in Africa.[7] In North America about 10,000 years ago, there was another wave of widespread animal extinction; at least 200 species, the vast majority of them mammals, became extinct or disappeared from their former range at this time.[8]

Not only did humans cause the extinction of numerous species; it is highly likely that a number of new species evolved in response to man's activities. For example, a number of fast-growing, fire-resistent tree species apparently evolved in response to man's use of fire. The very existence of these species depends on fire—if it were not for fire, they would be crowded out by the larger (but less fire-resistant) species of tree. Such fire-resistant species include the long-leaf pine, the Burmese teak, Cheer Pine of the Himalaya, and the Douglas fir of the Pacific Northwest.[9]

So even prehistoric and preagricultural humans were making increasing demands on the environment. While the damage caused by humans was limited, due to the small human population of the time, over the course of thousands of years human beings had a considerable cumulative effect on the environment. Indeed, such was the strain that humans made on natural resources that around 8000 B.C., humans experienced their first ecological crisis!

The Development of Agriculture

Man's hunting and gathering existence continued for many hundreds of thousands of years until suddenly, about 10,000 years ago, agriculture emerged as the dominant mode of production and hunting and gathering ceased almost completely. We say suddenly because, while agriculture seems to be perfectly normal and natural to us today, there is great puzzlement over exactly why agriculture developed and spread so rapidly.

Possible theories have been widely discussed. Some have suggested that agriculture developed because it conferred many advantages—enabling humans to stabilize their food supply and increase their leisure time. Unfortunately, this view is not tenable; some modern hunter-gatherers spend only 12 to 19 hours a week gathering food, thus spending a more leisurely existence than most modern Americans.[10]

Others postulate that agriculture developed out of necessity; worldwide adverse climatic changes may have rendered hunting and gathering obsolete, as humans discovered they had to cultivate the land in order to get anything out of it. This view is not tenable either; all the evidence indicates that there were no adverse climatic changes 10,000 years ago, and that in fact the land was more fertile then than it is now.

One particularly interesting theory has been advanced by Mark Nathan Cohen in his book *The Food Crisis in Prehistory*.[11] This view is startlingly simple: agriculture developed because the world was overpopulated. Relative to the existing hunter-gatherer technology, the environment was simply no longer capable of supporting the existing population.

It seems odd at first to think of the world as being overpopulated 10,000 years ago, when population was only a fraction of what it is today; or to think of the world as environmentally exhausted, when it was more fertile then than it is now. But we must remember that the hunter-gatherer technology is extremely inefficient with respect to land resources. It is estimated that each of the Kung bushmen (a modern hunter-gatherer society) requires over 10 km^2 of land—more than 2500 acres.[12] At this rate of land use, the world could hardly have supported more than a few million hunter-gatherers.

In the years preceding the adoption of agriculture, events took a strangely "modern" turn: the land came under increasing pressure from the population. The diet of hunter-gatherers utilized less and less palatable species. Many animal species formerly hunted became extinct. Fighting broke out between different groups of hunter-gatherers, presumably because of the scarcity of food resources.

Cohen is correct in believing that agriculture originated out of necessity, rather than because of any enlightened attitudes about the advantages of agriculture. It is not necessary to postulate that some wide-sweeping climatic change forced man to cultivate his food. Given the population of the day and the extremely inefficient hunter-gatherer technology, ancient man was simply responding to the law of supply and demand.

Sedentary and Nomadic Communities

Plant species were the first to be domesticated; early agricultural communities were thus largely, if not entirely, vegetarian. The first animal species to be domesticated was probably the dog. Other species, including the more traditional "meat" animals, were domesticated later.[13]

After the development of agriculture, but before the beginning of recorded history (usually put at about 3000 B.C.), there were some startling and revolutionary changes in human society. In the first place, population increased about sixtyfold.[14] Secondly, sedentary communities became the dominant form of human existence, prevailing over the nomadic form of organization.

From our point of view, the critical difference settled and nomadic communities is in the food supply. Nomads rely almost entirely on animal foods; they move their herds of animals from place to place as circumstances warrant. The sedentary communities—while sometimes consuming animal foods with great relish—have placed a heavy, increasing emphasis on plant foods. Settled communities have also, when they have survived, put limits on the use of land through various cultural or social institutions. This pattern is manifested worldwide today. Despite great advances in science and technology, two thirds of the world lives on a vegetarian or nearly vegetarian diet.

Why did sedentary communities become dominant over nomadism? The answer must lie in the food supply. Livestock agriculture, on which nomadism relies almost exclusively, is quite inefficient, so sedentary communities inevitably have had a stronger economic base. Sedentary communities were able to support a larger population on a smaller area, than nomadism.

Nomads still exist today, but for the most part only in desert regions. Much has been made of the pastoral nomads' knowledge of the deserts. If pastoral nomadism disappears, we hear some experts plaintively say today, vast desert areas of the world which are now productive will become entirely useless to mankind. Realistically, though, it is no accident that pastoral nomads exist only in desert areas. Desert areas cannot support sedentary agriculture; and in the more fertile areas, the sedentary communities have been able to successfully oppose the nomads. In addition, any form of livestock agriculture is bound to be quite destructive environmentally; and so any area in which pastoral nomads get the upper hand will inevitably be transformed into a desert, since they rely almost exclusively on livestock agriculture for food. The nomads' desert exist- ence is not caused by any mystical affection for the desert. Pastoral nomads would be quite happy to utilize the very best agricultural lands in the world for their herds; and when they get the chance, as they do on the southern edge of the Sahara today, nomads do just that—with the environment suffering tremen- dous damage.

So while historians are entitled, perhaps, to shed a nostalgic tear for the passing of pastoral nomadism from the scene, in social terms the triumph of sedentary communities was both inevitable and desirable. Without it, the entire world would probably today have already been reduced to a desert.

Dissenters may claim that settled communities have also contributed their share of environmental destruction. History is littered with examples of the most "civilized" societies in the world pillaging and destroying the land. But in such cases, these societies eventually suffered retribution: their environmental de- struction weakened their own economic base, and they were either occupied by foreign invaders or were destroyed by pastoral nomadic tribes from nearby des- erts.

So sedentary communities have not always been vegetarian or even largely vegetarian. But in sedentary communities, meat consumption quickly ran into serious natural obstacles, such as lack of resources to support such a resource- intensive diet, which limited this practice. Inevitably, there was either a turn towards a more vegetarian diet, or towards the ecological decline and depopula- tion of the region and the eventual victory of nomadism.

Agriculture and Desertification

The process of desertification—the turning of fertile areas into deserts by human or other causes—has been much studied in recent years. Many scientists now view the contemporary spread of deserts with great alarm. Much has been written on the causes of such massive deterioration of the land.[15] There is a growing consensus among the scientific community both that these effects are serious and increasing, and that the effects of man himself, and his livestock, have been throughout history the decisive factor. "The principle cause of deser- tification in the United States, as in the rest of the world, is overgrazing by livestock," concludes R. Neil Sampson in his book *Farmland or Wasteland*. Most scientists agree.[16]

Many areas of the world, now barren, were filled with vegetation prior to the rise of agriculture. The Sahara Desert is the most startling example of this. Most of the Sahara was not a desert at all 10,000 years ago. The desert is dotted with fossil remains of elephant, rhinoceros, hippopotamus, giraffe, and domestic animals; and with upper Paleolithic and Neolithic rock engravings of animals. None of these animals, of course, could have possibly existed without some sort of supporting vegetation. As late as 5000 B.C., hippopotamus and other swamp animals were living 400 miles north of Timbuktu; reliable rainfall must have extended hundreds of miles north of where it does today.[17]

Southwest Asia furnishes another case of this. The Fertile Crescent fully justified its name 4000 to 6000 years ago. In present-day Syria and Iraq, the discovery of prehistoric settlements outnumbers those of historic settlements by about 5 to 1, indicating that the area was already experiencing a considerable ecological decline by the time that written records began to be kept. Throughout the ancient Near East, vegetation has been progressively "slaughtered."[18] Many cities once flourished in Central Asia where there is today only sand; the Arabian peninsula supported an enormous population, which annoyed Babylon for thousands of years.[19]

These examples can be multiplied considerably. In 4000 B.C., Pakistan was well wooded and settled, and the center of what is today the Great Thar Desert was a jungle. In India, regions which are now desert were forested when Alexander the Great invaded the area. In Roman times, North Africa was the granary of the Empire; Hannibal got his elephants from the forests which then existed in Tunisia. The area around Tripoli was forested, and the land surrounding it was able to support a population of six million at the time of Mohammed. By 1935, the population of Tripoli had dwindled to 35,000, and the country surrounding it was largely barren.[20]

The inescapable conclusion must be that many desert regions were fertile and productive before the rise of modern agriculture. What happened? Some have speculated that this trend towards desertification is simply a product of adverse climatic conditions. But most scientists now are coming to believe that man and man's animals have been the most important factors. Both historical evidence and contemporary observations strongly support the view that human beings, rather than climate, bear the responsibility:

- There has been no postglacial dessication due to worldwide alterations in climate during the past 10,000 years or so. In some areas of the world, the climate has been getting drier, while in other parts, it has been getting wetter.[21]
- In many areas of the world, the process of desertification has taken place in the manifest absence of any change in climate at all. In the Mediterranean region, for example, where extensive devegetation has taken place in historical times, paleontological studies have shown that the climate in ancient times was not different than the climate today. Obviously, then, climate cannot account for the degradation of the land in that part of the world.[22]
- The advance of deserts in recent times, when the climate was not going through any great fluctuations at all, has been well documented. Even 100 or 200 years ago, areas of Africa which are now desert had been observed

to have trees and wild animals. We cannot attribute this to the effects of climate.[23]

- Even in those areas where climate has changed, it does not follow that climatic change was the cause of desertification. It is quite probable that the reverse is true: that desertification is the cause of climatic change.

    a. In Chapter 11 ("Forests") we saw that forests increase precipitation. Deforestation, then, could alter climate by decreasing precipitation.

    b. Air subsidence (sinking or falling air currents) may contribute significantly to local alterations of climate. Upward air currents or updrafts are favorable to increased precipitation; sinking air currents create dryness. Albedo (reflectivity) of the soil appears to increase air subsidence, and devegetation, by making the land surface lighter rather than darker, contributes to increasing the albedo of the surface.[24]

    c. Dust in the air also tends to cause air subsidence. Since lack of vegetation to hold the soil in place increases dust in the air, devegetation contributes to the alteration of the climate.[25]

It would not be an exaggeration to conclude, as does W.C. Lowdermilk, that "the history of civilization is a record of struggles against the progressive dessication of civilized lands."[26]

Patterns in Recorded History: India

The Indus Valley civilization, which flourished around 2500 B.C., may have been one of the first recorded casualties of environmental problems. It was an urban civilization in which meat-eating and animal sacrifice were common. We do not know exactly what caused the destruction of the Indus Valley civilization. We do know that there was extensive deforestation in the area, and that extensive migration out of the cities occurred well before the final blow—destruction due to barbarian, probably nomadic, invaders.[27]

The rest of India continued to consume meat during the Vedic period which followed. There are frequent allusions to the sacrifice and cooking of cows, buffaloes, bulls, and even horses. There were slaughterhouses for cattle. Early Hindu scriptures make explicit references to when and how animals were to be sacrificed, slaughtered, and eaten,[28] a fact which causes great consternation among some modern Hindu vegetarians.

Beginning about 1000 B.C., however, we can detect the beginnings of change. Meat eating began to be restricted. The sutras of this period stated that one may only eat meat when the animal is sacrificed. Then, around the sixth century B.C., several dramatic changes took place. Vegetarianism was advocated by some Hindu sages, and Jainism and Buddhism came on the scene, preaching doctrines of general nonviolence towards living creatures.[29]

During the reign of Asoka in the third century B.C., India became officially vegetarian. Asoka outlawed the killing of most animals at the royal court, and of some animals under any circumstances. The official religion changed from Hinduism to Buddhism. Asoka also enacted laws to protect the forests. It is quite likely that Asoka took these actions in order to halt the general deterioration of the land at the time. It appears that large-scale cattle-rearing and dairy farming had already become quite difficult, and animal produce very expensive, because of the limitations of the land.[30]

Meat-eating continued in India, though less conspicuously. Hinduism returned, and Buddhism almost completely disappeared from India. From the third century A.D., the use of beef was discouraged among Hindus, though the upper castes abandoned it only as late as the ninth and tenth centuries. By the sixteenth century A.D., the Krishna cult, whose devotees were strict vegetarians, completely dominated the Hindu religion. No orthodox Hindu would then kill a cow or eat beef.[31]

The widespread influence of vegetarianism in India is frequently attributed to cultural and religious influences. But if this is true, then it must be equally true that these religious influences were inextricably linked to environmental problems caused by livestock agriculture. India came under the influence of vegetarianism only due to a gradual process over thousands of years, and which cannot be separated from the changing environmental and economic situation.

Patterns in Recorded History: The Mediterranean

The Mediterranean region affords an even more striking example of the interplay of ecology, economics, and diet. Many settled communities sacrificed much to livestock agriculture. The consequent overgrazing and deforestation led to their decline or collapse, weakening them beyond the point at which they were able to resist pastoral nomadism.

All areas of the Mediterranean suffered from deforestation in ancient times, and lumber became a critical commodity fairly early. Even states with abundant timber usually permitted export only by treaty. Athens at its height prohibited the export of timber altogether. The cedars of Lebanon became a focal point of the Mediterranean over which Egypt and Babylonia frequently fought.[32]

Deforestation was not isolated from the agricultural situation. There was frequent competition between land for grazing and land for forests. Many forests in Yugoslavia were destroyed in ancient times by goats, sheep, and cattle. Incredibly, mountain forests throughout the region were being burned to provide pastures for the animals of mountain herdsmen.[33]

The result was a "squeeze" on both the supplies of wood and the supplies of meat. In the seventh century B.C. in Greece, beef and swine meat were quite common; but by the fifth century B.C., they were becoming increasingly rare.

Throughout the Greek and Roman period, in fact, meat consumption became less and less frequent.[34]

The single exception to the rule of declining meat consumption was Italy, where meat consumption of all kinds was quite common after the Punic wars. The Romans in Italy converted their farms to livestock ranches, importing grain from their exploited provinces.[35] This exploitation of the countryside by the Roman cities, which provided nothing of economic value in return, was probably one of the chief factors behind the fall of Rome. It was an economically artificial system, maintained by military force.

On the other hand, the influence of Rome was not all bad. Roman agricultural techniques were the most advanced of their day, and they spread to places as distant as Ireland, western Siberia, and the Arabian peninsula. They were the basis of the traditional attitudes toward the land of the Eurasiatic peasant, who had few options to find new land if the old land was misused.[36] These traditional values had the effect of preserving soil resources. The decline of the Empire, indeed, cannot be regarded as a decline as far as agriculture or the countryside is concerned. The Roman provinces, and the countryside generally, were largely self-sufficient.[37]

After the fall of the Roman Empire in the West, though, livestock agriculture made a big comeback in the Mediterranean. This was a consequence of the Arab conquests. In the Muslim world the pastures were considered public. The Arabs were stock herdsmen, and all herd-owners were accorded equal rights to the land. Restrictions on forest-cutting were nonexistent. This turned the region into an ecological disaster area.[38]

Overgrazing and deforestation led to a severe environmental and economic decline. The area was laid open for nomadic invasions—pastoral nomadism, it seems, was undergoing something of a renaissance. Many flourishing farmlands and cities in the eastern Mediterranean, southwestern Arabia, and North Africa were abandoned as a consequence of this instability. "The effect of the nomadic invasions, particularly those in the late sixth century," states Karl Butzer, "has not been made good even today."[39]

Spain and Italy survived until the Middle Ages without experiencing these kinds of environmental problems. But Spanish destructive methods of sheep-breeding after A.D. 1300 created an emptiness in the Spanish countryside which endures even today.[40] For some reason, sheep-herding spread to Italy about two centuries later, with (curiously enough) the same destructive effects. Demands for wood for manufacturing of glass and iron, in tandem with livestock agriculture, finished off what was left of the productive forested land.[41]

The consequences of this environmental destruction can be seen today. All of the Mediterranean has a very low percentage of forested land: Spain has a forest cover of 20.8%; Portugal, 5.2%; Italy, 15.7%; and Greece, 9.3%. The southern and eastern Mediterranean are covered with large areas which would qualify as desert. This degree of forest cover is much lower than what is found in

Germany, Switzerland, Norway, or even Japan; and yet even much of the land counted as forest in the Mediterranean represents a low scrub rather than a genuine forest.[42] Livestock agriculture has played the dominant role in engineering these "accomplishments."

Northern Europe generally escaped this ecological decline. Southern Europe, while subject to intense damage, seemed to escape the even more disastrous consequences of which northern Africa and the eastern Mediterranean were victims. The differences among the environmental conditions of these areas are directly correlated with the extent to which livestock agriculture—and especially pastoral nomadism, its most vicious variant—were practiced. Neither pastoral nomads nor any of the people who practiced livestock agriculture with such relish ever really made it into northern Europe. The Mongols got as far as Poland and Hungary. The Moors were in Spain. The Turks got even further, and besieged Vienna in 1683. The supremacy of modern Europe is largely a consequence of the stable agricultural base which made Europe naturally the economically strongest area in the Old World.

Patterns in Recorded History: The United States

The United States began its history with an incredible quantity of natural resources—land, water, and forests. Many areas of the North American continent had scarcely been touched by modern agriculture, existing in practically virgin condition at the time of the Constitution. Not surprisingly, the United States has since become one of the world's great powers; and much of this must be attributed to its great natural resources.

Unfortunately, the United States has utilized these natural resources to support what is certainly the largest system of livestock agriculture in history. Heavy consumption of meat has always been part of the typical U.S. diet. It was not invented in the last fifty years. And the agricultural system which has supported these habits has taken a terrible toll on the land.

Karl Butzer describes what has happened in the following words:

> The American colonization of the mid-central U.S.A. may be the most flagrant example of land abuse . . . In about 150 years the agricultural soil resources of the United States have been cut by perhaps a half, and in some areas such as Oklahoma, a single generation sufficed to destroy almost 30 percent of the soil mantle. Such a systematic if unconscious rape of the land has had an impact that rivals or exceeds that of 6 to 10 millennia of cultivation in the Mediterranean world.[43]

The first attempt to measure the extent of land resources and land degradation in the United States was done by H.H. Bennett and his colleagues in the USDA, in 1934. This study revealed that over 900 million acres in the United States—

more than twice the total amount of cropland currently under cultivation—had suffered moderate, serious, or severe soil erosion.[44] Despite charges of exaggeration, these results have stood up pretty well compared with later studies of the soil conservation problem.[45] Soil erosion in the United States is now estimated at about 12 tons per acre on cropland, and deterioration of rangelands threatens at least 60% of all land used for grazing. Almost all of this soil erosion can be attributed to livestock agriculture. While much good land still remains, many experts are now warning of cropland scarcity in the year 2000, if present trends continue.[46]

Conclusions

It is a mistake to suppose that meat eating is more prevalent today than it ever was in the past. Meat was in plentiful supply in much of the ancient world, much to the detriment of the land which supported its production. During the era of the Roman Empire, meat consumption actually declined throughout most of the Mediterranean; after the fall of the Empire in the West, meat consumption and pastoral nomadism returned with a vengeance.

We can learn from the ebb and flow of livestock agriculture that a resource-intensive agriculture depletes natural resources. Ostensibly, this is not a terribly startling conclusion. Still, our resource-intensive diet not only flourishes but appears to be gaining momentum in many parts of the world. Attitudes toward land in today's America have not noticeably advanced since the Neolithic period. Land is still regarded as an economic commodity, the only limitation on its use being the ability to acquire it and the expense of exploiting it. The consequences of such attitudes have been devastating.

16
Social and Political
Implications

Meat production makes tremendous demands on natural resources and the environment. These demands have frequently led to social crises in societies in which livestock agriculture has played a prominent role, and have forced these societies to make social adjustments. Such social adjustments have not always been pleasant—societies have sometimes been overwhelmed by the crisis, or destroyed by pastoral nomads or other "barbarians" from abroad after they became hopelessly weakened.

A vegetarian food economy would be much more efficient in its use of natural resources than the present agricultural economy of the Western world. But what are the social and political implications of these ecological realities? These can be summarized fairly quickly.

Any economy that relies on meat production is in serious trouble. Any social system which persists in putting an emphasis on meat production will be progressively weakened until it is destroyed or until its policies are changed. The amount of time which will pass before a serious social disaster sets in, of course, will vary from region to region. In the case of the United States, which still has abundant agricultural resources, there are probably many decades left. In the case of Africa, the disaster is there today.

The ecological effects of meat consumption affect all social systems equally. Regardless of social system or ideology, any country that emphasizes meat production is going to make its food situation worse. The way in which these problems will be manifested may vary considerably, though. In the richer nations, food may simply become somewhat more costly. If the livestock industry is subsidized by the government—as is the case in both the United States and the Soviet Union—then other areas of the economy may suffer, as they are sacrificed to keep agriculture afloat. In the poorer nations, food may become unavailable to many and starvation may result. So the effects of meat consumption vary depending on how close to the end of the rope a particular area of the world is.

Some people believe that our food problems can be dealt with by redistributing food supplies, or by ending economic mismanagement, or by increasing the total production of food. These are at best stopgap measures as they do not address the fundamental problem. By redistributing food supplies, or by famine relief, we could probably feed many of the world's hungry, given enough goodwill in the world. But this can only postpone a disaster for a matter of years. The food problems created by meat consumption affect both rich *and* poor nations. The difference is that for the rich a food problem is an inconvenience; for the poor, it may be fatal. Since the agricultural systems of all countries emphasizing meat production are going downhill, redistribution can only postpone matters.

The same problem applies to economic management and increasing production as means of solving the food crisis. Even relatively well-managed agricultural systems, such as those in the U.S., suffer from serious depletion of resources by meat production. Increasing production of total food supplies would perhaps increase meat availability for a short time, but it would also accelerate the rapid depletion of agricultural resources.

We can explore these social and political implications in more detail by examining the current world food situation, by looking at the tremendous social pressures and tensions generated by meat production, and by looking at the end of the road for meat production—a world in which we are much poorer and hungrier than we would be on a vegetarian diet.

Food Problems in Current Social Crises

Many major and minor crises around the world are directly related to the wasteful system of meat production. The most important example is in Africa. In Ethiopia and Mozambique, to name only the two countries most recently affected, we have two cases of very poor countries which have relied heavily on livestock agriculture with tragic results. In both countries, thousands have died and tens of thousands more are in danger of dying. In both countries, livestock agriculture has played a key role in crippling the ability of the food system to produce food.

Ecological disaster is not new in Africa. Northern Africa, once the granary of the Roman Empire, was reduced to a barren wasteland by the pastoral nomads which entered the area after the Empire's collapse. The march of the Sahara desert southward, preceded by large herds of livestock animals, has been observed for decades. Numerous independent observers have confirmed that soil erosion today is rampant in Africa. The destruction has been savage. Fifty years ago, 40% of Ethiopia was covered with trees, while only 2% to 4% is covered with trees today.[1]

So the current (1985-86) famine in Ethiopia should not be that much of a surprise. Many blame the drought, the civil war, or governmental incompetence in pushing the country over the edge into starvation; and certainly these factors have played a role. But we cannot ignore the ecological realities which are the underlying conditions responsible for Ethiopia's getting to the brink of disaster in the first place. Overgrazing by cattle has played a key role in Ethiopia's decline. Incredibly, while the people are starving, Ethiopia today has a larger livestock population than any other country in Africa, though it is only ninth in total land area![2]

Similar problems have affected Mozambique. Here we have a country which recently liberated itself from colonialism. Yet Mozambique then proceeded to import beef from abroad to satisfy the demands of the urban elite for meat. Perhaps even worse, they are intensifying their production of corn—one of the most erosive of all plant foods—and feeding it to their cattle! This is, of course, a recipe for disaster; and disaster is now precisely what Mozambique has on its hands. This is a most depressing pattern throughout many third world countries. They throw out colonialism, but they keep or even intensify the colonial system of food production.

Africa is not the only area of the world directly affected by problems related to meat production. Eastern Europe and the Soviet Union are also experiencing serious problems in this regard. In Poland, prior to the workers' riots in 1979 over rising meat prices, the per capita meat consumption was nearly as high as it was in the United States. In 1979 the government allowed the price of meat to rise, and the workers expressed their intense dissatisfaction. Regardless of what else one can say about the situation in Poland, there is no question that meat consumption has placed a severe strain on the Polish economy. No matter what kind of the government the Poles have, they will have to recognize economic realities; and these realities are, that the Polish economy simply cannot sustain the level of meat consumption which approaches the "American" level. They could subsidize meat production or import meat or feed for meat animals; and this is, of course, precisely what the government has been doing for some time. At best, however, this can only shift their economic problems from agriculture to those sectors of the economy which are subsidizing agriculture.

The Soviet Union is affected with similar problems of resource availability due to the wastefulness of their diet. Today, their agricultural system is a serious burden to their economy, and they are forced to import vast quantities of wheat from their chief ideological opponent, the United States, in order to keep it afloat. But the Soviet Union's well-publicized agricultural difficulties only arise because it tries to feed its citizens a Western-type diet high in meat and animal products. The Soviet Union would not have the slightest difficulty in feeding itself from its own resources, but grain has to be imported for their cattle.

Other countries are hardly doing better. Another example of contemporary attitudes towards livestock agriculture can be found in Israel. Because of its reliance on livestock agriculture, Israel's economy depends heavily on groundwater use. You can't make the desert bloom through sheer hard work; it requires water. Today Israel is heavily dependent on water from the West Bank, and the Israeli press is full of talk of retaining the West Bank in order to protect water supplies from encroaching Arab wells. One analyst gloomily concludes that water in the West Bank region—which the Israelis captured from the Arabs in the 1967 war—is "fast becoming the most ominous obstacle to any peaceful settlement in the region."[3]

Latin America provides us with yet another example of how food problems contribute to social tensions. Throughout Latin America, land availability is a prominent social issue. Revolutionaries as well as reform-minded moderates have made land reform a major issue. Yet in many Latin American countries, forests are being leveled in order to create pastures for cattle grazing land. In a region where land availability is a central social issue, existing land is being gobbled up by livestock agriculture. The resulting social tensions have resulted in civil wars, repression, and violence.

And finally, what about the United States? Despite its vast resources, even this country is not immune from the ecological effects of livestock agriculture. The resources which have up to now so generously supported agriculture are becoming scarcer, harder to get, and therefore more expensive. It is becoming increasingly expensive to farm in the United States. As in Eastern Europe and the Soviet Union, it is always possible to subsidize meat production in order to maintain the availability of meat; but this does not really alter the problem, it merely shifts it somewhere else—in this case, to the federal budget deficit. In the meantime, the soil erosion, deforestation, and groundwater depletion, increasing dependence on energy-intensive fertilizers, all brought on by meat production and livestock agriculture, will increasingly undercut the food base of the United States.

How quickly do nations abandon their ideals in order to consume meat! The third world countries copy the methods of their former colonial oppressors; the socialist countries strive to imitate the foods of the decadent West; and the United States throws its free enterprise system aside in favor of government subsidies. We are closer to the Orwellian "1984" than ever, in which everything becomes its opposite for the sake of meat consumption: colonial methods become liberation, decadence becomes the progressive future, and government intervention becomes free enterprise.

Further Down the Road: World Hunger

Even if the art of famine relief alleviates (to a certain extent) the possibility of mass starvation, thousands of unfortunate hunger victims are quietly dying in remote corners of the earth, beyond the reach of TV cameras. Some have estimated the total number of deaths due to lack of food as being 15,000,000 each year. The link between meat consumption and world hunger has been frequently debated. If there is such a link, then this is easily the most serious social consequence of meat consumption, with significant moral and ethical implications.

The two most commonly advanced theories about the cause of hunger are:

- That it results from a scarcity of food supplies in relation to the population to be fed. The solution would therefore be to increase food supplies, decrease population growth, or both.
- That world hunger results from inequalities—roughly speaking, from the divisions between the rich and the poor. According to this theory, the solution to the problem of hunger is political and social equality.

Both of these theories contain an element of truth. But both of them are also flawed, for they leave out the role of a wasteful and destructive diet.

It may be true that a relative scarcity of food supplies causes world hunger. But what exactly is there a scarcity of? What kinds of foods are scarce? If we define scarcity in terms of the typical Western diet, then the world has been hopelessly overpopulated for many years. The average American requires 6 to 7 acres of cropland and grazing land. If everyone in the world required this kind of extravagance, the land required would exceed that available by a factor of nearly three—with much of the land available not being nearly of the quality of that in the United States. But if we define scarcity in terms of a healthy vegetarian diet, there is no scarcity of food at all. On a vegetarian diet the world could undoubtedly support a population several times its present size.

Neither overpopulation nor underproduction can be the basic cause of hunger in the world or the cause of food scarcity. At most, there is only overpopulation or underproduction relative to the need for a diet high in meat and other animal products.

It may also be true that social inequalities result in hunger in the world. The paradigm of this theory could easily be the Irish potato famine of the nineteenth century. Because of the potato blight, many people starved to death in Ireland, yet at the same time Ireland was exporting wheat. Lack of food was not the problem, rather the lack of access to that food. Likewise today, it may be argued, we need to redistribute food in a more equitable way, rather than increasing production or decreasing overpopulation.

Certainly inequalities can be one of the causes of world hunger; in the poor countries, inequalities can be fatal to those at the bottom rungs of the social ladder. But would eliminating social inequalities—even if we could define what a "social inequality" was—necessarily end hunger? No, it would not. If the resources which are the base of the food system are systematically destroyed, redistributing food so that everyone gets an equal share will only temporarily solve the problem. In the end, the food system would deteriorate to the point at which everyone was equal but everyone was starving.

Nor would ending social inequalities necessarily have the effect of conserving resources. A democratically organized, free people, with almost unlimited access to some of the most fertile soils in the world—namely, those in the late nineteenth century United States—caused some of the most catastrophic soil erosion in history. And today, many "revolutionary" governments fully pledged to social equality have great difficulty conserving their resources or feeding their people.

Regardless of the social system a region may adopt, erosion of the resource base on which food supplies depend makes food more difficult and expensive to obtain. Thus, meat production cannot help but contribute to rising social tensions in the world in which conflict, violence, or social chaos will increase. A vegetarian economy would both increase food availability and decrease social tensions, thus alleviating or solving the problem of world hunger.

The Next One Hundred Years

Let us look down the road and try to imagine what the world will be like in the next hundred years. Of course, we can't hope to encompass all possibilities; there are many things, both good and bad, which we cannot really hope to anticipate. On the one hand, there might be a nuclear war which would largely or entirely destroy the human race. On the other, we might discover an unlimited and free source of energy. But barring the unforseen and the unforeseeable, what can we imagine the world to be like 100 years from today?

We could imagine three possible worlds: a world in which meat consumption (in per capita terms) is about what it is today; a world in which meat consumption has decreased considerably but has not been entirely eliminated; or a world in which virtually everyone is a vegetarian. (Of course, there are actually a continuum of possibilities, but these three are the most important alternatives.)

We can immediately discard the first possibility as completely unworkable. Within the next two to four decades, if present trends continue, vast quantities of land will be lost to soil erosion; forests in most parts of the world will be greatly decimated or entirely gone; U.S. cropland reserves will be gone; the Ogallala aquifer will be largely gone; and many parts of the third world will be reduced to desert. We face a serious crisis. Our supplies of agricultural resources are dwindling just as the demand on them is increasing. The human race is on a major collision course with reality. The only question is, what form will this collision take and when is it going to come?

So we turn to the second possibility—a world in which meat consumption has decreased considerably but has not been eliminated. The question at this point would be, just how much of a decrease would be enough to maintain a sustainable agricultural system. In practical terms, a decrease in absolute meat consumption, coupled with an increase in population, would mean an even greater decrease in per capita meat consumption. If, for example, meat consumption is cut to 50% of today's levels, and the population triples in the next 100 years, then per capita meat consumption would be only $1/6$ of what it is today. And it is not even clear that a reduction of world meat consumption to 50% of current consumption would be ecologically sustainable. It might merely mean that resource destruction was slowed down but not halted, and thus merely postpone an inevitable further unpleasant adjustment.

The second possibility, therefore, does not entail just a marginal social adjustment. It is not going to be sufficient just to eat a little less meat; it is going to be necessary, over the next one hundred years, to reduce per capita meat consumption by at least 80%. We are not talking about what would be practical or socially desirable, either—only about what would be, from a technical point of view, theoretically possible.

At this point we can reasonably pass from ecological considerations to social considerations. Even if there were an ecologically acceptable level of meat consumption, it is clear that this would be (in terms of today's meat consumption) rather low in per capita terms. What are going to be the *social* costs of propping up such a system?

The social costs are likely to be tremendous. In the first place, it is highly unlikely that everyone is going to eat just a little meat. If meat consumption were to drop by 50% over the next 25 years in the United States, it is most unlikely that everyone would be eating 50% less meat. Rather, it is likely that meat would become a "luxury item" and that those who were able to afford it, would continue to consume meat at roughly the present day levels; and those who could not, would become nearly or entirely vegetarian. The same sort of thing would doubtless occur in other countries. We would then have a social practice which would increasingly become the exclusive property of an ever shrinking privileged minority.

Secondly, even this reduced level of meat production would threaten food resources, which would have to be constantly protected. Anyone who imagines that meat producers are going to voluntarily protect natural resources when there is a continuing demand for their products by a privileged minority able to pay for them, is deluding themselves. There will have to be some social or legal pressure to conserve resources, to prevent rangelands from being overgrazed, and so forth. This will become another focal point of social tension.

For example, how could overgrazing be dealt with? Should we send out federal inspectors to these rangelands and levy fines for overgrazing, or what? The regulation of livestock agriculture, without eliminating it, would introduce a whole nest of practical problems which would be absent in a vegetarian economy. At best, such regulation would be burdensome; more likely, it would be completely ineffective.

Thirdly, there are non-ecological resources at stake as well. We are spending hundreds of billions of dollars each year on health care, mostly to treat the final stages of degenerative diseases which are perfectly preventable on a vegetarian diet—heart disease, cancer, and the rest. Don't these form part of the social costs of meat consumption? And another cost of a livestock agriculture reduced to ecologically acceptable levels is cruelty to animals. Many are very distressed over the suffering inflicted by the "factory farm" system on farm animals themselves; and this would continue to be a source of social tension under such a system.

A vegetarian economy, by contrast, would promote social equality; it would protect natural resources simply and easily; and it would eliminate many of the other financial and social costs of a meat oriented diet as well. Even if there were an ecologically acceptable level of meat production, we can only conclude that the social advantages of eliminating meat consumption would greatly outweigh the social costs of preserving this unnecessary and wasteful food for an ever-shrinking, privileged minority.

This is not to say that perfect social equality is feasible or even desirable. But food is one of the most basic of all human needs. And when there are such gross disparities among the resources available for such a basic human need, one tends to lose confidence that all human beings share certain basic common interests. The differences in land, water, and energy requirements of a meat-oriented diet and a vegetarian diet are quite large—varying by factors of from 5, 10, or 20, to 100. When food resources are the focal point of so many world tensions, a more equitable allocation of food resources would unquestionably promote world peace. And such an allocation of resources would best be achieved on a vegetarian diet.

Conclusions

In the long run, we are all going to be vegetarians. Doubtless, through further exploitation of the environment, we can prolong the period in our history in which we think it necessary to kill animals for food. But the ecological limitations of this procedure will soon make manifest to all that a vegetarian economy is both necessary and desirable.

Only a small minority of the world's citizens will ever be able to consume meat at current American levels: the resources to support a more intensive livestock agriculture simply don't exist. We will probably not feel the real effects of our present actions in the realm of agriculture for another twenty or thirty years. In the interim, things will merely become slightly less pleasant, year after year. To continue to maintain a meat economy can only make matters increasingly difficult for everyone, and can only adversely affect the goals of health for everyone and world peace.

III
VEGETARIAN ETHICS

17
Ethics, Animals, and Reality

One result of the world's meat-eating habits is incalculable suffering and death in the animal world. Each year, over 200 million cattle and calves are slaughtered throughout the world. In the United States alone, over three billion chickens are killed for food.[1] There is little question but that animals want to live, that animals have feelings, and that animals suffer—just as humans do.

This has led many vegetarians to conclude that there is no ethical justification for eating meat. In this chapter we will survey the ethical issues surrounding the use of animals for food.

The Ethical Question

If one attempts to justify meat consumption, or any use of animals for food purposes, there are two basic directions one could take:

- To deny or to minimize the suffering and death of animals, or its ethical significance;
- To claim that the ethical drawbacks are outweighed by the benefits of meat-eating.

Most people who eat meat, if they think about this question, probably advance both lines of argument. They might think that animals suffer pain, but not very much, and that in the case of animals slaughtered for food, the advantages of meat consumption justify the inevitable pain and death animals suffer.

What about these benefits of meat consumption? Our desire for meat and the pleasure we get from eating it are sufficient justification for many. Others will cite what they believe are the health advantages of a meat-oriented diet, or maintain that meat is a necessary part of our diet. In the first section, on vegetarian nutrition, we have dealt at length with these "benefits," and shown not only that there are no advantages to eating meat, but that meat consumption is actually a danger to health, increasing the chances of getting heart disease and cancer. Regardless of how one feels about these controversies, though, one thing is quite obvious: eating meat is not necessary for human life.

If meat consumption is not necessary, then it can only be justified by minimizing or denying the suffering or death which it causes—or by admitting that animals do suffer, but denying that their suffering is ethically significant. First, then, we need to deal with the facts concerning what animals experience; then we will deal with the ethical significance of killing animals for food.

The Facts

Animals do not want to be killed, of course; but in addition to being killed, they suffer a great deal of pain in the process of being turned into food. Of course, their slaughter itself causes a certain amount of pain (more or less, depending on the method of slaughter used). But the process by which the animals are raised in Western societies also causes suffering. Indeed, given the suffering of many animals' day-to-day life, slaughter itself is practically an act of mercy.

In most Western countries, animals are raised on "factory farms." The treatment animals receive in them is solely connected with price. While it is not necessary to be cruel to animals prior to their slaughter, it does save money.

There is no disagreement about the basic facts concerning the ways animals are treated on these factory farms. The nature and types of pain endured by animals in the process of being raised on such farms have been detailed frequently before, most notably in Peter Singer's *Animal Liberation*.[2] I will spare the reader too many of the grisly details, but will indicate the broad outlines of the issue Singer treats so well in his book.

Crowding is the worst problem. Indeed, it is the main cause of the high mortality rate among many factory farm animals. Chickens typically lose 10% or 15% of their population before they ever get to the slaughterhouse. Veal calves suffer a 10% mortality in their brief 15 weeks of confinement. It makes more economic sense to crowd the animals together and increase mortality than to pay the money necessary to maintain all of the animals in more humane conditions.

Chickens are probably the most abused animals. Near the end of its 8 or 9 week life, a chicken may have no more space than a sheet of notebook paper to stand on. Laying hens are crowded into cages so small that none can so much as stretch its wings. This inevitably leads to feather-pecking and cannibalism—the chickens attack and even eat each other. Obviously, such chickens are under a great deal of stress.

The manufacturer's response to this is de-beaking—cutting off most or all of the chicken's beak. Of course, this causes severe pain in the chickens, but prevents the cannibalism.

A similar problem arises when pigs are kept in confinement systems. Pigs, under the stress of the factory farm system, bite each other's tails. The solution, of course, is tail-docking, whereby the tail is largely removed.

About 75% of all cattle in the industrialized countries spend the last months of their lives in feedlots, where they are fattened for slaughter. Cattle usually have at least some degree of freedom for the first months of their lives, veal calves being the exception. Veal calves are kept in very small stalls, prevented even from turning around, and kept deliberately anemic. They are denied any roughage or iron. The purpose of this is solely to keep the flesh pale-looking. It has no effect on the nutritional value of the meat (except perhaps to make it less nutritious); it does not even alter the taste. The only effect this cruel diet has is to produce a pale-colored flesh.

Transportation of animals is frequently another traumatic event in the life of any animal destined for slaughter. Cattle may spend one or two days in a truck without any food, water, or heat—which can be terrifying, and even deadly, in winter time. It is not unusual for cattle to lose 9% of their body weight while being transported. About twenty-four hours or so before slaughter, all the animal's food and water is cut off—there is no point in feeding an animal food which won't be digested before it is killed.

The act of slaughter is not necessarily painful. In many slaughterhouses in the United States, animals must be stunned before having their throats slit. After being rendered unconscious, they are bled to death. The animals must experience awful terror in the minutes or hours before they are killed, smelling the blood of those who have gone before. But the moment of death itself need not be painful at all. Unfortunately, not all slaughterhouses utilize such stunning devices. It is probable, in such cases, than an animal bleeds to death while fully conscious.

The fact of death is almost impossible to minimize in most systems which produce animals for food. In our culture, the use of animals for food in any way usually means putting the animals to death. Even dairy cows and laying hens are likely to wind up in someone's soup once they cease producing. Efficient production of milk, eggs, or meat for humans invariably entails substantial suffering for the animals and—sooner or later—death.

The ugly reality of modern factory farms is an open book, and for this reason I have not gone into detail.[3] Peter Singer's comments are worth quoting at this point:

> Killing an animal is in itself a troubling act. It has been said that if we had to kill our own meat we would all be vegetarians. There may be exceptions to that general rule, but it is true that most people prefer not to inquire

into the killing of the animals they eat . . . Yet those who, by their pur-
chases, require animals to be killed have no right to be shielded from this or
any other aspect of the production of the meat they buy. If it is distasteful
for humans to think about, what can it be like for the animals to experience
it?[4]

Ethical Significance of These Facts

Among vegetarians there is certainly no consensus on what ethical system,
philosophy, or religion one ought to have. Most ethical vegetarians, though,
agree on these two points:

- Animals suffer real pain at the hands of meat producers, both from their
  horrible living conditions and, in some cases, from the way they are slaughtered; and in no case do animals want to die.
- Animals are our fellow creatures and are entitled to at least some of the
  same considerations that we extend to other (human) fellow creatures: specifically, not to suffer or be killed unnecessarily.

Very few have seriously attacked the first view, that animals suffer real pain or
have real feelings. Some have questioned whether animals suffer quite as much
pain as humans do, perhaps because animals (allegedly) cannot foresee future
events in the same way that humans do. Only one major philosopher, Descartes,
is said to have held the extreme view that animals have no feelings whatsoever—
that they are automatons.

The second issue, though—whether animals are our fellow creatures, entitled
to the same considerations that we accord other human beings or even pets—is
less obvious. This issue requires a more thorough examination.

Are Animals Our Fellow Creatures?

Most people recognize a set of living beings whom they acknowledge to be
entitled to a certain amount of consideration on their part. The inhibitions
against killing or mistreating one's own family or near relations may very well
have a biological basis.[5] Most human beings extend the idea of a "fellow creature" to other humans of their own race or nationality, and often to all humans
anywhere. The most logical ethical vegetarian position is that this idea should
be extended to include animals as well as humans.

Animals are like us in many ways. They have the senses of sight, taste, touch,
smell, and hearing. They can communicate, though usually on a more rudimen-
tary level than humans. They experience many of the same emotions that humans do, such as fear or excitement. So why shouldn't animals be considered
our fellow creatures?

There are three frequently heard attacks on the idea that animals are our fellow creatures. These kinds of attacks can be summarized as follows:

- Killing for food is natural: "Animals kill other animals. Lions kill zebras, and spiders kill flies. Killing for food is part of nature; it can't be wrong for us to do something which is natural."
- Animals are significantly different from people, so it's all right to kill animals: "We can only have equal consideration for those who are our equals. Animals are not our equals; they are weaker than we are, and they are not rational. Therefore they are not our fellow creatures, and it can't be wrong to eat them."
- To abstain from killing is absurd: "Plants are living creatures too. Perhaps plants have feelings. If one objects to killing, logically one ought to object to eating all living creatures, and thus ought not to eat plants either."

Let us examine these arguments one by one.

Is Killing for Food Natural?

The first argument, perhaps the most sophisticated, concedes that animals may be in some sense our fellow creatures and that animals suffer real pain. But because of the dictates of nature, it is sometimes all right to kill and eat our fellow creatures; or alternatively, it is all right to eat those of our fellow creatures which, as a species, are naturally food for us.

This is quite an admirable argument. It explains practically everything; why we do not eat each other, except under conditions of unusual stress; why we may kill certain other animals (they are, in the order of nature, food for us); even why we should be kind to pets and try to help miscellaneous wildlife (they are *not* naturally our food). There are some problems with the idea that an order of nature determines which species are food for us, but an examination of human history indicates the broad outlines of just such an order, though inhibitions against eating certain species may vary from culture to culture.

The main problem with this argument is that it does not justify the practice of meat-eating or animal husbandry as we know it today; it justifies *hunting*. The distinction between hunting and animal husbandry probably seems rather fine to the man in the street, or even to your typical rule-utilitarian moral philosopher. The distinction, however, is obvious to an ecologist. If one defends killing on the grounds that it occurs in nature, then one is defending the practice as it occurs in nature.

When one species of animal preys on another in nature, it only preys on a very small proportion of the total species population. Obviously, the predator species relies on its prey for its continued survival. Therefore, to wipe the prey species out through overhunting would be fatal. In practice, members of such predator species rely on such strategies as territoriality to restrict overhunting, and to insure the continued existence of its food supply.

Moreover, only the weakest members of the prey species are the predator's victims: the feeble, the sick, the lame, or the young accidentally separated from the fold. The life of the typical zebra is usually placid, even in lion country; this kind of violence is the exception in nature, not the rule.

As it exists in the wild, hunting is the preying upon isolated members of an animal herd. Animal husbandry is the nearly complete annihilation of an animal herd. In nature, this kind of slaughter does not exist. The philosopher is free to argue that there is no moral difference between hunting and slaughter, but he cannot invoke nature as a defense of this idea.

Why are hunters, not butchers, most frequently taken to task by the larger community for their killing of animals? Hunters usually react to such criticism by replying that if hunting is wrong, then meat-hunting must be wrong as well. The hunter is certainly right on one point—the larger community is hypocritical to object to hunting when it consumes the flesh of domesticated animals. If any form of meat-eating is justified, it would be meat from a hunted animal.

Is hunting wrong? A vegetarian could reply that killing is always wrong, and that animals have a right to live. This would seem to have the odd consequence that it is not only wrong for humans to kill, but that it is wrong for lions to kill zebras, spiders to catch flies, and so on. If animals have a right not to be killed, then they would seem to have a right not to be killed by any species, human or nonhuman.

There are two ways of replying to such an apparent paradox:

- To draw a distinction between necessary and unnecessary killing. Humans have an alternative; they do not have to eat meat. A tiger or a wolf, on the other hand, knows no other way. Killing can be justified only if it is necessary, and for humans it is not.
- To accept the challenge, and to agree that the most desirable state of the world is one in which all killing, even between nonhuman animals, has ceased. Such a world would, perhaps, be like that envisioned by Isaiah, in which the wolf would lie down with the lamb, the lion would eat straw like the ox, and so on. To implement this, we should start by eliminating as much killing as is possible by changing the habits of that one species whose habits can most easily be changed, our own. After humans become vegetarian, we can start to work on the lions and tigers.

Are Animals Different from People?

The second argument justifying meat consumption is usually expressed as a sort of reverse social contract theory. Animals are different from people; there is an unbridgeable gulf between humans and animals which relieves us of the responsibility of treating animals in the same way that we would treat humans.

David Hume argues that because of our great superiority to animals, we cannot regard them as deserving of any kind of justice: "Our intercourse with them could not be called society, which supposes a degree of equality; but absolute command on the one side, and servile obedience on the other. Whatever we covet, they must instantly resign: Our permission is the only tenure, by which they hold their possessions . . . This is plainly the situation of men, with regard to animals . . ."[6]

Society and justice, for Hume, presuppose equality. The problem with this theory is that it justifies too much. Hume himself admits in the next paragraph that civilized Europeans have sometimes, due to their "great superiority," thrown off all restraints of justice in dealing with "barbarous Indians"; and that men, in some societies, have reduced women to a similar slavery. Thus, Hume's arguments appear to justify not only colonialism and sexual discrimination, but probably also racism, infanticide, and basically anything one can get away with.

If we were to reply to Hume that some superior creatures from another planet might find us a tasty morsel, Hume would probably bravely reply that there would be nothing wrong with this. But this seems to undermine the very possibility of an ethical community. At best, Hume has convinced us not merely that ethical distinctions should not be applied to animals, but that they should not be applied at all—to animals, humans, or anything else.

Thomas Aquinas provides a different version of the unbridgeable gulf theory. This time it is the human possession of reason, rather than superior force, that makes us so different from animals. Aquinas states that we have no obligations to animals because we can only have obligations to those with whom we can have fellowship. Animals, not being rational, cannot share in our fellowship; thus, we do not have any duties of charity to animals.[7]

There are two possible responses to this: that the ability to feel, not the ability to reason, is what is ethically relevant; or that animals are not all that different from humans, being more rational than is commonly supposed.

Both of these objections are expressed briefly and succinctly by Jeremy Bentham: "a full-grown horse or dog is beyond comparison a more rational, as well as a more conversable animal, than an infant of a day, or a week, or even a month, old. But suppose the case were otherwise, what would it avail? The question is not, Can they *reason*? nor, Can they *talk*? but, Can they *suffer*?"[8]

The problem is that none of the differences between humans and animals seem to be ethically significant. Animals are just as intelligent and communicative as small children or even some mentally defective adult humans. If we do not eat small children and mentally defective humans, then what basis do we have for eating animals? Animals certainly have feelings, and are aware of their environment in many significant ways.[9] So while animals may not have all the same qualities that humans do, there would seem to be no basis for totally excluding them from our consideration.

Equal Rights for Plants?

A third kind of argument seeks to reduce ethical vegetarianism to absurdity. If vegetarians object to killing living creatures (it is argued), then logically they should object to killing plants and insects as well as animals. But this is absurd. Therefore, it can't be wrong to kill animals.

Fruitarians take the argument concerning plants quite seriously; they do not eat any food which causes injury or death to either animals or plants. This means, in their view, a diet of those fruits, nuts, and seeds which can be eaten without the destruction of the plant that bears the food.

Finding an ethically significant line between plants and animals, though, is not particularly difficult. Plants have no evolutionary need to feel pain, and completely lack a central nervous system. Nature does not create pain gratuitously, but only when it enables the organism to survive. Animals, being mobile, would benefit from having a sense of pain; plants would not.

Even if one does not want to become a fruitarian and believes that plants have feelings (against all the evidence to the contrary), it does not follow that vegetarianism is absurd. We ought to destroy as few plants as possible. And by raising and eating an animal for food, many more plants are destroyed indirectly by the animal we eat than if we merely ate the plants directly.

What about insects? While there may be reason to kill insects, there is no reason to kill them for food. One distinguishes between the way meat animals are killed for food and the way insects are killed. Insects are killed only when they intrude upon human territory, posing a threat to the comfort, health, or well-being of humans. There is a difference between ridding oneself of intruders and going out of one's way to find and kill something which would otherwise be harmless.

These questions may have a certain fascination for philosophers, but most vegetarians are not bothered by them. For any vegetarian who is not a biological pacifist, there would not seem to be any particular difficulty in distinguishing ethically between insects and plants on the one hand, and animals and humans on the other.

Reductionism

The realities of the modern factory farm have led many meat eaters to question the morality of the present system of raising animals for food. The simplest solution would be to eliminate the practice of raising animals for food. However, some have suggested that—morally reprehensible as the present system is—modifications to today's factory farms would make the process ethically acceptable.

These reductionists generally come in two varieties: those who suggest that we abolish the death of animals, but not the suffering; and those who suggest easing the suffering of animals, while still killing them.

Lacto-ovo-vegetarians are sometimes accused of being reductionist. Animals who provide dairy products and eggs suffer just as much—if not more—than animals raised specifically for slaughter, and most dairy cows and laying hens wind up at the slaughterhouse anyway. The dairy industry and the veal industry are closely related: breeding dairy cows sometimes results in male calves. These calves obviously can't provide milk, nor do they have the characteristics of good beef cattle, so these male calves typically wind up as veal.

One way to get around this argument is to maintain that one only has an obligation not to eat foods which directly and necessarily cause the death of animals. If the only ethical question were the killing of animals, this argument would have a certain amount of force, but what is one to do about the undeniable pain and suffering which dairy cows and laying hens suffer along the way? Once one admits that what the suffering animals experience while they are still alive is an important ethical issue, it is hard to escape the total vegetarian or vegan position, that one ought to abstain from dairy products, eggs, or any other products (including of course meat) which are the result of modern factory farms. And virtually all animal products in the United States today are products of the factory farm system.

Some lacto-ovo-vegetarians obtain their eggs and milk from "free range" animals, or raise the cows and chickens themselves. Such animals are not kept in small cages or factory farms; they are, as far as is possible, allowed to live out their normal lives in normal surroundings. However, it is often hard to find such free range dairy products and eggs, and they are always much more expensive than the regular factory farm products. But a lacto-ovo-vegetarian who gets his eggs and milk from free range animals can scarcely be faulted on ethical grounds.

Another type of reductionist is the conscientious omnivore. Such a person will maintain that causing pain to animals is wrong, but that an instantaneous, painless death at the end of a more-or-less normal life is morally acceptable. In other words, we have a right to kill the animals, but not a right to cause undue or unnecessary suffering.

Sometimes conscientious omnivores live on farms; they may eat only animals which they themselves have raised humanely. Or, they may eat only wild animals which they have killed. Finally, they may buy meat in a regular grocery store, but avoid the types of meat associated with the very worst abuses. Such a person, for example, would avoid all poultry, veal, and eggs.

While most ethical vegetarians would object to these kinds of reductionism, the reductionist at least admits that animals are entitled to some kind of consideration.

Conclusions

There is no real disagreement over the facts of the ways that animals are treated today. Nor is there any doubt that animals experience real suffering, and experience death in much the same way that a human might experience it. The consumption of meat and of all animal products thus creates a great moral dilemma for those who are concerned about the suffering and death of animals.

The dictionary defines ethics as "the study of standards of conduct and moral judgment." The remainder of this section will consist of a study of the major standards of conduct familiar to those in Western societies, as they pertain to meat consumption and the treatment of animals generally. In most such systems, the treatment of animals is a footnote, if it is considered at all. The real problem, it is suggested, is how to treat other humans; and such systems explore this question at great length.

But sometimes animals are a significant topic in these ethical systems. The study of the role animals play in religion could be endless. Innumerable religions deal with animals in innumerable ways; we will limit ourselves to those religions which are most familiar to Westerners: Hinduism, Buddhism, Jainism, Judaism, and Christianity.

As far as philosophy is concerned, few philosophers give a major place to the consideration of animals at all. The big exceptions here are the Platonists, who provide us with the philosophical tradition most strongly identified with vegetarianism. Finally, any consideration of vegetarian ethics must include the attitudes and opinions of vegetarians themselves, and the section will conclude with a brief history of vegetarianism.

18
Hinduism, Buddhism, and Jainism

Hinduism, Buddhism, and Jainism are all frequently cited as examples of vegetarian religions. In fact, all three of these Indian religions have large numbers of vegetarian adherents—largely, probably, than the relative numbers of vegetarians which one would find in any Western religion. However, it is unclear whether this vegetarianism is more a product of cultural and economic factors than of the religion itself. Even today, only the Jains forbid the eating of meat as a question of doctrine.

In the West, ethical vegetarians frequently act out of a heightened respect for animals; in the Indian religions, asceticism is sometimes a motive. It's not always the only motivation—Hindus have a very high regard for the cow, and Buddhist scriptures reflect a positive conception of animal existence. But asceticism is more of a motivation than it is for the typical Western vegetarian.

Religions are frequently mixtures, in different proportions, of doctrine, ritual, story-telling, and cultural beliefs. This is as true for Indian religions as it is for Western religions, and all these factors play a part in the religious phenomena which attract our attention.

Hinduism

Hinduism can be characterized as being difficult to characterize. It is a very resilient religion which has, over a period of centuries, managed to absorb the elements of many other religions without losing its distinctive character. Hindus believe in many gods and accept the doctrines of reincarnation and *karma*—the moral effect of one's actions in previous lives on the current cycle of existence. The cow is a sacred animal, and no orthodox Hindu will kill a cow or eat beef.

Vegetarianism has a long history within Hinduism, going back many centuries before Christ.

Almost none of the things which distinguish Hinduism today were present in its oldest forms. During the Vedic period in India (after about 2000 B.C.), Hindus ate meat with great delight. There was extensive practice of animal sacrifices. There was a simple idea of an afterlife—a heaven, where those who had acquired merit through the bestowal of numerous sacrificial gifts were most likely to wind up.[1]

Vegetarianism only emerged in Hinduism over a long period of time. After about 1000 B.C., meat-eating was restricted. There was an increasing identification between animal slaughter and animal sacrifice: the sutras of this period state that one may eat meat only when the animal is sacrificed.[2] The Upanishads of this period are the first Hindu scriptures to mention doctrines suggestive of reincarnation.[3]

There was a major upheaval around the sixth century B.C. in India, which not only deeply affected Hinduism, but also led to the formation of the Buddhist and the Jain religions—both of which put increased emphasis on the sanctity of all life, including animal life. In the third century B.C. the great Indian king Asoka converted to Buddhism, and Buddhism became the official religion. Asoka himself gave up most, if not all, meat consumption. Meat was almost entirely done away with at the royal court; and the killing of some kinds of animals was prohibited entirely. It is said that he was converted to Buddhism after viewing the carnage that resulted from one of the great battles of the day.[4]

But economic factors, as well as religious factors, were making meat consumption increasingly rare. It was becoming more and more expensive to produce meat because of the pressure overgrazing and deforestation were placing on the land.[5] Given the economic situation in India at the time, it is quite possible that Asoka had one eye on the Buddha and another eye on the condition of the land. Some of Asoka's other decrees—such as restrictions on forest-cutting— also demonstrate an acute awareness of the relationship between ecology and human prosperity.[6]

Hinduism had begun to exhibit vegetarian tendencies at this time as well. Around the seventh century B.C., some Hindu sages first began to advocate vegetarianism,[7] though they were probably a minority. Hindu vegetarianism got its greatest push from the Krishna cult, which originated the prominent position of the sacred cow in Hinduism, which persists to this day. The followers of Krishna, who began propagating their views in the first few centuries A.D., were strict vegetarians, and Hinduism came increasingly under their influence. From the third century A.D. onward, the use of beef was increasingly restricted. In the fourth century, the Law of Manu restricted meat-eating to sacrificial occasions. In the fifth century, the life of Krishna was committed to writing in the *Bhagwat Purana*. The upper castes in India resisted this trend, and probably continued to eat beef as late as the ninth or tenth centuries. After the translation of the *Bhagwat Purana* into Hindi (fifteenth century A.D.), Krishna's cow became the cow mother of every Hindu, and from then on no orthodox Hindu would kill a cow or eat beef.[8] This does not mean that all Hindus therefore became vegetarian—though the orthodox followers of Krishna's teaching undoubtedly were. John L. Kipling, writing in the nineteenth century, makes these comments:

> Even Hindus are not, as is commonly believed, universally vegetarian. Nearly all eat fish, vast and yearly increasing numbers eat mutton and kid, Rajputs and Sikhs eat wild boar, and most low-caste Hindus are only vegetarian when flesh food is not within their reach . . . A Levitical code is naturally a mother of hypocrisy, so Hindus living among Hindus of upper caste will call mutton *lal sag*—red vegetable; and fish, water beans; while prawns are ennobled as Shiva biscuits, but they are eaten all the same.[9]

Kipling also noted that flesh food had been eaten by Hindus in some parts of India for centuries.[10] Kipling probably exaggerated the extent to which Hindus ate meat. In other passages, he ridiculed the Hindu respect for animals, which resulted in animals eating crops, animal hospitals to prolong the lives of suffering animals, and the sacred cows which were truly sacred. Some of the meat-eating he described is probably due to the influence of British colonialism.

While many Hindus today and in the past have not been vegetarian, there is nevertheless a strong vegetarian tradition within Hinduism. It can hardly be held against the religion itself if not all its professed followers obey all its precepts. As Kipling himself wryly noted, it is rare to see Christians in Western countries selling all their goods and following Jesus.

Buddhism

Buddhism and Hinduism have many similarities. Both originated in India; both assert the reality of a multiplicity of gods; both accept the ideas of karma and reincarnation. The Buddhist rejects the idea of the self or soul, however, believing it to be an illusion brought about by our attachment to worldly things. He believes that life is essentially suffering, that desire is the cause of suffering, and that the path to Nirvana (or salvation) is the cessation of all desire.

There are two chief branches of Buddhism, the Theravada and the Mahayana. The Theravada tradition is the older, original tradition, today found in Burma, Ceylon, Laos, Thailand, Cambodia, Tibet, and Malaya; while the Mahayana tradition is found in China. Both traditions are found in Vietnam, while Japan has yet another tangent which was originally brought from China.

Attitudes toward meat consumption are markedly different within these two traditions. In Theravada Buddhism, meat-eating has come to be largely condoned, while in Mahayana Buddhism, meat consumption is frowned upon. Interestingly enough, though, no great theoretical doctrinal dispute gives rise to these differences, but rather cultural differences and differences in rituals through which the Buddhist monks acquire their food.

Any standard of behavior which is acceptable to Buddhist monks tends to be acceptable to the rest of the Buddhist community as well. This is only natural; it would be hard to enforce a standard of behavior in the general community when the monks—supposedly the upholders of the moral standard—are permitted to do otherwise.

In Theravada Buddhism the monks beg for food. Moreover, they are not supposed to be particularly picky about what they are given. To accept part of their food but to reject part of it is to be too attached to the world, a trait which monks are supposed to suppress. Thus, when a monk is offered meat for food, he may accept—indeed, he *should* accept—what is given to him.[11]

This principle has many restrictions. First of all, no monk can kill an animal. Secondly, no monk can accept meat which has been specially prepared for him. Thirdly, certain kinds of meat cannot be eaten under any circumstances.

The Buddha clearly enjoins monks to abstain from killing animals. When a monk is killed by the bite of a snake, the Buddha blames this event on the fact that the monk "never suffused the four royal families of the snakes with his friendliness." The Buddha expresses the desire that all creatures of whatever kind be allowed to live.[12]

On the other hand, if a monk is offered meat, the Buddha is represented as having ruled that a monk should accept it, provided that the animal was not killed or prepared especially for him.[13] The Buddha went on to impose further restrictions. One story relates how a monk asked a female lay-devotee for some broth. There was no meat available, so the female lay-devotee secretly cut off part of her own flesh and made a broth out of that. The Buddha, needless to say, was none too pleased about these developments when he discovered what happened. Miraculously, the female lay-devotee's self-inflicted wound healed, and the Buddha forbade the eating of human flesh thereafter. In a similar manner, the Buddha forbade the eating of the meat of elephants, horses, dogs, serpents, lions, tigers, bears, hyenas, and panthers, even if they have died natural deaths.[14]

Like all scriptures, these are subject to interpretation. It would appear to make the acceptance of meat bought in a meat market perfectly all right for monks (or anyone else), since the butcher could not have had any idea at all who was going to buy it when he slaughtered the animal. On the other hand, the prohibition against eating meat "specially prepared" for them could be regarded as forbidding the eating of any animals which did not die a natural death. In most Theravada countries today, though, lay Buddhists eat meat with great relish whenever they get the opportunity.[15] Ironically, a vegetarian in a Theravada country would have no problem with Buddhism itself, but could not become a monk—given the present necessity of monks accepting whatever food is given them.

In the Mahayana countries, the custom regarding monks is completely different, reflecting a different attitude towards meat consumption. The Mahayana Buddhist monks do not beg for food at all; they prepare their own food, which is either bought, grown, or collected as rent. The Mahayana monks in China were strictly vegetarian in ancient times and remain so today.[16]

According to some traditions, the Indian monks who first brought Buddhism to China many centuries ago were vegetarian. Could this mean that, perhaps, vegetarianism was the oldest tradition, and that the rule permitting monks to accept meat was a later aberration? This is possible but unlikely. Dietary abstinence from meat was an ancient Chinese tradition that antedated the arrival of Buddhism.[17] In China, all animal foods, onions, and alcohol were either forbidden or customarily avoided. Animal products were avoided in dress as they were in diet. There was a prohibition on the use of silk or leather (not observed in Theravada countries).

Not only are the Mahayana Buddhist monks vegetarian, but so are many Buddhist lay people in China. Lay people usually receive a lay ordination, in which they must take from one to five vows. Almost everyone takes the first vow, which is not to take the life of any sentient creature. Usually this is interpreted to mean or imply vegetarianism. Sometimes there is disagreement even on this point; some argue that the injunction not to take the life of sentient creatures only means that one should not personally slaughter animals, or eat an animal expressly killed for his benefit.[18]

The devout feelings of the Chinese Buddhists are well illustrated by one well-known story concerning a pious mother and her two sons. The mother is sick. One of her sons offers her a meat dish, but she (being pious) refuses. The first son finally manages to persuade the mother to eat the dish by cleverly disguising the meat as a kind of plant food. The second son, who is also a pious Buddhist, finds out about this and tells his mother that she has eaten meat.

The mother denies this vehemently. "If I have eaten meat," she says, "I pray that all the gods may cast me down into the deepest hell!" Immediately blood streams from her nose, mouth, and eyes, and devils drag her away to hell. The pious son does everything possible to save her. Eventually he goes to hell himself, where he finds his mother about to be dismembered and cooked. He offers to take her place, and this is allowed for a while. However, the Buddha appears. The Buddha declares that the mother can be saved if (!) the monks will perform a mass for her soul. A group of monks do so, and the gates of hell release both the son and his mother.[19]

Buddhism spread to Japan from China, but Japanese Buddhism appears to have gone off on yet another, completely different tangent. Interviews with modern Japanese Buddhist leaders reveal a curious reluctance to deal with the issue of meat consumption. One leader states that ideally we should not even kill plants, let alone animals; but that "in reality, we cannot but do so. Here is one of the sorrows of mankind."[20] In this way, the tradition of nonviolence and vegetarianism is both upheld and denied at the same time.

Animals have clearly achieved a certain kind of status in Buddhism; the Buddhists are worried about the problem of the place of animals in the world order, and of how Buddhists should behave towards animals. An animal's status is somewhat limited—it may have to go through eons of existences before finally accumulating enough good karma to be reborn as a human. A plant may have to go through even more eons to achieve an animal existence. No animal or plant can achieve Nirvana directly; that is something only humans can do. (On the other hand, gods cannot achieve Nirvana directly either).

However, it is evident that animals *can* achieve salvation. There are innumerable birth stories of the Buddha in which prior existences of the Buddha are related. In many of these stories, the Buddha is an animal. Usually, he spends his animal existence doing characteristically Buddha-like things—teaching the other animals about the Buddhist doctrine and precepts, leading them to greater enlightenment.

In one amusing story the Buddha (as a human) is teaching doctrine to some villagers. A frog is in their presence, and a cow-herd accidentally steps on the frog and kills it. Instantly, the frog is reborn as a god in the Heaven of the Thirty-three, "in a golden palace twelve leagues in length."[21]

While not all Buddhists are vegetarians, there is obviously a very strong tradition of vegetarianism in Buddhism. The Buddha commands his followers not to kill animals; and in many segments of Buddhism, it is counted as meritorious to abstain from meat.

Jainism

The Jain religion came into existence at about the same time that Buddhism did—around the sixth century B.C. Jainism shares several ideas with Hinduism and Buddhism; it accepts the ideas of reincarnation, karma, and nonviolence.

According to the Jains, the entire universe is alive. One should abstain, as much as is possible, from violence towards any living creature—and all beings, including rocks and stones as well as plants and animals, are in some sense alive. The idea of *ahimsa,* or nonviolence, is heavily stressed by the Jains, and it has far-reaching implications.

There are five types of beings in the Jain universe, each type having either one, two, three, four, or five senses. These beings are arranged according to the following schema:

Five-sensed beings—human, gods, infernal beings, some animals.
Four-sensed beings—most larger insects, which lack hearing.

Three-sensed beings—small insects and moths, ants, fleas, and bugs, which lack both hearing and sight.

Two-sensed beings—worms, leeches, shellfish, etc., which possess only taste and touch.

One-sensed beings, or *nigodas*—vegetable bodies, earth bodies, water bodies, fire bodies, and wind bodies; these all possess only the sense of touch.[22]

While harm to a higher being is worse than harm to a lower being, the Jains carry the doctrine of ahimsa to its furthest extreme: ideally, one should not harm any kind of being. This can only be accomplished by the Jain monks, who do as little as possible and are entirely supported by the lay community. The path to salvation is that of purifying the soul of its contaminations with matter. As long as the soul is enmeshed in matter, some violence is inevitable, as countless nigodas would be destroyed even in the simple act of taking a walk.[23]

Dietary restraints are very important to the Jains. Forbidden to the Jain are meat, alcohol, honey, or any of five kinds of figs. The single-sensed nigodas are especially present wherever sweetness or fermentation is involved. Thus, consuming honey or alcohol brings untold millions of these nigodas to an untimely and violent end.[24]

Of course, since violence against higher beings is worse than violence against lower beings, Jain lay people may on occasion consume medicine with honey or wine in it; but they may *never* consume meat. Even meat from an animal which has died a natural death contains innumerable nigodas and must be absolutely avoided.[25]

Vegetarians will be pleased, then, to find that there is at least one major religion which unequivocally enjoins vegetarianism for all of its adherents. Before vegetarians go out en masse and convert to Jainism, however, they should probably cast a casual glance at the rest of the Jain religion. The Jains are decidedly ascetic. Their vegetarianism does not arise so much from the discovery that animals are worthwhile beings worthy of respect as from the necessity of purifying the soul of its attachments to matter. This is not to say that they would not make an issue of kindness to animals; undoubtedly they would. But the ultimate objective is denial of the body and purification of the soul, as a necessary step to win the soul's release from matter.

It is interesting to contrast the Buddhist attitude towards asceticism in this regard. The Buddhists describe their doctrine as "the Middle Way." They reject both the followers of bodily pleasure and the followers of asceticism. The Buddha himself, we are told, went through an ascetic phase, in which he deprived himself of food, fasting until his body became black and emaciated in the last degree.[26] Having tried this, though, the Buddha decided that it was not the path to enlightenment. Asceticism was attachment to the body, in a negative way. Probably the Jains, or groups like them, are what the Buddha had in mind when he rejected asceticism. Logically, it would appear that the only way a person could achieve salvation in the Jain scheme of things would be to become a Jain monk in one of his existences, rid himself of desire, and then starve to death.

Conclusions

The Indian religions present a great difficulty for Western vegetarians who are looking for a religious example to emulate. That difficulty is that religions encompass a great many things other than an attitude towards food. While a vegetarian can find much to admire in all three of these religions, the surrounding cultural and religious milieu may seem quite foreign.

One gets the impression from all three of these religions that the vegetarian tradition is sometimes more an expression of asceticism than of a positive ethical conception of the dignity and worth of animals. This is most obvious in the case of the Jains, though it is certainly present in Hinduism and Buddhism as well.

Despite these problems, and despite the tendency for theory and practice to diverge (a problem shared with most other major modern religions), vegetarianism is a very strong force in all three of these religions. Certainly there are more vegetarians among the ranks of Hindu, Buddhists, or Jains than there are among any religion of the West. How much of this is due to the influence of the religion itself, and how much to the influence of culture or economics, is a question for other scholars to determine.

19
The Jewish Tradition

In Judaism, animals have received close and detailed attention. The verdict of the Jewish tradition on animals has not always been favorable. Meat-eating, for example, is clearly permissible provided that the appropriate procedures are followed. But the problem of the ethical status of animals within God's creation has been greatly worried over.

Among present-day Jews, only a minority are vegetarian. The views of most Jews were probably well represented by one Jewish authority on the ritual slaughter of animals for food (*Shehitah*), who states, "Judaism has always looked upon the eating of meat as a wholly justified indulgence. Cases made out from scanty talmudic references for a Jewishly inspired vegetarianism are labored. To Judaism meat eating and wine drinking are natural and sanctioned by God."[1]

Despite this, a vegetarian would feel quite comfortable with the Jewish tradition, and there are within Judaism numerous well-defined practices, customs, or writings relating to the ethics of human treatment of animals.

Original Ideal and Ultimate Hope

According to Genesis, the first diet of humanity was a vegetarian diet—even the animals were to be vegetarian:

> God also said, "I give you all plants that bear seed everywhere on earth, and every tree bearing fruit which yields seed: they shall be yours for food. All green plants I give for food to the wild animals, to all the birds of heaven, and to all reptiles on earth, every living creature." So it

was; and God saw all that he had made, and it was very good. (Genesis 1:29-31)

However, after the flood, meat consumption was permitted:

Every creature that lives and moves shall be food for you; I give you them all, as once I gave you all green plants. But you must not eat the flesh with the life, which is the blood, still in it. (Genesis 9:3-4)

Some vegetarians have argued that this passage actually supports vegetarianism, since it is impossible to drain the blood entirely from an animal. Others have only quoted the phrase "But you must not eat the flesh" out of context. Both the Ebionites in the first century A.D., and the Society of Bible Christians in the nineteenth century, argued that blood could never be entirely drained from the animal.

In the context of the rest of the Bible this argument is questionable. The prohibition in Genesis 9:3-4 is clearly against eating blood, not against eating flesh; and there is no indication that the draining of blood would be a particularly difficult task. Parallel passages in Deuteronomy (12:23-24, 27-28) imply that the injunction against eating blood is fulfilled if you pour the blood "out on the ground like water." The talmudic commentators concur on this interpretation. Adam, they state, was not permitted to eat flesh; but after the flood, with the advent of the sons of Noah, meat-eating was permitted (Sanhedrin 59b).

One could argue, however, that the original diet of humanity (the total vegetarian diet in Genesis 1:29) was the diet which God truly intended us to have; and that permission to eat meat was granted by God only after it became apparent that humans were going to go their own way regardless of what God told them. One Jewish writer comments, "Only after man proved unfit for the high moral standard set at the beginning was meat made part of the humans' diet."[2] According to this interpretation, while it would not be a violation of the law to eat meat, it would be morally better to abstain.

There is considerable biblical evidence for the view that God's ultimate hope is for a world in which no animals are killed, even by other animals—a world which, in respect to diet, is like that envisioned in the Garden of Eden. The most striking example of this is in Hosea:

Then I will make a covenant on behalf of Israel with the wild beasts, the birds of the air, and the things that creep on the earth, and I will break the bow and sword and weapon of war and sweep them off the earth, so that all living creatures may lie down without fear. (Hosea 2:18)

It would appear from this statement that God hopes for a future era in which animals need not fear the bow, the sword, or the weapon of war. It is striking that God states his intent to make his covenant *with the animals themselves*. This is not the only time in the Bible that God deals directly with animals; his covenant with the animals in Hosea is very much like a similar covenant which is made after the flood:

> God spoke to Noah and to his sons with him: "I now make my covenant with you and with your descendants after you, and with every living creature that is with you, all birds and cattle, all the wild animals with you on earth, all that have come out of the ark. I will make my covenant with you: never again shall living creatures be destroyed by the waters of the flood . . ." (Genesis 9:9-11)

While this covenant is limited in extent (the animals are only protected against God's wrath, not man's), it indicates that animals are part of God's concerns; that, in the words of the Psalmist, "his tender care rests upon all his creatures" (Psalms 145:9).

This future world of peace is also outlined in Isaiah. The wolf, sheep, leopard, calf, lion, cow, bear, cobra, and little child will all be at peace with each other, and—

> They shall not hurt or destroy in all my holy mountain; for as the waters fill the sea, so shall the land be filled with the knowledge of the Lord. (Isaiah 11:9)

This prophecy is repeated further on (Isaiah 65:25); and it would seem to indicate that the ultimate hope of God is for a world in which all creatures live in peace with each other, and where not even the carnivorous animals (like lions) will kill other animals.

Compassion for Animals

In many other places in the Bible, the obligations of humans towards animals is made clear. It is apparent that animals are entitled to consideration, even if they are to be used for farm work or to be slaughtered. While humans are allowed to use and eat animals, they do not have the right to be cruel to them or cause unnecessary suffering.

The process of slaughter itself is carefully regulated. The procedures are dealt with in the Talmud. Only specially trained slaughterers, who must be God-fearing, observant Jews, can be employed. The knife must be sharper than a razor, without the slightest indentation. The killing consists in cutting the esophagus and the trachea, severing the jugular vein and carotid arteries. This causes practically instantaneous unconsciousness. The only pain experienced by the animal is the cutting of the skin, a pain minimized by the sharpness of the knife.[3]

And whatever the ultimate destiny of the animal, the well-being of the animal itself is a concern of both the law and of God himself:

- In Proverbs it is stated that, "A righteous man cares for his beast" (12:10).
- Animals, as well as humans, are involved in the observance of the Sabbath (Exodus 20:10, 23:12).
- Humans have an obligation to relieve the suffering of animals. Deuteronomy 22:4 enjoins the individual to assist a fellow-countryman's ass or ox which is lying in the road; and in Exodus 23:5, this obligation is extended to the ass or ox of an enemy or of someone who hates you. Several talmudic commentators conclude that one can infer from these passages that relieving the suffering of an animal is a biblical law (Baba Mezia 32b). One does not, that is, merely have an obligation to help other human beings; one has an obligation toward animals, even the animals of an enemy.

  Probably the most famous talmudic passage along these lines is the story of Rabbi Judah (Baba Mezia 85a). A calf was being taken to slaughter when it broke away and hid its head under the Rabbi's skirt, crying out in terror. The Rabbi said: "Go, for you were created for this purpose." The response in heaven to the Rabbi's indifference is, "Since he has no pity, let us bring suffering upon him." After this, the Rabbi suffered from disease for thirteen years. But one day the Rabbi's maid-servant was sweeping the house and was going to sweep away some young weasels lying there. The Rabbi said to leave them be, quoting the Psalms—"and his tender care rests upon all his creatures" (Psalms 145:9). After this, the Rabbi's heavenly judges relented.

- Finally, man is like the animals and suffers a common fate. Ecclesiastes 3:19 states, "For man is a creature of chance and the beasts are creatures of chance, and one mischance awaits them all: death comes to both alike. They all draw the same breath. Men have no advantage over beasts; for everything is emptiness. All go to the same place: all came from the dust, and to the dust all return."

  In Proverbs the ant is praised for its industriousness (6:6-8), and ants, rock-badgers, locusts, and lizards are said to be "wise beyond the wisest" (30:24-28). The ox and the ass are favorably compared to Israel by Isaiah (1:2-3). The Lord's protection of his people is compared to that of an eagle toward its young (Deuteronomy 32:10-12). Animals are held responsible for their actions (Exodus 21:28-32) and look expectantly to God for their food (Psalms 104:24-30).

This by no means exhausts the biblical references to man's relationship to animals.[4] But the inescapable conclusion is that humans do have some obligations toward animals. Animals are like humans in many ways; they are our fellow creatures, and God cares for them in much the same way that God cares for us.

The Rejection of Animal Sacrifices

The question of animal sacrifices must have been a pretty hot topic in ancient times. The Mosaic law is full of references to the times, occasions and circumstances under which it is appropriate to offer sacrifices of all kinds. On the other hand, there are numerous passages in the Bible and the Talmud in which sacrifices are either downgraded in importance or rejected. In still other passages, the sacrificial tradition is denied altogether.

What relevance does any of the biblical discussion of animal sacrifice, pro or con, have to do with vegetarianism? Certainly, not all sacrifices involved eating animals for food. "Whole-offerings" were entirely given up, with nothing left behind, but the "shared-offering" involved a sacrifice of part of the animal, while the rest was eaten.

But did all slaughtering of animals for food necessarily involve a sacrifice? The evidence of the Bible is that there was such a connection in biblical times. While not all sacrifices involved slaughtering for food, all slaughtering for food (in accordance with the law) implied a sacrifice. In Leviticus 17:3-4 it is stated that "any Israelite who slaughters an ox, a sheep, or a goat, either inside or outside the camp, and does not bring it to the entrance of the Tent of the Presence to present it as an offering to the Lord shall be guilty of bloodshed: that man has shed blood and shall be cut off from the people."

In short, any slaughtering exclusively for the sake of food was bloodshed. One scholarly commentator on this passage remarks that "the import of the old tradition is that eating the flesh of a domestic animal must be accompanied by a rite."[5] There is the implication that the slaughter of animals without such a sacrifice is idolatry, for further down the biblical writer states, "They shall no longer sacrifice their slaughtered beasts to the demons whom they wantonly follow. This shall be a rule binding on them and their descendants for all time" (Leviticus 17:7).

It is interesting that much the same thing was taking place in other parts of the world at this same time. Both in India and Greece there was an increasing identification between meat consumption and a religious sacrifice; meat could only be eaten if the animal was sacrificed.

This gives an entirely different meaning to the discussions of animal sacrifice in the Bible. It is not only a discussion of the sacrificial rite; it is a discussion of meat consumption as well. And in many of the prophetic books, sacrifices are strongly attacked:

I hate, I spurn your pilgrim feasts; I will not delight in your sacred ceremonies.

When you present your sacrifices and offerings I will not accept them,
nor look on the buffaloes of your shared-offerings.

Spare me the sound of your songs; I cannot endure the music of your
lutes.

(Amos 5:21-23)

Similar strong language can be found in Isaiah 1:11-16. Other, somewhat
more conciliatory passages include Hosea 6:6, Micah 6:6-8, and Makkoth 10a
in the Babylonian Talmud. These passages suggest that sacrifices, while not
necessarily inspiring God's hatred, are unnecessary.

Now of course these passages are subject to interpretation. Were the prophets
attacking the practice of making sacrifices? Or were they attacking other behavior by the people of Israel, and saying that making sacrifices was hypocritical or
inadequate due to this previous offense against God? This is hard to answer. The
anger of Isaiah, though, must at least partially be directed against the making of
sacrifices at all: "The reek of sacrifice is abhorrent to me" (Isaiah 1:13), and
"There is blood on your hands; wash yourselves and be clean" (1:15-16).

Still other parts of the prophetic books deny the sacrificial tradition in different ways. Jeremiah 7:21-22 denies that God gave any commands at all about
sacrifices at the time of Moses. In Ezekiel 20:21-26 there is the suggestion that
God was having second thoughts about the Mosaic statutes, or at least some of
them. In Amos 5:25-26 it appears that the children of Israel never presented any
sacrifices to the Lord while they were in the wilderness.

The destruction of the Temple in 70 A.D. by the Romans renders the relationship of meat-eating to sacrifices even more problematic. This made it impossible for the Jews to offer sacrifices at the Temple. Was the slaughtering of
animals thereafter necessarily bloodshed? Did the Jews find some other location
to make their sacrifices? Did it release them from obligations to make sacrifices
at all?

Apparently there was considerable debate about these points among the Jews
of the day. In Babba Bathra 60b we have one account of such a debate, in which
it is related that Rabbi Yishmael said, "From the day that the Holy Temple was
destroyed it would have been right to have imposed on ourselves the law prohib-
iting the eating of flesh."[6]

It is not clear what the debates which took place subsequently were all about.
We do not have precise knowledge of what the sacrificial tradition was when the
Temple was destroyed; it is possible that the tradition itself was in some ways
ambiguous or undefined. It would appear quite likely, though, that a number of
Jews at the time identified meat consumption with sacrifice (or as entailing
sacrifice), and identified the Temple as the only possible sanctification for such
sacrifices. We do know that after the destruction of the Temple, many Jews gave
up meat-eating altogether, and that, in fact, meat consumption nearly died out at
the time.[7]

The Jewish Folk and Literary Tradition Since Biblical Times

Is the concern for animals merely a passing aberration in the history of the Jewish religion? Or does it find expression within Jewish communities and writings down to the present day? Folk and literary traditions since biblical times give evidence that there is a continuing concern for animals within Judaism—it was not simply a passing thought which somehow found its way into the Bible.

The Jewish historian Josephus, who participated in the Jewish wars against Rome, described the basic principle of all the Jewish laws as mercy. The laws, he says, do not neglect the care of animals; "Ill-treatment even of a brute beast is with us a capital crime."[8]

In the *Tanchuma*—a set of homilies from the fifth century A.D. written by Tanchum Bar Abba—we find the following:

> If men embark on a sea voyage and take cattle with them, and should a storm arise, they throw the cattle overboard, because people do not love animals as they love human beings. Not so is the Lord's love. Just as he is merciful to man, so is he merciful to beasts. You can see this from the story of the flood. When men sinned the Lord decided to destroy the Earth. He treated both man and beast alike. But when he was reconciled, he was reconciled to both man and beast alike.[9]

In the Middle Ages Yehudah Ha-Chassid wrote, "The greatest sin is ingratitude. It must not be shown even to the brute. That man deserves punishment who overloads his beast, or beats or torments it, who drags a cat by the ears, or uses spurs to his horse . . . "[10]

It is said of the Kabbalist Rabbi Isaac Luria, who lived in the sixteenth century, that his respect for life was so great that he would avoid treading on iinsects or on grass.[11] In the nineteenth century Shalom Rabinowitz (1859-1916) wrote a story entitled "Cruelty to Living Creatures," devoted to a child's sorrow at the fate of a little fish which is shortly to be eaten.[12]

The Jewish vegetarian movement crystallized in the nineteenth century with the publication of Aaron Frankel's book *Thou Shalt Not Kill, or the Torah of Vegetarianism*. Since that time numerous Jewish vegetarian societies have sprung up all over the world. This has evoked great respect among many Jews; the late Rabbi M. Kossowsky, who was not himself a vegetarian, stated that vegetarianism was "the highest pinnacle of ethical achievement."[13]

Conclusions

Judaism does not unequivocally condemn meat eating as a sin. But a strong case can be made that Judaism does revere vegetarianism as an ethical ideal. All

Jews are enjoined to have respect and compassion for animals. Even if an animal must be killed for food, it should not be caused to suffer unnecessarily. Jews would have absolutely no problem in becoming vegetarians, while still remaining loyal to their religion.

20
Christianity

Christianity presents a problem for a religiously motivated vegetarian. That problem is that the New Testament says so very little about animals or about vegetarianism. To be sure, a vegetarian who wanted to find a place within Christianity could certainly do so. Seventh-day Adventists recommend vegetarianism and have a large vegetarian contingent among their membership. The Trappist monks of the Catholic Church are vegetarian. But exactly what place would vegetarianism have in the teachings of Christianity?

Jesus' teachings focus on nonviolence and poverty. It could hardly be otherwise for anyone who recommends loving one's enemies, and selling everything one owns and giving it to the poor. Would it not be a logical extension of the principles of nonviolence to extend these principles from humans to animals? Should we not love animals and care for them? And isn't meat a wasteful luxury item, a food for the rich? Shouldn't we be making more food available for the poor and the hungry by eating plant foods? While all of these ideas seem plausible enough, there does not seem to be very much direct support for such views in the New Testament.

Sometimes it is difficult to reestablish the context of Jesus' teachings as we try to understand their meaning. The fact that Jesus opposed the sacrificial cult, for example, is largely unnoticed today. Yet Jesus made a point of driving the sellers of livestock out of the temple (John 2:14-16). He also quoted on two occasions the Old Testament saying, "I require mercy, not sacrifice" (Matthew 9:13 and 12:7). In the first century, many Jews thought of meat eating as being part of these sacrifices—all meat-eating, that is, requiring or implying a sacrifice. In such a case, doing away with animal sacrifices would appear to imply doing away with meat eating as well.

Such reasoning would seem remote to most Christians today. That is because the question of animal sacrifice is remote; it is a question, at best, for scholars of ancient history. But things were very different in the first century. For many of those who first heard the message of Jesus, Christianity had directly vegetarian implications.

The Bible, the Church, and Vegetarianism

Our knowledge of a vegetarian tradition within Christianity comes from several places. There is first of all the Bible; secondly, the history of the early church; and thirdly, the evidence given by figures in the Christian tradition themselves. These sources are not always in agreement and this frequently provokes consternation among Christians today, not only on questions of food and the treatment of animals, but on innumerable other practical and ethical issues too numerous to mention. We must look at the evidence as a whole and use our common sense.

The New Testament is sometimes cited as proving that Jesus was not a vegetarian. First, there are references to "meat" on several occasions; second, to Jesus eating the passover lamb, and third, to Jesus eating fish after the resurrection. However, none of these references prove that Jesus was not a vegetarian.

Most of the references to "meat" in the New Testament are due to a misunderstanding of the vernacular of the King James Version of the Bible. When Jesus' disciples "were gone away unto the city to buy meat" (John 4:8), this means, in the language of the day when the King James Version was distributed, merely that the disciples had gone away to buy food. The Revised Standard Version translates this same passage as "his disciples had gone away into the city to buy food." So much for the references to meat.

In the case of the passover lamb which is thought to have been eaten at the last supper, there are no references to Jesus having eaten the lamb itself. In fact, there are no references to lamb at all, only to bread and wine. Moreover, in John's gospel it is clear that the last supper is not the passover. The chronology would put the last supper on Thursday night, with the Passover on the Sabbath (i.e. beginning on Friday night), which would make it impossible for the last supper to have been the passover.

Finally, the references to Jesus eating fish (Luke 24:43), and other references to Jesus catching fish or distributing fish. The fish was a well known mystical symbol among the early Christians; the Greek word for "fish" (Ichthys) was an acronym whose initials in Greek stood for "Jesus Christ, Son of God, Savior."[1] The earliest and favorite representations of the Eucharist in the catacombs were inspired by the story of the multiplication of the loaves and fishes—which were taken to symbolize the Eucharist. A bishop of the early church wrote as his own epitaph of the fish symbolically, saying: "Faith hath provided as my food a fish of exceeding great size, and perfect, which a holy virgin drew with her hands from a fountain." And Tertullian, also in the second century, wrote similarly: "We little fish, after the image of our Ichthys (Fish) Jesus christ, are born in the water."[2] Clearly the use of the term "fish" is symbolic, not literal, in these cases. It is quite likely that such symbolism has managed to get into the gospels; and that all of the "fish stories" which we find there are not even *intended* to be taken literally, but rather are intended symbolically.

Neither the Bible nor the church can be cited as necessarily proving anything on these matters. The Bible is neither complete nor consistent on numerous matters both of detail and of substance. Compare, for example, Genesis 1:29-30 with Genesis 9:2-3, in which contradictory accounts of what it is acceptable to eat are given. Or compare the detailed description of the proper methods of making animal sacrifices, with the prophetic denunciations of those same practices. Or, in the New Testament, compare the repeated attacks on meat offered to pagan idols (Acts 15:20, 29; Revelation 2:14) on the one hand, with Paul's assurances that eating such meat is all right if no one is offended, on the other (I Corinthians 10:14-33).

Nor have the various churches always been consistent with each other. Even fundamentalists are unable to agree on what the "literal" interpretation of the Bible is. There were innumerable schisms and heresies both in ancient and in modern times. Today we have the division between Protestant and Catholic, and within Protestantism there are further countless divisions into various churches and denominations, all varying from one another on this or that matter of detail or substance.

If neither the Bible nor the church can give automatic answers, then what reasons can we have that indicate that vegetarianism is part of the Christian tradition? There are basically three: (1) Jesus' rejection of animal sacrifices; (2) the lifestyle of Jesus and the early Christians; (3) the Christian traditions since ancient times which indicate a continuing interest in Christian vegetarianism.

Jesus' Rejection of Animal Sacrifices

If we commit a sin, is it necessary—or helpful at all—to go out and sacrifice an animal? The answer of Christianity is clearly "no." Indeed, this is one question of belief which unites all Christians, from Catholics to Baptists to Unitarians. The rejection of the sacrificial cult is central to Christianity. No Christian today entertains the slightest thought that any degree of virtue, merit, or forgiveness, to any extent or to the faintest degree, can be derived from the practice of sacrificing animals.

Animal sacrifice is not a very controversial topic today, because the practice of sacrificing animals for religious reasons has pretty much gone out of style. Things were considerably different in the first century, however. There is abundant evidence that the sacrificial cult was very controversial even before Jesus' time. The prophetic books are full of attacks on sacrifices which are so strong that some have questioned whether or not the so-called "sacrificial cult" was originally ever part of the Law of Moses.

For us, the interesting aspect of the controversy over sacrifices is the connection between sacrifices and meat eating. In the first century, when Jesus lived and taught, there was a very close connection between the two. Indeed, all slaughter of animals was considered a sacrifice of a certain sort. In this context, the rejection of the sacrificial cult acquires an even more radical meaning— entailing the rejection not only of making sacrifices, but of slaughtering animals at all.

What exactly was the link between meat eating and sacrifices? We cannot be certain, but there is no doubt that such a connection was made. As discussed in chapter 19, it appears that sacrificial offerings could entail meat consumption; and a strict reading of Leviticus 17 would imply that all meat consumption necessitated a sacrifice. Not only is this implied by a reading of the laws relating to sacrifice, it is also the view that many persons shared in Biblical times.

For example, consider the prophet Isaiah. He strongly denounces the practice of animal sacrifice; but he also endorses a vegetarian world view in which the wolf, lamb, little child, and the snake will all lie down without fear, and none of the creatures will hurt or destroy one another (Isaiah 11:1-9). Many Christians interpret this passage in Isaiah as prophesying the coming of Jesus. If this is true, then some of the best evidence that Jesus was a vegetarian is in the Old Testament, as it would then appear that Jesus is to bring about or work for a future vegetarian world of peace.

The Essenes, one of the three major groups of Jewish adherents in Jesus' time, also shared this view of the connection between sacrifices and meat eating. Josephus states of the Essenes, "they did not make sacrifices," and adds that the Essenes live in the same way that the Pythagoreans did among the Greeks (that is, they were vegetarian). Philo states, "they did not slaughter living creatures"; while Porphyry says that "all meat is forbidden for the Essenes."[3] Clement of Alexandria, an early leader of the church and a noteworthy vegetarian, also clearly understood that meat eating and animal sacrifice were interconnected; he states flatly, "Sacrifices were invented by men to be a pretext for eating flesh."[4]

What did Jesus say about animal sacrifices? He does not explicitly condemn animal sacrifices in the New Testament, but there are several indications of what his position was. On two occasions Matthew's Jesus quotes Hosea 6:6, saying at one point "Go and learn what this means, 'I desire mercy, not sacrifice' " (Matthew 9:13). At another point, he says, "And if you had known what this means, 'I desire mercy, and not sacrifice,' you would not have condemned the guiltless" (Matthew 12:7). In both of these passages he indicates that God does not desire sacrifices at all, and rather wants us to show mercy.

The celebrated confrontation of Jesus in the Temple gives us further evidence. This incident is found in all four gospels. John states, "In the temple he found those who were selling oxen and sheep and pigeons, and the money-changers at their business. And making a whip of cords he drove them all, with the sheep and oxen, out of the temple" (2:14-15). Obviously, the oxen and sheep were not being sold as companion animals; they were being sold to be sacrificed and eaten. Jesus clearly felt that this was a desecration of the Temple.

In the Gospel of the Ebionites, there is even stronger and less equivocal language. In this gospel, the full text of which is now lost to us, Jesus says: "I am come to abolish the sacrifices; and if ye cease not to sacrifice, the wrath of God will not cease from you."[5] It is quite likely that this saying is genuine. Since the Temple sacrifices necessarily ceased with the destruction of the Temple in 70 A.D., a forger fabricating such a saying after 70 A.D. could probably not have resisted the temptation to turn this saying into an exact prediction of the destruction of the Temple. Therefore, this saying must be one of the earliest known of Jesus' teachings, earlier than the accepted canonical gospels, which were not finalized until the third century A.D.[6]

Jesus, then, must have opposed the sacrificial cult. Jesus was very much in the prophetic tradition, and attacked the sacrificial cult in much the same way that the prophets did. His confrontational style in making clear his opinions on this subject is doubtless one of the key factors responsible for his death. Today, no Christian church gives the slightest credence to the idea that sacrificing animals could possibly do anyone any good. Since we have gone far beyond the Jewish context of the first century, however, this rejection does not carry any great implications for modern-day Christians. The evidence indicates that for those who first heard the message of Jesus, though, the rejection of animal sacrifices had directly vegetarian implications.

The Lifestyle of Jesus and the First Christians

What do we know of how Jesus and the first Christians lived? In order to answer this question, we must examine three groups which existed at or after the time of Jesus: the Essenes, the Nazoreans, and the Ebionites. The Essenes were one of the three major Jewish religious groups at the time of Jesus. The Nazoreans were the first Christians; the term "Nazorean" is frequently mistranslated as "Nazarene," or resident of Nazareth. Finally, the Ebionites, as the Jewish Christians were called, were the successors to the Nazoreans, forming a group distinct from the rest of Gentile Christianity after the destruction of Jerusalem in 70 A.D.

We have no mention at all of the Essenes in the New Testament, but we have quite definite knowledge of their existence from other sources. The Essenes were Jews who bore remarkable similarities to the early Christians. Like the early Christians, the Essenes lived in the cities on the periphery of Israel, rather than in and around Jerusalem, which was the stronghold of their chief adversaries, the Pharisees and the Saducees. Like the early Christians, they abhorred property and riches. Like the early Christians, they practiced a primitive sort of communism, owning all their goods in common. And like the early Christians, they rejected animal sacrifices.[7]

The similarities between the Essenes and early Christianity is so striking that many scholars have concluded that Jesus must have been an Essene. Martin Buber, the Jewish philosopher of religion, thought Jesus was an Essene; and so did Ernest Renan, the great nineteenth century author of *The Life of Jesus*.[8] Renan drew other conclusions from this view: Jesus sought "the abolition of the sacrifices which had caused him so much disgust," and said that "The worship he had conceived for his Father had nothing in common with scenes of butchery."[9] Heinrich Clementz, the German translator of the works of Josephus, concluded: "The Essenes were the ones who created the popularity and following for Jesus Christ's teachings because of their high reputation with the people. . . . The Essenes were the forerunners and the pioneers of the 'sect of the Nazoreans' (Acts 24:5), as Jesus and the first Christians were called."[10] If Jesus was an Essene, or drew upon Essene teachings for his following, then it would be almost certain that Jesus himself was a vegetarian, since the Essenes were vegetarians.

The name by which the first Christians were known is the "Nazoreans." In the Bible this term has already become somewhat confused with the name "Nazarene," or resident of Nazareth. But even in the Bible the term "Nazorean" is the one most frequently used in the original Greek: "Nazarene" is used six times, while "Nazorean" is used twelve times.[11] In Eastern Syria, the term was used to refer to all Christians; but in the areas west of Palestine, it referred specifically to the Jewish Christians, the descendants of the original Christian community.[12]

Scholars differ on the derivation of the term "Nazorean." In the English speaking world, the Biblical references to "Nazorean" have been mistakenly and blandly translated as "Nazarene." According to Hans-Joachim Schoeps, a Jewish scholar, the term derived from "nozrim," meaning "to keep" or "to observe," and designated those who kept to secret traditions.[13] According to Carl Skriver, a Protestant theologian, the term derives from the reference to the Hebrew "nezer" or "branch" referred to by the prophecy of Isaiah 11:1: "There shall come forth a shoot from the stump of Jesse, and a branch shall grow out of his roots."[14]

After the flight from Jerusalem at the beginning of the Jewish War against Rome, the Nazoreans fled to Pella in eastern Palestine. At that time, or shortly thereafter, they took up the title of "Ebionim," or "the poor." From this they became known as "Ebionites." Thus, the Ebionites and the Nazoreans constitute a single group. The Ebionites had their own gospel, which is now lost to us except in fragments. Most importantly, the Ebionites were vegetarian; the Ebionite Jesus taught and practiced vegetarianism, which was not merely recommended but required of its adherents.[15]

Here we have direct testimony of the central role which vegetarianism once played in Christianity. But unfortunately, this role did not spread to the church at large. The Ebionites were Jewish and tried to maintain their status both as Jews and as Christians. Unfortunately, they failed at both tasks. Despite their professed loyalty to the law of Moses, they were persecuted by many in the Jewish community of the day; and despite their devotion to the teachings of Jesus, they were eventually condemned as heretical by the larger Christian church, which was dominated by Gentile Christianity. This latter condemnation goes far in explaining the absence of any references in the New Testament which would demonstrate Jesus' Jewish origins. Thus, it is likely that Gentile Christians removed any references to the Essenes, since such references would have underscored the Ebionite position.

But they did not remove all such references. When Jesus himself speaks to Paul on the road to Damascus, he states that he is "Jesus the Nazorean, whom you are persecuting" (Acts 22:8)—thus declaring himself a member of the very group that the Church condemned as heretical! And there are numerous other references to the "sect of the Nazoreans" which make it clear that the early Christians were, in fact, identical to this "heretical" sect.[16]

For those who hesitate to believe on the basis of the testimony by "heretical" witnesses, there is ample evidence from the most "orthodox" of sources that vegetarianism was a central facet of the very earliest Christians. The letters of Paul testify to this inadvertently. Paul warns against those who "inculcate abstinence from certain foods" (I Timothy 4:3), advance outlandish teachings concerning "scruples about what we eat" (Hebrews 13:8-9), or try to "take you to task about what you eat or drink" (Colossians 2:16). In Romans, he is even more specific; Paul frankly advises the Romans not to offend the "weaker" brethren who are vegetarians (Romans 14:2-22). They should abstain from meat in order to avoid offending the vegetarians, not because eating meat is in itself bad (Romans 14:20).

Since Paul, at every turn, is constantly dealing with these "trouble-making" vegetarians, the conclusion is inescapable: there are apparently a great number of people in the early church who disagreed with Paul, and who were not only vegetarian, but felt that vegetarianism was a demand of their faith. This vegetarian faction must have been quite widespread, existing all the way from Palestine to Rome, and probably included the leadership of the early church.

There is further evidence of vegetarianism in the earliest Christian communities. According to Clement of Alexandria, the disciple Matthew was a vegetarian; and the Clementine Homilies and Recognitions attest that Peter was a vegetarian as well.[17] In the New Testament, Peter uses the term Nazorean, saying at Acts 3:6, "In the name of Jesus Christ the Nazorean, rise up and walk."[18]

Even more importantly, James the Just, the brother of Jesus and the first head of the church in Jerusalem after the death of Jesus, was a vegetarian. Both Hegisuppus and Augustine, "orthodox" sources, testify that James was not only a vegetarian but was *raised* as a vegetarian.[19] If Jesus' parents raised James as a vegetarian, why would they not also be vegetarians themselves, and raise Jesus as a vegetarian?

Even Paul himself, the great opponent of the Ebionites, was himself a vegetarian. In I Corinthians 8:13 Paul states that "if food is a cause of my brother's falling, I will never eat meat, lest I cause my brother to fall." Since there were many Christians at that time who were offended by meat consumption, if Paul took his words seriously he must have been a vegetarian. There is external evidence that Paul was a vegetarian as well: according to the Toldot Jeschu, an anti-Christian Jewish polemic, Paul states that "Jesus commanded me not to eat meat and not to drink wine, but only bread, water, and fruits so that I will be found pure when he wants to talk with me."[20] This not only suggests that Paul was a vegetarian, but that he had other motives for being a vegetarian besides simply appeasing the vegetarian faction in the early church.

Even using the most "orthodox" of sources, vegetarianism extends back to the very beginnings of Christianity, being part of the way of life of the disciple Matthew, the apostle Paul, and James the Just, the brother of Jesus. Indeed, it appears that vegetarianism must have had its source with Jesus himself, for the orthodox fourth-century Christian Hieronymus connects vegetarianism both with the original diet given by God in Genesis 1:29 and with the teachings of Jesus:

"The eating of animal meat was unknown up to the big flood, but since the flood they have pushed the strings and stinking juices of animal meat into our mouths, just as they threw quails in front of the grumbling sensual people in the desert. *Jesus Christ, who appeared when the time had been fulfilled, has again joined the end with the beginning, so that it is no longer allowed for us to eat animal meat.*"[21]

Christian Traditions Since the Earliest Times

Is vegetarianism a passing aberration in earliest Christianity? Or is it reflected in Christian traditions down to the present day? The evidence of history is that vegetarianism is a tradition within Christianity down to the present day.

The most important manifestation of Christian vegetarianism in ancient times was in the Ebionites, or the Jewish Christians. The Ebionite community was the direct descendant of the original "sect of the Nazoreans" (Acts 24:5) whose leaders were themselves descendants of Jesus' relatives. The Ebionites tried to maintain both their loyalty to Moses and to Jesus. They were strict vegetarians, requiring abstinence from all animal flesh. They were closely related to the Essenes, and most of the Essenes were eventually absorbed into Ebionite Christianity. They rejected Paul and sought to reconcile Christianity with the law of Moses.

Their conception of Moses was substantially different from that of other Jews of their day or of modern day Jews. They not only rejected the sacrificial cult in the strongest possible terms, they denied that God had ever commanded sacrifices in the first place. The insertion into the scriptures of commandments to make sacrifices was a grave error; such insertions, or "false pericopes," had to be purged from the Bible.[22] Such assertions cannot have been unique to the Ebionites alone; there are many passages in the Old Testament which suggest such an idea. Jeremiah says, "Add whole-offerings to sacrifices and eat the flesh if you will. But when I brought your forefathers out of Egypt, I gave them no commands about whole-offering and sacrifice; I said not a word about them" (Jeremiah 7:21-22). Amos 5:25 and Ezekial 20:21-26 also suggest such a "revisionist" approach. There is an echo of the theory of "false pericopes" in the speech of Stephen, the first Christian martyr. Stephen quotes Amos 5:25-27 (at Acts 7:42-43), which implies that no true sacrifices were made by the Israelites in the desert.

Like the Essenes and other early Christian groups, the Ebionites rejected the accumulation of material wealth as a meaningful goal in life. They held all their goods in common and endorsed the value of poverty. The Ebionites were pacifists and fled from Jerusalem at the beginning of the Jewish revolt against Rome, which led to the destruction of the Temple in Jerusalem in 70 A.D. They emigrated to Pella, in the eastern part of Palestine. They returned at the end of the war, only to leave again for good at the beginning of the Bar Cocheba revolt, which ended in 135 A.D. The Ebionites persisted into the fourth or fifth centuries; it is not clear why or how they perished. It is possible that the persecutions of Diocletian were largely directed at them and virtually eliminated them. Or, it is possible that they were absorbed into the larger Church.

But many others, both orthodox and heterodox, testified to the vegetarian origins of Christianity. Both Athanasius and his opponent Arius were strict vegetarians. Many early church fathers were vegetarian, including Clement of Alexandria, Origen, Tertullian, Heironymus, Boniface, and John Chrysostom. Many of the monasteries both in ancient times and at the present day practiced vegetarianism. Basilius the Great, in the fourth century, was a vegetarian who attacked the morality of eating meat: "The steam of meat meals darkens the light of the spirit. One can hardly have virtue if one enjoys meat meals and feasts. . . . In the earthly paradise there was no wine, no one sacrificed animals, and no one ate meat. As long as one lives frugally, the luck of the house will increase; the animals will be safe; no blood will be shed; no animal will be killed."[23] Boniface (672-754) wrote to Pope Zacharias that he had begun a monastery which followed the rules of strict abstinence, whose monks do not eat meat nor enjoy wine or other intoxicating drinks.[24]

Legends have sprung up concerning several saints of the Catholic Church who practiced compassion towards animals. Hubertus (656-727) was originally a hunter who stopped hunting after a stag which he had been pursuing turned and confronted him, a cross growing out of his horns, saying "Hubertus, Hubertus, why are you hunting me?"[25] Aegidius was a vegetarian (around 700) who lived on herbs and water and the milk of a deer which God sent to him. One day the deer was being hunted by a king and his entourage, and fled to Aegidius for protection. Aegidius stopped with his right hand the arrow intended for the deer but which only perforated his hand.[26]

Perhaps the most famous friend of animals was Francis of Assisi, who lived in the 11th and 12th centuries. It is said of Francis that he bought two lambs from a butcher and gave them the coat from his back to keep them warm; and that he bought two fish from a fishwoman and threw them back into the water. Francis said: "All things of creation are children of the father and thus brothers of man. . . . God wants us to help animals, if they need help. Every creature in distress has the same right to be protected."[27]

The Trappist monks of the Catholic Church are vegetarian even today. According to the Trappist rules, as formulated by Armand Jean de Rance (1626-1700), "In the dining hall nothing is layed out except: pulse, roots, cabbages, or milk, but never any fish. . . . I hope I will move you more and more rigorously, when you discover that the use of simple and rough food has its origin with the holy apostles (James, Peter, Matthew). We can assure you that we have written nothing about this subject which was not believed, observed, proved good through antiquity, proved by historians and tradition, preserved and kept up to us by the holy monks."[28]

Perhaps the largest and most significant group of Christian vegetarians today are found in the Seventh-day Adventists. The Seventh-day Adventists, a Protestant denomination, recommend vegetarianism to their members, of whom nearly one half or more are vegetarian. Because of their dietary practices, the Seventh-day Adventists have frequently been the object of scientific studies relating diet to health; and these studies have consistently found that Adventists live longer and enjoy greater health than the rest of the population.

Conclusions

Though it is not obvious from a survey of the present day Christian churches, vegetarianism occupies an ancient and important place in the Christian tradition. The earliest Christian communities, including Jesus himself, were vegetarian, and vegetarianism was an important part of the Christian lifestyle.

The Ebionites, or Jewish Christians, the first Christian community after the death of Jesus, were not only vegetarians but held vegetarianism as a tenet of their beliefs. But many other Christians, both in the earliest times and down through the centuries until the present day, have practiced vegetarianism both for health and for ethical reasons. The requirement to be vegetarian has been diluted considerably since the earliest days, but the practice of vegetarianism was continued by many saints, monks, and laymen. Vegetarianism is at the heart of Christianity.

21
Plato and Ancient Philosophy

There was a strong vegetarian tradition in ancient philosophy, at the center of which was Plato. Plato defends or advocates vegetarianism at several points in his famous *Dialogues*. Even more striking is the adoption of vegetarianism by others—both before and after Plato—who were of the Platonic school of thought. This indicates that Platonism was a single tradition incorporating numerous beliefs, one of which was vegetarianism.

Indeed, Plato's role in the Platonic tradition may not be primarily that of an originator at all—he probably originated very few of the beliefs which we would today describe as part of his system. He was, though, the one who with greatest success compiled these ideas, wrote them down, and systematically undertook to spread them. To these ends, he wrote the *Dialogues* and founded the Academy which undertook to spread Platonic ideas.

Besides Plato, we will consider the most famous of the philosophers closely associated with Platonism—Pythagoras, Empedocles, Plutarch, and Porphyry. In ancient times, the opponents of Plato were Aristotle and his "rationalistic" followers and predecessors: Anaxagoras, Epicurus, and the Stoics. With the single exception of the late Stoic philosopher Musonius, these individuals were distinguished by being non-vegetarian, or even anti-vegetarian, and by taking a hostile attitude toward animals. The Platonists, by contrast, believed in the essential moral worth of animals. Unfortunately, modern philosophers have generally followed Aristotle rather than Plato on these and numerous other points—even on the question of how to interpret Plato.

Pythagoras

Pythagoras was one of the most famous pre-Socratic philosophers living in the sixth century B.C. He left no writings at all, though he did leave a highly organized band of followers who passed on the teachings of their master orally. By the time of Plato, they had produced a large number of writings, almost all of which are lost to us today, as is much of ancient philosophy. From what remains, though, the broad outlines of the philosophy of Pythagoras can be determined.

Pythagoras was a vegetarian. This is the conclusion to which Plutarch, Ovid, Diogenes Laertius, and Iamblichus all came to in ancient times; and modern scholars also concur.[1] Indeed, vegetarianism is one of the doctrines which is distinctively Pythagorean. Some ancient writers tried to deny this, claiming that Pythagoras on occasion sacrificed an ox, or occasionally ate meat. These reports apparently stem from Aristoxenus, who in turn seemed to be relying on yet other reports that certain of Pythagoras' followers ate meat two centuries after Pythagoras' death.[2] Even in ancient times, Diogenes Laertius—who dutifully reports all the various contradictory writings along these lines—dismissed these reports, concluding that Pythagoras was a vegetarian.[3]

Another key doctrine of Pythagoras was the transmigration of souls, or reincarnation. Pythagoras taught that the soul was immortal, and that when a plant or animal died, it was reborn as another living organism. Once upon hearing a dog's yelping, Pythagoras remarked that he could recognize the voice of a friend.[4] Pythagoras' belief in the transmigration of souls and in vegetarianism are obviously linked: if one killed an animal for food, one was causing pain or death to an organism that was just as worthy of moral concern as a human being, and who may have been a human being in a previous life.

Pythagoras believed that the essence of reality was number, and that in studying mathematics, one was studying the nature of ultimate reality. Though probably not the originator of the famous Pythagorean theorem often attributed to him, he was intensely interested in mathematics. For Pythagoras, mathematics was the key to reality; indeed, mathematics *was* reality.[5]

Vegetarianism has not been merely tacked on to Pythagoras' philosophy; it is an integral part of it. His philosophy provides several excellent reasons to be a vegetarian. If animal souls can be reborn as humans (and vice versa), then it must be just as wrong to kill animals as to kill humans—their souls are essentially of the same nature. We may speculate further that Pythagoras saw an uncomfortable similarity between human relations with animals and the gods' relations with humans. Just as we would not appreciate the gods' manipulating or killing humans, so we should not manipulate or kill animals.

Empedocles

Empedocles was another pre-Socratic philosopher of ancient Greece who was a vegetarian. We do not know if he was a member of the Pythagorean society, but it is obvious that he was greatly influenced by Pythagoras or Pythagorean views.

We have today only fragments of Empedocles' writings.[6] Nevertheless, even from these brief sayings we can tell much of what Empedocles thought. Empedocles believed in the transmigration of souls:

> For I was once already boy and girl,
> Thicket and bird, and mute fish in the waves. (Fragment 117)

> All things doth Nature change, enwrapping souls
> In unfamiliar tunics of the flesh. (Fragment 126; *see also* Fragment 127)

Empedocles draws significant moral conclusions from the transmigration of souls. He felt that we were eating human beings in a changed form when we ate meat:

> Will ye not cease from this great din of slaughter?
> Will ye not see, unthinking as ye are,
> How ye rend one another unbeknown? (Fragment 136)

> The father lifteth for the stroke of death
> His own dear son within a changed form . . .
> Each slits the throat and in his halls prepares
> A horrible repast. Thus too the son
> Seizes the father, children the mother seize,
> And reave of life and eat their own dear flesh. (Fragment 137)

It seems that Empedocles once ate meat, and that this caused deep guilt subsequently:

> Ah woe is me! that never a pitiless day
> Destroyed me long ago, ere yet my lips
> Did meditate this feeding's monstrous crime! (Fragment 139)

Empedocles also describes a Golden Age, in which human beings lived simpler and better lives and in which everyone was vegetarian (Fragment 128). While we do not know very much about Empedocles, we have several striking examples of his ethical thought.

Plato

Was Plato a vegetarian? And if so, what role did this belief play in his philosophy? We know very little about Plato's life; both biography and history were ill-defined disciplines in Plato's day. Diogenes Laertius, the first (and perhaps the last) true biographer of Plato, lived centuries after Plato died and probably knew little more about Plato than we do today.

Plato began as a follower of Socrates, whom he subsequently made the chief character in most of his famous *Dialogues*. We will probably never know if Socrates was a vegetarian—unless it turns out that the *Dialogues* are a faithful depiction of the more or less historical Socrates. Most modern scholars are inclined to think, though, that the Socrates of the *Dialogues* is mostly a spokesman for Plato's own views.

After the death of Socrates, Plato became a pupil of the then greatest living Pythagoreans—Philolaus, Eurytas, and Archytas, among others. Moreover, Plato was the greatest collector of Pythagorean materials in antiquity. He had ample funds, and bought all the Pythagorean books that could be had.[7] It is clear that Plato was greatly influenced by Pythagoras.

The role of vegetarianism in Plato's thought shows itself both in the statements that Plato directly makes on the subject and in the other striking resemblances—much too great to be coincidental—between Plato's ideas and those of Pythagoras. On most essential points, in fact, Plato is a Pythagorean.

The most important discussion of vegetarianism is found in the *Republic*. Socrates is discussing the ideal republic, and Socrates describes a vegetarian diet as the nourishment of its citizens: "And for their nourishment they will provide meal from their barley and flour from their wheat, and kneading and cooking these they will serve noble cakes and loaves on some arrangement of reeds or clean leaves . . ." (*Republic* 372b).

Glaucon breaks in and objects that there are no "relishes" (*opson*) for the citizens which Socrates describes as "feasting." The word *opson* is a bit ambiguous—it is usually, but not always, composed of meat or fish.[8] Probably Glaucon wants meat on the table; but Socrates misunderstands him on purpose, replying that of course the citizens of this republic will have "relishes":

> Salt, of course, and olives and cheese, and onions and greens, the sort of things they boil in the country, they will boil up together. But for dessert we will serve them figs and chick-peas and beans, and they will toast myrtle berries and acorns before the fire, washing them down with moderate potations. And so, living in peace and health, they will probably die in old age and hand on a like life to their offspring. (372d)

These relishes, though, lack meat; and this isn't good enough for Glaucon, who indignantly demands to know if Socrates is founding a city of pigs. Glaucon insists that the citizens of the ideal state have "dishes and sweetmeats such as are now in use," leaving little doubt that he wants meat on the menu. Socrates replies, "I understand. It is not merely the origin of a city, it seems, that we are considering but the origin of a luxurious city . . . *The true state I believe to be the one we have described* [italics mine]—the healthy state, as it were. But if it is your pleasure that we contemplate also a fevered state, there is nothing to hinder." (372e)

Socrates then proceeds to stock the ideal state with swineherds, huntsmen, and "cattle in great number," not to mention various other extravagances. He then argues that this "fevered state" will require more doctors, more territory to support the increased food requirements, and an army to acquire and defend this territory; and that war is an inevitable consequence of such policies. Critics of Plato, reading the rest of the *Republic*, have complained that what Plato gives us is a militaristic or proto-fascist state, with censorship and a rigidly controlled economy. Plato would hardly disagree with these critics; what they have overlooked is that the state which he describes is not his idea—it is merely a consequence of Glaucon's requirements which Socrates himself disavows. Greed for meat, among other things, produced the character of the second state Plato describes.

Plato indicates his vegetarianism in other dialogues as well. In the *Timaeus* Plato describes a total vegetarian diet as divinely ordained. According to the *Timaeus*, the gods created certain kinds of beings to replenish our bodies (i.e., to be food): "These are the trees and plants and seeds which have been improved by cultivation and are now domesticated among us; anciently there were only the wild kinds, which are older than the cultivated" (*Timaeus* 77a). These kinds of beings had been created "to be food for us" (77c). Also, he refers in passing to "the fruits of the earth or herb of the field, which God planted to be our daily food" (80d). In all of these passages, Plato indicates his belief that a total vegetarian diet is divinely ordained.

Finally, Plato refers to an ideal or Utopian Golden Age, now long gone by, in which humans were vegetarian. In the *Statesman*, the Eleatic Stranger (who is the "hero" of the dialogue, Socrates sitting on the sidelines) describes an era in which "God was supreme governor" of the entire universe: "So it befell that savagery was nowhere to be found nor preying of creature on creature, nor did war rage nor any strife whatsoever. . . . they had fruits without stint from trees and bushes; these needed no cultivation but sprang up of themselves out of the ground without man's toil." (*Statesman* 271e, 272a)

This is remarkably similar both to the Garden of Eden story in Genesis, and to Empedocles, who refers to a similar ideal vegetarian age in the past.

Besides these specific references to food in Plato's thought, there are other striking resemblances between Plato's ideas and those of Pythagoras. Most conspicuously, there are frequent references to the transmigration of souls. All souls—whether of humans or animals—were thought to be of equal moral worth. This is most strikingly illustrated in the story of Er (*Republic* 614-621). In this story, many souls which were human choose to become animals in their next existence; and many souls which were animals choose to become human. Other references to the transmigration of souls leave no doubt that this is not an aberration (*Phaedrus* 248c; *Phaedo* 81-83, 85a; *Meno* 81b; etc.). This is remarkably similar to the formulations found in both Pythagoras and Empedocles. These are not the only similarities between Plato and Pythagoras, either: both accepted the recollection theory of knowledge, and believed in the equality of women.[9]

Clearly, both Plato and Pythagoras advocate a simple life and a vegetarian diet.

Plutarch

Plutarch was a Platonist who also acknowledges his own debt to Pythagoras and Empedocles.[10] His main claims to fame today are his famous biographies of Greek and Roman personalities, and his essays. Three of these essays bear on vegetarian ethics and show that Plutarch, like his predecessors, was a vegetarian.

The most obviously relevant of these essays is the fairly brief essay entitled "Of Eating of Flesh."[11] Here, he forthrightly argues for vegetarianism. He claims that it is not natural for human beings to eat flesh, and that man's anatomy is not that of a flesh-eater: there are no sharp talons, no rough teeth, no hawk's bill. Plutarch invokes the possibility of transmigration of souls as a warning against flesh-eating, as we might be killing a friend or relative in a different form when we kill an animal for food. Even in his one short essay, we can see elements which can be traced back to Pythagoras, Empedocles, and Plato.

A second, more amusing essay also deals with the moral status of animals. In "That Brute Beasts Make Use of Reason,"[12] Plutarch gives us a satirical dialogue between Ulysses, the goddess Circe, and Gryllus—formerly one of Ulysses' men, now recently bewitched by Circe and turned into a hog. But Gryllus argues that Circe has done him a great favor by turning him into a hog, for animals are superior to humans in many ways: they fight fair, they are not cowards, they are temperate, they do not value money. Humans, on the other hand (Gryllus argues), indulge unnatural and excessive appetites. This is Platonism in an accessible and accommodating form. But there is an underlying serious tone to the essay; the Platonic belief in the moral worth of animals is implied in the whole discussion.

A final essay relevant to vegetarianism is the "Rules for the Preservation of Health."[13] In this essay, Plutarch is concerned with the question of health, not ethical standards of action. The essay is in the form of a dialogue between three characters who are very likely fictional. One of the characters, Glaucus, states that one should abstain from the "heavy" meats on grounds of health. He is willing to admit, as a matter of scientific fact, that the "light" meats (such as fish and fowl) would not be damaging to one's health; but he concludes that "it would be best to accustom one's self to eat no flesh at all, for the earth affords plenty enough of things fit not only for nourishment, but for delight and enjoyment . . ."

In these three essays in which Plutarch discusses the ethical and practical aspects of vegetarianism, Plutarch indicates that his own personal beliefs were vegetarian. In this respect Plutarch is very much in the Platonic tradition.

Porphyry

Vegetarianism also manifested itself in the "neo-Platonist" school, which flourished in the third and fourth centuries A.D. The leaders of the neo-Platonists were Plotinus, Porphyry, and Iamblichus, all of whom were vegetarian.

Plotinus, generally considered the founder of neo-Platonism, brought a distinctly ascetic tinge to his philosophy. Plato advocates a simple life, but Plato is hardly an ascetic. The citizens of Plato's ideal republic are vegetarian, but they can drink wine, marry, and have families.

However, Plotinus is a different character altogether. He was deeply ashamed of his body, never took a bath, and could never be induced to tell of his ancestry, his parentage, or his birthplace. He was a strict vegetarian, rejecting not only meat as food, but also any medicines containing animal products.[14] Plotinus left no writings concerning vegetarianism; and the writings that have been given to us (edited by Porphyry after Plotinus' death), would be considered quite esoteric today.

Porphyry was Plotinus' closest disciple and quite possibly a greater philosopher than his teacher. He has given us the earliest surviving book on vegetarianism, called *On Abstinence from Animal Food*.[15] In this work, Porphyry restates many of the arguments used by Plato, Empedocles, and Plutarch to justify vegetarianism—transmigration of souls; the equal moral worth of all souls, whether human or animal; the natural repugnance of humans to animal flesh; and the adverse effects of meat on health.

Curiously, Porphyry is ambivalent on the relationship of vegetarianism to health. On the one hand, Porphyry wants us to believe that a vegetarian diet is healthier. Such a diet would liberate us "from many and vehement diseases, from medical assistance"; and "neither does animal food contribute, but is rather an impediment to health."

On the other hand, Porphyry wants to show himself a disciple of Plotinus. He is concerned with the idea of the purification of the soul, and freeing the soul from the concerns of the everyday material world. So he claims that an advantage of a vegetarian diet is that it does *not* contribute as much to the strength of the body! He goes out of his way to say that his arguments are solely addressed to those pursuing the philosophic life, and not to athletes, soldiers, or sailors. Porphyry could resolve this apparent contradiction by saying that meat makes one physically stronger in the short run, but more susceptible to disease in the long run. But Porphyry has come a considerable distance from Plutarch on the question of the relationship of a vegetarian diet to health.

Porphyry is also concerned with the moral status of animals. He wants to show that animals are very much akin to human beings; and his discussion of the relationship between language and rationality in animals is interesting and thought-provoking. He maintains that "every soul which participates of sense and memory is rational."

Animals do have language, Porphyry argues; crows, hyenas, magpies, etc., all have ways of communicating. Animals understand their masters: "Our opponents," he notes, punish their dogs and horses, "and not in vain." He claims that animals use strategy, acquire knowledge necessary to their survival, and think logically. Animals may not possess as much reason as we do, he states, but just because their thinking is more disordered or dull doesn't mean that they lack it altogether.

Porphyry's assertion that everything that has sense and memory is rational is very much analogous to Hume's analysis of "impressions" and "ideas." Modern science has largely confirmed Porphyry's observations. There is now broad agreement among many scientists that there is evolutionary continuity of mental experience and mental abilities, and that animals have many of the same mental abilities that humans do, though not always to the same degree.[16]

There is much else in Porphyry's *On Abstinence* as well; there is a discussion of animal sacrifices, and answers to many commonly made objections to vegetarianism. Porphyry has made a genuine contribution to the literature of Platonism, and also to the literature of vegetarianism.

Conclusions

We have not exhausted the topic of vegetarianism in ancient philosophy— Ovid, Musonius, and Iamblichus, among others, were also vegetarians and worthy of mention. However, we have shown that Platonism forms a single tradition in ancient philosophy, and that the tradition surrounding Plato forms the chief source of vegetarianism in philosophy in ancient times.

This is not to say that there are not variations in the Platonic outlook: Plutarch's easygoing and popular style of Platonism is radically different from the esoteric and ascetic doctrine of Plotinus. But in all of their writings, the Platonists give evidence of their endorsement of a simple, natural life; and all of them hold that animal life is to be respected, just as human life is to be respected. The traditions of their lives and the evidence of their writings indicate that all of the ancient Platonists were vegetarians.

22
Modern Philosophy

What does modern philosophy have to say about human standards of conduct toward animals? What does modern philosophy have to say about vegetarianism? As it turns out, not much. There are very few philosophers who make animals a problem for their philosophies at all. Animals typically appear as a kind of footnote to the System, if they appear at all. They are the victims, usually, of whatever assumptions and theories have already been worked out.

Modern philosophy is usually dated from Descartes. From our point of view—that of tracing the philosophy of animals—modern philosophy really begins with Aristotle. For Aristotle first develops the idea that humans are radically different from animals. Humans differ from animals, Aristotle argues, in that they possess reason or "mind" (*De Anima* II, 3); furthermore, animals exist for the sake of man—either for work or for food (*Politica* I, 8).[1]

Aristotle does not try to carefully define what mind is; nor does he advance very many arguments to support his contention that animals do not have minds or reason. However, in Aristotle, at least these assumptions are explicitly stated. Many modern philosophers do not even get as far as Aristotle.

Rationalists

Modern philosophy starts out with the realization that philosophy requires some sort of justification; it can't be just dogma. Bravely, the modern philosophers set out to tear away the assumptions Aristotle made and demand justification for them; but then, one by one, the assumptions of Aristotle are reaccepted. Aristotle's influence on modern philosophy is astonishing; and this largely accounts for the anti-vegetarian bias of modern philosophy.

The rationalists hold that reason must be the basis for human knowledge: the empiricists maintain that experience must be the basis. The rationalists are generally considered to be Descartes, Leibniz, and Spinoza (among others), while the empiricists include at least Locke, Berkeley, and Hume. Kant falls somewhere in between. Then, in the nineteenth and twentieth centuries, it becomes harder to categorize philosophers, though there are some who are clearly in the rationalist or the empiricist camp.

Descartes gives the tendencies of modern philosophy their classic expression. He begins by doubting everything, but winds up by accepting much of the Aristotelian world view. His views on animals are indicative of Descartes' general approach. In the *Discourse on Method*, Descartes makes a number of statements that have usually been read to mean that animals are machines—that they have no feelings and are automatons. He makes his argument on the basis of the fact that animals lack language. He grants that they may have the ability to externalize some of their feelings, but argues that (as in the case of parrots) this results from instinct, not reason.

Actually, Descartes only suggests the theory that animals are machines; he does not endorse it. He states that such a theory would explain all the evidence and goes no further. In letters to some of his philosophical correspondents, he retreats from the idea that animals are machines: animals do have feelings and sensations, he admits, but they entirely lack the ability to think.[2] Descartes was frequently ridiculed for even suggesting that animals are automatons; Voltaire and Gassendi both questioned his views on these points.

The other rationalists shy away from the extreme position that animals are machines. Spinoza states that we cannot doubt that animals have feelings, but falls back on the Aristotelian idea that animals are there for humans to use as they please.[3] Liebniz states that "one cannot reasonably doubt the existence of pain among animals, but it seems as if their pleasures and the pains are not so keen as they are in man."[4] Leibniz then distinguishes between the different kinds of creatures by dividing them into three categories: those lacking distinctness, memory, or consciousness (e.g., plants); those possessing memory and sensation, but lacking consciousness (e.g., animals); and those possessing consciousness (e.g., humans, or "rational souls").[5] This three-way division of animate nature is basically a rehash of the Aristotelian explanation of the three types of souls (*De Anima* II, 3).

So far as the theory of animals is concerned, modern rationalism—at least as represented by Descartes, Leibniz, and Spinoza—does not really offer us anything except a slightly warmed-over version of Aristotle.

Empiricists

Empiricism emphasizes the role of experience and sensation, rather than reason, as the basis of human knowledge. Since animals are generally acknowledged by both rationalists and empiricists to have just as much experience and sensation as humans, we would expect the status of animals to be somewhat higher. To a certain extent, this is true. However, the power and extent of Aristotelianism is not eliminated, only subdued. Aristotle has a way of exerting, as it were, an unconscious, repressed influence on empiricist philosophy.

As far as Locke and Berkeley are concerned, it is difficult to tell if they have *any* views on animals. Locke does recommend (for health reasons) that young children not eat meat until they are older, and only a very sparing amount of meat after that.[6] Since Berkeley maintains that to be is to be either a perceiver or perceived, it would seem that animal existence would be on a par with human existence in Berkeley's philosophy. Animals must be just as good at perceiving things or at being perceived as are humans. Berkeley, however, never deals with the question of animal souls or animal awareness in any detail.

At last, however—in Hume, the most famous empiricist philosopher—we have a substantial amount of material concerning animals. Hume maintains that animals are just as rational as humans. He states:

> Next to the ridicule of denying an evident truth, is that of taking much pains to defend it; and no truth appears to me more evident, than that beasts are endow'd with thought and reason as well as men. The arguments are in this case so obvious, that they never escape the most stupid and ignorant.[7]

Does this mean, perhaps, that humans have moral obligations toward animals? Apparently not. Hume adopts the ethics of utilitarianism, maintaining that in all determinations of morality, the circumstance of public utility or "the true interests of mankind" are the final arbiters.[8] Animals are excluded from this "public," because we cannot form a society with them. We are greatly superior to them, and only where there is equality can there be a society and can the idea of public utility be put into practice.

If equality of strength is the basis of society, then this would seem to justify many things other than just meat-eating; it would also justify colonialism and the exploitation of women. To his credit Hume acknowledges these difficulties,[9] but most modern readers would regard this as just a variation on the might-makes-right theory.[10] So, by a very circuitous route, we are back to the Aristotelian idea that humans have no ethical obligations to animals and can use them for their own purpose.

In the utilitarianism of Bentham and Mill, the concept of utility is carried further. Both maintain that the pleasures and pains of animals should be considered in any moral calculations of the good or evil of an action. Bentham, in an often quoted passage, states that the question of whether animals are rational or not is irrelevant; the real question is whether they can suffer.[11]

However, Bentham also states that the world is a better place because of our meat-eating habits. He claims that we are the better for eating animals, and the animals are never the worse, since they are protected from the uncertainties of living in the wild[12]—having only to surrender their lives at the end. There are problems with this view; most conspicuously, its total inapplicability to conditions on most factory farms. Also, would Bentham apply this same principle to humans? Would it then justify killing humans for food? These problems notwithstanding, it is remarkable that animals are mentioned at all by these modern philosophers, and that animals' pains and pleasures are actually considered to be morally significant.

Kant

Kant, in an off-handed and casual way, deals with the whole problem of our ethical obligations to animals in the following three sentences: "But so far as animals are concerned, we have no direct duties. Animals are not self-conscious and are there merely as a means to an end. That end is man."[13]

We find in this statement a reflection of the theories of Aristotle, Aquinas, and Spinoza. But does it fit in with the rest of Kant's moral theory?

The basic idea of Kant's ethics is that one ought to treat persons as ends in themselves, and never merely as a means to an end. Therefore, claims Kant, we do not kill for profit (or do any number of other reprehensible things), because such actions treat the other person as a mere means to getting money. Kant applies this ethical law to all rational beings: "For rational beings all stand under the *law* that each of them should treat himself and others, *never merely as a means,* but always *at the same time as an end in himself.*"[14]

Kant evidently did not think that animals are rational beings, and therefore they fall entirely outside of his moral system. But what is a rational being? And what is reason? From Kant's *Critique of Pure Reason,* it would seem that animals not only *could* be rational, but that they *must* be rational—because being rational is a condition of having any experience whatsoever. If animals have experience, this experience must be in space and time, must be subject to causality, and must be subject to all the other categories by which beings (according to Kant) experience the world. Indeed, Kant implies that self-consciousness itself is a condition of having any experience whatsoever.[15]

It would thus appear that animals must possess reason, and even self-consciousness, if they experience the world at all; and if they are rational, self-conscious beings, we must treat them as ends rather than means to an end. Now, of course, Kant might be able to save his distinctions between humans and animals by making some further arbitrary judgment. Perhaps animals really are machines, and have no sensations or experiences after all. It is obvious, though, that Kant hardly dealt with this problem. He simply borrowed the old Aristotelian idea about the role of animals, without giving the matter a second thought.

As long as animals are excluded from Kant's "kingdom of ends"—those beings which are rational and should be treated as ends in themselves—animals are a severe, and probably fatal, embarrassment to Kant's moral system.

Everybody Else

There are a great number of philosophers who say little or nothing of significance about animals, our ethical obligations towards animals, or vegetarianism. In fact, this forms the chief "school" of modern philosophy. Hegel, Nietzsche, Feuerbach, Kierkegaard, Sartre, Heidegger, Camus, Lukacs, Russell, Moore, Ayer, Carnap, Wittgenstein, Pierce, Santayana, James, and many others are almost completely silent on the subject. There are, however, a few footnotes to this philosophical disaster area:

- Schopenhauer. Schopenhauer makes numerous sympathetic references to animals. He was greatly influenced by Hinduism and Buddhism, and saw the world as the operation of a single, super-personal Will. Despite the solipsistic and monistic tone of his system, which would seem to imply sympathy towards all living creatures (who are really manifestations of the same Will), Schopenhauer defends meat consumption in his principal work. According to Schopenhauer, the animal suffers less in being killed and eaten than the human would suffer in being deprived of his flesh. To his credit, though, Schopenhauer opposes all animal experiments.[16]
- The Marxists. The Marxist-Leninist school of thought has a relatively enlightened philosophical view of animals. Marxists explicitly reject the extreme view of Descartes, maintaining instead that: "The high level of development of mental activity in animals shows that man's consciousness has its biological preconditions and that there is no unbridgeable gap between man and his animal ancestors; in fact, there is a certain continuity."[17] Engels also elaborates on the problem of animal intelligence in his *Dialectics of Nature.*[18]
- Singer. Peter Singer, a contemporary Australian philosopher, has advocated the view that humans do have obligations towards animals, and that becoming a vegetarian is a practical necessity for anyone opposed to cruelty to animals: "there is one other thing we can do that is of supreme importance; it underpins, makes consistent, and gives meaning to all our other activities on behalf of animals. This one thing is that we cease to eat animals."[19]

    His famous book *Animal Liberation* outlines his views on animals and ethics. He has subsequently elaborated on these views and given them philosophical and scientific justification in his books *Practical Ethics* and *The Expanding Circle*. Singer's books are required reading for anyone interested in the ethical aspects of vegetarianism; they cover many topics concerning all aspects of human behavior towards animals.

Singer distinguishes between conscious and self-conscious beings, and argues that some animals qualify as self-conscious beings (chimpanzees, dogs, pigs) and therefore should be treated as "persons." Other animals, according to Singer, are not self-conscious, but are nonetheless conscious and their suffering is significant on straightforward utilitarian grounds. He condemns the factory farming system outright—claiming that it cannot be justified for either conscious or self-conscious animals.[20]

He also tackles the issue of scientific experimentation on animals, stating that the majority of animal experiments are completely worthless: "to be opposed to what is going on now it is not necessary to insist that all experiments stop immediately. All that we need to say is that experiments serving no direct and urgent purpose should stop immediately, and in the remaining areas of research, methods involving animals should be replaced as soon as possible by alternative methods not involving animals."[21]

Who's a Vegetarian?

Having defined, such as it is possible, the intellectual positions of these various philosophers, we might now ask which of them are (or were) actually vegetarians? In most cases, it is impossible or difficult to answer this question since the philosophers in question make no references to the ethics of eating animals and their biographers make no references to their diet. In ancient times, such silence would be ambiguous, since there was very little meat-eating in some parts of the world. But in the modern world, silence probably means that the person is not a vegetarian.

In Descartes, oddly enough, it seems that we do have one isolated piece of information: Descartes preferred vegetables to meat.[22] Since we would presume that Descartes had a choice most of the time, it would be reasonable to conclude that he was a vegetarian most of the time. This would be quite ironic, considering that Descartes made the now infamous suggestion that animals do not have feelings. Perhaps, however, all the fuss about whether animals have souls was beginning to worry Descartes; perhaps he began to wonder if, after all, animals might not have souls (or at least feelings).

In the case of Berkeley and Hume, we have some indirect information about their diets. Berkeley suffered from gout.[23] Gout is commonly associated with a high-fat diet; and it is difficult to imagine anyone in the eighteenth century who could develop gout without eating meat. Hume suffered from extreme obesity and died of a disease which appears to have been colon cancer[24]—both are degenerative diseases caused by a high-fat, probably high-meat, diet. The evidence would seem to be that neither Berkeley nor Hume was a vegetarian.

Bentham was apparently not a vegetarian, since he expressly defends meat consumption. Concerning Mill, Kant, and most of the other modern philosophers, we have only silence—which in context probably means that they ate meat, since a vegetarian diet would have surely been considered sufficiently odd to be pointed out or noticed by their biographers or contemporaries.

Conclusions

This is not an exhaustive survey of the philosophy of animals in modern times; there are some minor philosophers here and there who have some things to say (one way or another) about animals. There are also some writers (e.g., Shelley, Salt) who have written about animals or vegetarianism in a philosophical vein—but they neither considered themselves philosophers, nor were their writings ever accepted into the corpus of philosophy. However, this brief examination of modern philosophy does cover most of the major philosophers, and the results are not encouraging.

Animals are hardly a topic for modern philosophy at all. For most modern philosophers, animals are a brief and quickly forgotten footnote to the System. With the exception of Descartes, Hume, Engels, and Singer, there is very little about animals in modern philosophy that is of interest one way or another. And the list of major philosophical advocates of vegetarianism in modern times can be narrowed down to one: Singer.

The basic problem is that modern philosophy has been unable to unlearn, or deal critically with, Aristotle. There is something to be learned here, even if it is only to discover what has been overlooked by the modern philosophers.

23
The History of Vegetarianism

Considering the history of vegetarianism presents a great problem. That problem is that the vegetarian movement (such as it is) has been extremely fragmented.

An impressive list of individuals who were vegetarians can be drawn up: Leonardo da Vinci, Leo Tolstoy, George Bernard Shaw, Mohandas Gandhi, and many others. But these individuals did not found any vegetarian school of thought, nor did they lead any vegetarian organization. They were distinguished, but isolated, examples of vegetarians, and it is difficult to speak of these vegetarians as having a history at all.

The most important manifestation of vegetarianism has not been as an independent movement, but as part of a larger social, cultural, or religious whole. Thus, the history of vegetarianism largely lies in the history of philosophy and religion. But in this case, one can only speak of the history of vegetarianism as a footnote to the history of something else. The Pythagoreans, the Hindus, and the Seventh-Day Adventists were all vegetarian or contained large vegetarian contingents. But there is much more to these philosophies and religions than abstention from meat. In previous chapters, we have focused on the role of vegetarian ideas in philosophy and religion.

In this chapter, we will discuss the history of vegetarianism as an independent movement. There are two facets to this history: the vegetarian literature and vegetarian organizations.

Modern Vegetarian Literature

The most concrete manifestation of vegetarian sentiment has been in the literature of vegetarianism. Fortunately for the English-speaking world, English is unquestionably the language of the vegetarian idea. The one non-English-speaking country in which a strong vegetarian tradition exists—India—has also been extensively exposed to the English language, since it was for many years a

Table 19. A partial list of works of interest to vegetarians, published in the modern era.

Year	Author	Title
1683	Thomas Tryon	The Way to Health, Long Life, and Happiness
1791	John Oswald	The Cry of Nature
1792	Thomas Taylor	A Vindication of the Rights of Brutes
1802	Joseph Ritson	An Essay on Abstinence From Animal Foods
1811	John Frank Newton	The Return to Nature
1815	Percy Bysshe Shelley	A Vindication of Natural Diet
1826	Sir Richard Phillips	Golden Rules of Social Philosophy (Appendix)
1839	Sylvester Graham	*Lectures on the Science of Human Life
1840	Antoine Gleizes	Thalysie: ou la Nouvelle Existence
1851	William Alcott	Vegetable Diet
1854	John Smith	Fruits and Farinacea, The Proper Food of Man
1861	Gustav von Struve	Pflanzenkost, die Grundlage einer Neuen Weltanschauung
1877	Gustav Schlickeysen	Fruit and Bread, a Scientific Diet
1883	Howard Williams	*The Ethics of Diet
1887	Leo Tolstoy	The First Step
1892	Henry Salt	*Animals' Rights
1897	Charles Forward	Fifty Years of Food Reform
1904	Anna Kingsford	The Perfect Way in Diet
1923	John Harvey Kellogg	The Natural Diet of Man
1956	Geoffrey L. Rudd	Why Kill for Food?
1964	Ruth Harrison	Animal Machines
1971	Frances Moore Lappé	*Diet for a Small Planet
1975	Robin Hur	Food Reform: Our Desperate Need
1975	Peter Singer	*Animal Liberation
1975	Janet Barkas	The Vegetable Passion
1976	Laurel Robertson, Carol Flinders, Bronwen Godfrey	Laurel's Kitchen
1977	Nat Altman	Eating for Life
1978	Vic Sussman	The Vegetarian Alternative
1979	Dudley Giehl	Vegetarianism: A Way of Life
1979	Richard Bargen	The Vegetarian's Self-Defense Manual
1979	John Scharffenberg	Problems with Meat
1980	Jim Mason, Peter Singer	Animal Factories
1982	Judith Dyer	Vegetarianism: An Annotated Bibliography
1983	John and Mary McDougall	The McDougall Plan
1984	Daniel Dombrowski	The Philosophy of Vegetarianism

"Classics" are denoted by an asterisk (*).

colony of Great Britain. While the literature of vegetarianism in English is not large, even less has ever been written on the subject in other languages.

A partial list of works published on or about vegetarianism and vegetarians since the seventeenth century is found in Table 19. Cookbooks have been excluded—to include these would have greatly expanded the list. These works represent a wide variety of material, both in quality and in subject matter. Five of these books, however, have definitely achieved classic status and deserve special mention.

Sylvester Graham's *Lectures on the Science of Human Life* is one of the best of the nineteenth century offerings. Graham was a well-known dietary reformer, and the inventor of the "Graham cracker" made from unrefined wheat. The *Lectures* contain much material on health and physiology, which was quite important in his day but which by now is dated. In addition to these matters, Graham also deals in a tantalizing way with broader philosophical questions, such as what a natural diet is, and how nature and ethics are related.

Howard Williams' book *The Ethics of Diet* is, even today, the best book on the history of vegetarianism. Leo Tolstoy was so impressed by it that he wrote a lengthy introductory preface for it ("The First Step"), and had the book translated into Russian. Gandhi also spoke highly of Williams' book. The book is subtitled *A Catena of Authorities Deprecatory of the Practice of Flesh-Eating*, and this very well describes the contents. Williams considers all of the writers and thinkers who have either been vegetarians or who have supported the case for vegetarianism through scientific or literary efforts. He considers thinkers as diverse as Hesiod, Musonius, Chrysostom, Cheyne, Metcalfe, Pope, and Cowherd—from the ancient Greeks to the nineteenth century.

In altogether a different category are the ethical books. These books largely bypass nutritional and social issues, focusing instead on the ethics of eating animals for food. The most famous book in this category is, of course, Singer's *Animal Liberation*, already discussed in some detail. An excellent earlier effort, recently reprinted, is Henry Salt's book *Animals' Rights*. Singer says of this book: "Defenders of animals, myself included, have been able to add relatively little to the essential case Salt outlined in 1892; but we can console ourselves with the fact that our opponents have been able to come up with few objections that Salt has not already dealt with."

Finally, we have *Diet for a Small Planet*, which is probably the best-selling book which makes a case for eliminating meat from one's diet. Ironically, though, the author herself is not a vegetarian. One cannot deny, though, that this book has been very influential; there are many vegetarians around today who date their "conversion" from around the time they came across this book.

Some of these books concentrate almost exclusively on nutritional issues (Hur, Bargen, Kingsford); others deal only or largely with ethical problems (Harrison, Salt, Singer). A good sense of the fragmented history of vegetarianism can be gotten from a critical reading of Williams, Forward, Barkas, and

Giehl. In the largest category of titles are the attempts at a survey of the vegetarian issues: this includes Alcott, Kellogg, Rudd, and more recently, Sussman and Altman.

Vegetarian Organizations

The history of the vegetarian movement has been quite uneven. In ancient times, various groups such as the Pythagoreans, Hindus, some Buddhists, Jains, and neo-Platonists, were vegetarian; but they were not groups specifically organized to further vegetarianism in the sense in which we think of them today. The history of these groups has been considered in the previous chapters on philosophy and religion (chapters 18 through 22). For all practical purposes, the history of vegetarian organizations begins in the nineteenth century.

The Bible Christian Church was instrumental in the development of organized vegetarianism in both England and the United States. This church was founded in 1807 in Salway, England. Its members took vows of abstinence from meat and from alcohol. In 1817, 42 members left England and travelled to America, where they founded a sister church in Philadelphia.

On September 29, 1847, the first Vegetarian Society was formed at Ramsgate, England. Three years later, members of the Bible Christian Church in the United States helped form the first Vegetarian Society in the new world. Between this time and the first world war, vegetarianism grew and flourished in both England and the United States. Indeed, in some respects this was the golden age of the vegetarian movement. In Great Britain, the society suffered greatly after the death of its first president, James Simpson, and nearly went out of existence. But it made a big comeback late in the nineteenth century. Many intellectuals, such as George Bernard Shaw, Henry Salt, Leo Tolstoy, and Mahatma Gandhi, became well-known advocates of a vegetarian diet. Numerous periodicals appeared which advocated or recommended a vegetarian way of life. In 1908, the International Vegetarian Union was formed to further the cause on an international scale.

The two world wars dealt a severe blow to the vegetarian movement. In England, the Vegetarian Society continued to function; but in the United States, the movement nearly died out completely, as the national vegetarian society went out of existence. In the 1960's and 1970's, however, vegetarianism underwent something of a renaissance, as vegetarianism once again became the concern of more than just a few and vegetarian organizations began sprouting up in the United States.

Today, there are vegetarian groups in many different countries of the world, including Australia, India, Germany, and various other European countries. The vegetarian movement in England is probably as strong as it is anywhere in the world. The Vegetarian Society of the United Kingdom claims a membership of over 10,000 and puts out a bimonthly magazine, *The Vegetarian*. In the United

States, there is no strong national movement, although there are signs that this is changing. There are several local and national vegetarian groups (see Appendix). There is also an independent vegetarian magazine, *Vegetarian Times*.

What has the impact of such groups been on the general population? There is no question that they have kept the spark of the vegetarian idea alive, and that they have influenced some individuals. Objectively, however, we can only conclude that such organizations have had little noticeable impact on the dietary habits of those in the United States. Up to now, the spontaneous spread of vegetarian sentiment has been a more potent force than any vegetarian organization. It is unlikely that even 1/10 of 1% of the estimated seven million vegetarians in the United States are in any vegetarian organization. This is not to say, however, that the situation will necessarily remain the same in the future. Several cities now have thriving vegetarian organizations, and many Americans are consuming less meat out of concern for their health. So we have every hope that the vegetarian movement will gain increasing strength in the coming years.

There are two undercurrents in this brief history of the vegetarian movement. One is veganism, the other is animal rights. Throughout the nineteenth and twentieth centuries, there have been groups which can be viewed alternatively as "splinter groups," or perhaps as groups expressing the true ideal of vegetarianism better than the established vegetarian groups—depending on one's point of view. The vegans on the one hand, and animal rights organizations on the other, are the most important of these groups.

Vegans do not use dairy products and eggs. Vegetarian organizations have historically sidestepped the issue of dairy products and eggs. They have left it as an issue for the individual vegetarian to decide. One can trace the antipathy of some vegetarians towards dairy products and eggs back into the nineteenth century, but it was not until 1944 that some British vegetarians decided to form a separate group, the Vegan Society, to advocate the ideals of a diet which uses no animal produce whatsoever. The vegans have been only a small proportion of the total vegetarian population, however, they are frequently very active and articulate out of proportion to their numbers.

Animal rights groups are not, strictly speaking, a splinter group of the vegetarian movement at all—since their organizational origins were from the animal welfare organizations. Animal rights groups are based on the belief that animals have rights not to be harmed or mistreated, not the least of which are the rights not to be killed and eaten by humans. Thus, these groups stress vegetarianism for ethical reasons, but address themselves to other issues as well: an end to experimentation on animals, an end to hunting and trapping, and similar problems.

There has been a great surge of interest in animal rights in recent years. Much of this can be specifically attributed to Peter Singer's book *Animal Liberation*. As a consequence, much media attention has been devoted to this topic, and many of the more traditional animal welfare groups—those organized to defend wildlife, save the whales, etc.—have become increasingly sensitive to the issues raised by animal rights groups. The difference between animal welfare and animal rights is not entirely clear. But in the context of the current debate, "animal welfare" has become associated with groups which support only limited action on behalf of animals, such as finding homes for stray dogs and cats. Animal rights groups, on the other hand, focus on issues which the more traditional groups shy away from, such as factory farms and animal experimentation. What the results of this interest will be, and what the interaction between animal rights and vegetarian groups will be in coming years, is still unclear. But there is no question that there has been increasing interest in animal issues of all kinds in recent years.

The Future of Vegetarianism

What is the future of the vegetarian idea? In the short run, the outlook for vegetarianism is not especially good. But in the long run, the chances are excellent. There are important social and economic factors which are making it increasingly costly to eat meat. We are spending hundreds of billions of dollars on medical care for problems such as heart disease and cancer, which are perfectly preventable on a vegetarian diet. In the third world, the flames of revolution and social chaos are being fanned by an agricultural system which squanders agricultural resources in order to provide meat for a few and starvation for millions. And there is moral outrage over the treatment of animals and the factory farms which produce a hell on earth for billions of animals each year—a hell which is only terminated by the slaughterhouse. Food is going to be the big social issue of the upcoming years, and it is likely to dominate everything else as an issue by the year 2000. A vegetarian world is within our reach.

What are the strategic objectives of the vegetarian movement? The ultimate objective, of course, is a vegetarian world. But how are we going to get there?

Numerous ideas as to how to accomplish this end are now being circulated. Legislative action to aid farm animals has been suggested. Others advocate attacking some of the worst abuses, such as veal, for which there might be some sympathy in the general public. Still others suggest a variety of approaches to the media and the public, including publication of magazines, demonstrations, and other media-oriented events.

All of these ideas have a place in our overall strategy. All of them lack the one common ingredient which could bind them all together: *the creation and strengthening of the vegetarian community.* Without this ingredient, none of these admirable tactics make any strategic sense. How can legislative action to aid farm animals do any good, as long as the public wants meat? How can attacking the worst abuses of the meat industry produce anything more than reformist sentiment? Shouldn't the agenda of the vegetarian movement be the abolition, not the reform, of the meat industry? And how can launching media campaigns, no matter how well thought out and well funded, overcome the tremendous media advantages of the well entrenched meat industry, and the "meat-eating press"—which is virtually the entire press everywhere?

In the absence of a strong vegetarian community, none of these tactics makes very much sense. They all are merely the expression of vegetarian sentiment *within* the existing meat-eating community. We can only overcome a community which slaughters billions of animals yearly with *another* community, a vegetarian community. We cannot accomplish this simply through an idea, a book, a magazine, or a media campaign. We must therefore ask how it is possible to strengthen the existing vegetarian community—or, in those places where there is no organized vegetarian sentiment, to create a vegetarian community in the first place?

Three things are needed for such a community: (1) an ecumenical viewpoint, representing all the various kinds of vegetarians; (2) an emphasis on local organizing at the grass-roots level; and (3) democracy within the vegetarian movement.

By an "ecumenical viewpoint," I mean that we need a community which includes as priorities all the various reasons for becoming a vegetarian, including nutrition, ecology, and ethics. There are many different and valid reasons for being a vegetarian; all of these should be utilized.

In the past, one failure of some vegetarian groups has been concentration on the health issues to the exclusion of all other issues. This in turn has led to the typical complaint of those interested in vegetarianism for ethical reasons, that such vegetarian groups were ignoring them, and the evolution of a strong animal rights movement independent of vegetarian groups. However, this problem does not seem to be a significant one in the United States at the present time, as ethical concerns have become an integral part of the vegetarian platform. On the other hand, one issue which has largely escaped both the health and the animal rights groups has been a discussion of vegetarianism in the context of ecology and world hunger. Today, most hunger groups have only the foggiest awareness of the relationship between meat consumption and world hunger. If vegetarian groups were to make world hunger a priority, they could contribute a great deal to public education on this issue.

The second ingredient which we need is local organizing at the grass-roots level. Local organizing is needed because we need to maximize the opportunities for personal contact between and with vegetarians. We ought to make it as easy and as pleasant as possible for vegetarians and the public to meet other vegetarians. It is hard to take a "radical" step such as rejecting meat consumption when you are completely alone in your beliefs, when none of your family or friends are vegetarians, and regard you as part of the lunatic fringe as a consequence of your diet.

It takes courage to be different. Perhaps those of us who are already committed vegetarians can demand such courage of ourselves. But there is no point in making excessive demands on those who are just struggling with a belief which will cause them to reorient their lives. That is one of the reasons that we need human contact. It is one thing to read about vegetarianism. It is quite another to meet vegetarians and talk with them personally. To be able to make contact with others who share your beliefs is one of the fundamental objectives of a vegetarian community. The presence of a strong vegetarian community can remove one of the major psychological obstacles to becoming a vegetarian. It is also a powerful tool with which to educate the general public and to encourage those who are already sympathetic to join with us. People sometimes become vegetarians without having had contact with other vegetarians, that is, in a "vacuum"; but usually, a person who becomes a vegetarian does so at least partially as a consequence of contact with other vegetarians.

Finally, there is a need for democracy within the vegetarian movement. A democratically organized vegetarian group can deal with problems which arise within the group in a mature fashion; it can speak with legitimacy on issues which confront the vegetarian community; and it can respect the rights of minority viewpoints within the community. Democracy is one of the most positive aspects of American culture, and vegetarians should utilize the democratic framework to their advantage. A democratic framework represents the best chance for promoting vegetarianism in the context of supporting and strengthening the vegetarian community.

A vegetarian world can be achieved. We can achieve it in this generation. We have people, we have ideas, and we have something even more important: the truth. Let us strengthen the democracy within the vegetarian movement. Let us strengthen the vegetarian community. Let us work together for a vegetarian world.

Appendix:
Becoming a Vegetarian

So you want to become a vegetarian? Congratulations on your new healthy, ecological, ethical lifestyle.

To start with, all you have to do is say to yourself out loud the following five words: "Now I am a vegetarian." Then stop eating all meat, fish, or fowl. That's simple enough. However, be prepared for physical and social changes.

Physical Changes

The physical reality is the food you will eat: no meat, fish or fowl in any manner, way, shape, or form. This means you will have to start reading the ingredients on the food you buy. You will probably be alert enough to avoid such things as "Beans and Franks" but sometimes things are not so obvious. The sneakiest offenders are the animal fats (such as lard) and gelatin. Animal fats are part of the flesh of the animal and you can't eat them. Gelatin is usually made from bones and hoofs and other animal tissues. Sometimes lard is found in certain kinds of cookies or margarines. Read the ingredients to be sure.

If you decide to become a total vegetarian, or vegan, you must avoid meat, fish, fowl, and also all dairy products and eggs. Some people who consider themselves total vegetarians eat honey; it doesn't matter so much whether you do this or not, just as long as you are clear in your own mind what you are eating and what you aren't. Cookies and bread frequently contain nonfat dry milk or eggs. In fact, the most inconvenient aspect of being a total vegetarian is finding commercially made pastry and bakery products. Most breads have milk in them. The sneakiest ingredient of all, though, is whey, which is the thinner part of milk which separates from the thicker part (curds) during coagulation, usually produced in making cheese. Margarine is another problem. Butter is obviously out, but almost all commercially made margarines now contain whey or nonfat milk. Health food stores can sometimes help you find total vegetarian products, but you'll have to look harder.

If you make a mistake, and discover to your horror that you have just eaten something with animal fat or lard in it, don't be discouraged. Make a mental note and try not to repeat your error. As a vegetarian you are obligated to take all reasonable precautions to insure that you are not eating meat, fish, or fowl; as long as you make the effort sincerely, you can forgive yourself if you fail through oversight or haste.

Figuring out the ingredients is the first problem. The second problem is realizing how *much* you are going to eat. A major mistake of would-be vegetarians is misjudgment of how much food they need. This is amazing, but true. If you become a vegetarian, the amount of fiber in your diet will increase and the amount of fat will decrease, and you will doubtless be eating a lot more vegetables which have a high water content. Thus, *the physical volume of your food must increase if you want to take in the same amount of calories.*

This is nothing to be alarmed about—low-fat, high-fiber diets contains lots of fresh vegetables are much healthier. And, if you are trying to lose weight, this is great news—you will probably be able to stuff yourself with vegetables and still take in fewer calories than you did when you were eating meat. It is a common and pleasant experience of overweight people that they lose weight when they switch to a vegetarian diet. This is especially true if you are a total vegetarian.

However, some would-be vegetarians of normal weight do not increase the quantity of their food. They ate small portions of meat before, and they substitute an equally small portion of salad. Then they are left with a feeling of weakness which they blame on "not getting enough protein," or something like that. "How can vegetarians possibly get enough protein?" they complain to themselves, and soon they go back to a meat-oriented diet.

There are several ways of handling this problem. The first is to eat dairy products and eggs, or plant foods (like tofu, soymilk, or nuts and seeds) which are relatively high in calories per unit volume. You could add liberal doses of foods cooked in vegetable oils. The advantage of this tactic is that the total volume of your food will probably not have to change all that much. If you are becoming a vegetarian primarily for ethical reasons, this might not be a bad way to start. The disadvantage of this process is that it carries the same health disadvantages as the typical American diet—too much fat and not enough fiber.

If you are becoming a vegetarian for health reasons, you will simply have to change your eating habits. Your dinner meal will just have to take a bit longer to finish. A pound of potatoes has a bit over 300 calories, while a pound of steak has over 1,000 calories. You won't be able to stuff yourself with 1,350 calories in 6 1/2 minutes like you used to be able to at McDonald's. We are living in a "fast food" society, and becoming a vegetarian may involve relearning a lot of your food habits—such as how and what to eat. Eat lots of high-carbohydrate, high-fiber, unprocessed plant foods, and don't forget those green leafy vegetables.

The third aspect of the physical changes you will have to confront is adjusting to a new pattern of cooking. Actually, this is the least traumatic adjustment. If your style was to cook interesting recipes and dainty dishes before you became a vegetarian, well, you can just keep on fixing interesting vegetarian recipes and dainty vegetarian dishes afterwards. It won't cramp your style a bit. On the other hand, if you were the type that just threw a hamburger into the pan before you became a vegetarian, you will probably just throw some potatoes into the oven afterwards.

Social Changes

And now, for the social aspects of becoming a vegetarian. In the final analysis, this is probably the greatest obstacle to becoming a vegetarian. There just aren't that many vegetarians in the United States, and people may treat you as if you've just converted to Zoroastrianism.

Social interactions frequently involve food. How should vegetarians act when invited to dinner or out to lunch, or in a restaurant? The author's advice (in case anyone is interested) is as follows: strive to satisfy the demands of one's conscience, but with the least amount of fuss. If you're unsure of what is in a prospective food item, never eat it until you have taken all reasonable precautions to insure that the item in question does not contain meat, fish, or fowl. On the other hand, do not make a spectacle out of yourself in getting the required information.

If you are offered food which you know contains meat, or anything else you object to for any reason, the proper response is (smile) "No, thank you." If, in order to be polite, you eat meat offered to you, then you aren't a vegetarian. On the other hand, you shouldn't make a big deal out of declining such a dish either. No lengthy lectures on the poisons and chemicals meat contains are proper.

A corollary of this is that when you are the host, you should never serve meat, or anything else which you find objectionable in principle. You might want to serve things which you don't eat for other reasons—e.g., you might serve onions even though you don't personally like the taste of onions. But you should never serve anything which compromises your vegetarian principles. The single exception to this might be cooking for members of your own family, or possibly for your very close friends. You might be willing to do this on the grounds that you entered into your relationship with (say) your parents before you had the wisdom or the opportunity to choose vegetarianism.

The above social rules seem to me to be good guidelines of how to mix socially in a non-vegetarian society. Since so many relationships center around sharing food, becoming a vegetarian can easily isolate you socially. It is greatly to the advantage of the vegetarian cause, however, for vegetarians to mix socially with non-vegetarians. Even if it were possible for vegetarians to live a life apart from non-vegetarians, it would not be desirable; the spread of vegetarian ideas is greatly facilitated by a social mixing of vegetarians in the larger non-vegetarian population.

Cookbooks

There are, by now, numerous excellent vegetarian cookbooks. These are a valuable resource for the new vegetarian who may find himself staring at his plate and saying, "What now?" The following list is by no means complete, but should provide a guide to many of the most commonly used cookbooks.

The Moosewood Cookbook, by Mollie Katzen (Berkely, CA: Ten Speed Press, 1977).

The Enchanted Broccoli Forest, by Mollie Katzen (Berkeley, CA: Ten Speed Press, 1982).

Laurel's Kitchen: A Handbook for Vegetarian Cookery and Nutrition, by Laurel Robertson, Carol Flinders, and Bronwen Godfrey (Petaluma, CA: Nilgiri Press, 1976).

The Vegetarian Epicure, by Anna Thomas (New York: Vintage Books, 1972). This book leans heavily toward eggs and dairy products.

The Vegetarian Epicure, Book Two, by Anna Thomas (New York: Alfred A. Knopf, 1981). See comment on previous book.

Recipes for a Small Planet, by Ellen Buchman Ewald (New York: Ballantine Books, 1973).

The Cookbook for People Who Love Animals, by World of God (P.O. Box 1418, Umatilla, Florida 32784; 1983). This book is vegan.

The Complete Vegetarian Cookbook, by Karen Brooks (New York: Pocket Books, 1974).

Cooking for Consciousness by Joy McClure and Kendall Layne (Denver, CO: Ananda Marga Publications, 1976).

Sunset Menus and Recipes for Vegetarian Cooking, by the editors of Sunset books and Sunset Magazine (Menlo Park, CA: Lane Publishing Co., 1981).

Follow Your Heart's Vegetarian Soup Cookbook by Janice Cook Migliaccio (Santa Barbara, CA: Woodbridge Press, 1983).

The McDougall Plan Recipes, Volume I, by Mary McDougall (available from McDougall, P.O. Box 1761, Kailua, Hawaii 96734). Vegan.

The Farm Vegetarian Cookbook, edited by Louise Hagler (available from The Book Publishing Company, 156 Drakes Lane, Summertown, TN 38483). Vegan.

Ten Talents by Frank and Rosalie Hurd (Collegedale, TN 37315: College Press, n.d.). Almost entirely vegan.

Oats, Peas, Beans, and Barley Cookbook, by Edith Young Cottrell (Santa Barbara, CA: Woodbridge Press, 1976). Vegan.

I think you'll find that the physical aspects of vegetarianism (which foods you eat) will soon become second nature; the social aspects (how you deal with food in social situations) will probably be more trying. With these helpful hints, I wish you great success in your brand-new existence as a vegetarian.

Vegetarian Organizations

How does one get into contact with organized vegetarian groups? For many people, especially new vegetarians, this is an easy and enjoyable way to meet other vegetarians, or to find out what is going on in the vegetarian movement. The vegetarian movement in the United States is not large at the present time (1986). In many areas there is no vegetarian organization at all. However, there are some thriving vegetarian organizations, and this list should provide a brief guide to some of them:

Friends Vegetarian Society
P.O. Box 474
Beverly, MA 01915

American Vegan Society
Box H (Old Harding Highway)
Malaga, NJ 08328

Vegetarian Society of Queens
150-39 75th Ave., Apt. 2A
Flushing, NY 11367

North American Vegetarian Society
P.O. Box 72
Dolgeville, NY 11329

Philadelphia Vegetarians
Box 175
Philadelphia, PA 19105

The Vegetarian Society of the District of Columbia
P.O. Box 4921
Washington, DC 20008

International Vegetarian Union
North American Regional Office
P.O. Box 9710
Washington, D.C. 20016
U.S.A.

Vegetarian Information Service
P.O. Box 70123
Washington, D.C. 20088

Baltimore Vegetarians
P.O. Box 1463
Baltimore, MD 21203

Vegetarian Dietitians and Nutrition Educators (VEGEDINE)
1225 Lenox Ave.
Miami, FL 33139

East Tennessee Vegetarian Society
P.O. Box 1974
Knoxville, TN 37901

Vegetarian Information Service of Minnesota
5049 Thomas Ave. S.
Minneapolis, MN 55410

Vegetarian Times Magazine
P.O. Box 570
Oak Park, IL 60303

Vegetarian Society of Colorado
765 S. Pennsylvania St.
Denver, CO 80209

San Francisco Vegetarian Society
1450 Broadway
San Francisco, CA 94109

Toronto Vegetarian Association
28 Walker Avenue
Toronto M4V 1G2
Ontario, Canada

Vancouver Island Vegetarian Association
9675 Fifth Street
Sidney, B.C. V8L 2W9
Canada

International Vegetarian Union
10 Kings Drive,
Marple,
Stockport,
Cheshire SK6 6NQ
England

The author is himself a member of the Vegetarian Society of D.C. in Washington, D.C., which has the distinction of being the oldest vegetarian organization in the United States (founded in 1927). He is also a member of the Baltimore Vegetarians, the North American Vegetarian Society, and the International Vegetarian Union.

Notes

All references to journal or magazine articles are cited in the form "magazine name, volume (number): page, date." For example, "*Journal of Vitamin C* 24(14): 301, April 1971" would refer to volume 24, number 14, page 301 of the *Journal of Vitamin C*, dated April 1971. Sometimes the number of the journal will be omitted.

I. VEGETARIAN NUTRITION

2. Protein

1. S. Davidson and R. Passmore, *Human Nutrition and Dietetics,* 3rd ed. (Edinburgh and London: E. & S. Livingstone, 1966), p. 13.

2. National Research Council, *Recommended Dietary Allowances,* 9th ed. (Washington, D.C.: National Academy of Sciences, 1980), p. 46.

3. (a) For corn: C. Kies, E. Williams, and H. M. Fox, "Determination of First Limiting Nitrogenous Factor in Corn Protein for Nitrogen Retention in Human Adults," *The Journal of Nutrition* 86: 350, August 1965.

    (b) For wheat: S. B. Vaghefi, D. D. Makdani, and O. Mickelsen, "Lysine Supplementation of Wheat Proteins," *The American Journal of Clinical Nutrition* 27: 1231, 1974.

4. C.-J. Lee, J. M. Howe, K. Carlson, and H. E. Clark, "Nitrogen Retention of Young Men Fed Rice With or Without Supplementary Chicken," *The American Journal of Clinical Nutrition* 24: 318, 1971.

5. (a) P. Markakis, "The Nutritive Quality of Potato Protein," in *Protein Nutritional Quality of Foods and Feeds,* pt. 2, ed. M. Friedman (New York: M. Dekker, 1975).

    (b) E. Kofranyi, F. Jekat, and J. Müller-Wecker, "The Minimum Protein Requirement of Humans Tested with Mixtures of Whole Egg Plus Potato and Maize Plus Beans," *Hoppe-Seyler's Zeitschrift für Physiologische Chemie* 351 (12): 1485, 1970.

6. P. Markakis, op. cit.

7. T. B. Osborne and L. B. Mendel, "Amino Acids in Nutrition and Growth," *The Journal of Biological Chemistry* 17: 325, 1914.

8. These points and others are discussed in S. B. Vaghefi et al., 1974.

9. P. V. Sukhatme, "Size and Nature of the Protein Gap," *The Nutrition Review* 28: 223, 1970.

10. B. M. Nicol and P. G. Phillips, "The Utilization of Proteins and Amino Acids in Diets Based on Cassava (Manihot Utilissima), Rice or Sorghum (Sorghum Sativa) by Young Nigerian Men of Low Income," *The British Journal of Nutrition* 39(2): 271, March 1978.

3. Vitamin B-12

1. V. Herbert, "Nutritional Requirements for Vitamin B-12 and Folic Acid," *American Journal of Clinical Nutrition* 21: 743, 1978. Cited in A. M. and C. L. Thrash, *Nutrition For Vegetarians* (Seale, Alabama: Thrash Publications, 1982), p. 68.

2. A. M. and C. L. Thrash, *Nutrition For Vegetarians* (Seale, Alabama: Thrash Publications, 1982), p. 68.

3. C. R. Das Gupta, J. B. Chatterjea, and P. Basu, "Vitamin B-12 in Nutritional Macrocytic Anaemia," *The British Medical Journal* 2: 645, 19 September 1953.

4. (a) F. V. Cox, M. J. Meynell, and W. T. Cooke, "Interrelation of Vitamin B-12 and Iron," Abstract, *The American Journal of Clinical Nutrition* 9: 375, 1961.

   (b) B. F. Chow, "The B-Vitamins: B-6, B-12, Folic Acid, Pantothenic Acid, and Biotin," in *Nutrition: A Comprehensive Treatise*, vol. 2, ed. G. H. Beaton and W. E. McHenry (New York: Academic Press, 1964).

5. J. D. Green, "Megaloblastic Anemia in a Vegetarian Taking Oral Contraceptives," *The Southern Medical Journal* 68(2): 249, February 1975.

6. R. J. Harrison, C. C. Booth, and D. L. Mollin, in *The Lancet* 1: 727, 19 May 1956.

7. J. D. Hines, in *The American Journal of Clinical Nutrition* 19(4): 260, October 1966.

8. M. C. Higginbottom, L. Sweetman, and W. L. Nyhan, in *The New England Journal of Medicine* 299(7): 317, 1978.

9. R. Bargen, *The Vegetarian's Self-Defense Manual* (Wheaton, Illinois: Theosophical Publishing House, 1979), p. 97.

10. The studies most commonly cited are:
    (a) F. Wokes, J. Badenoch, and H. M. Sinclair, "Human Dietary Deficiency of Vitamin B-12," *The American Journal of Clinical Nutrition* 3(5): 375, September-October 1955.

    (b) A. D. M. Smith, "Veganism, A Clinical Survey with Observations of Vitamin B-12 Metabolism," *The British Medical Journal* 1: 1655, 16 June 1962.

    (c) J. A. Halstead, J. Carroll, A. Dehghani, M. Loghmani, and A. S. Prasad, "Serum Vitamin B-12 Concentration in Dietary Deficiency," *The American Journal of Clinical Nutrition* 8: 374, 1960.

    (d) F. R. Ellis and V. E. M. E. Montegriffo, "Veganism, Clinical Findings and Investigations," *The American Journal of Clinical Nutrition* 23(3): 249, March 1970.

11. A. D. M. Smith, op. cit., 1962.

12. A. M. and C. L. Thrash, op. cit., p. 67.

13. A. M. and C. L. Thrash, op. cit., p. 67.

14. Anonymous, "Contribution of the Microflora of the Small Intestine to the Vitamin B-12 Nutriture of Man," *Nutrition Reviews* 38(8): 274, August 1980.

15. B. C. Parker, "Rain as a source of vitamin B-12," *Nature* 219: 617, 10 August 1968. Cited in A. M. and C. L. Thrash, op. cit., p. 69.

16. A. M. and C. L. Thrash, op. cit., p. 68.
17. A. M. and C. L. Thrash, op. cit., p. 69.

4. Other Nutrients

1. National Research Council, *Recommended Dietary Allowances,* 9th ed. (Washington, D.C.: National Academy of Sciences, 1980), pp. 120-129.
2. Ibid., p. 126.
3. D. Narins, in A. Bezkorovainy, *Biochemistry of Nonheme Iron* (New York: Plenum, 1980), pp. 47-126.
4. Ibid.
5. R. Hur, *Food Reform: Our Desperate Need* (Austin, Texas: Heidelberg Publishers, 1975), p. 151.
6. C. B. Taylor and S.-K. Peng, "Vitamin D—Its Excessive Use in the USA," in *Nutritional Elements and Clinical Biochemistry,* ed. M. A. Brewster and H. K. Naito (New York: Plenum, 1980).
7. National Research Council, *Recommended Dietary Allowances,* p. 34.
8. F. R. Ellis and T.A.B. Sanders, "Angina and Vegan diet," *The American Heart Journal* 93(6): 803, June 1977.

5. Diet and Degenerative Disease

1. M. Hindhede, "The Effect of Food Restriction During War on Mortality in Copenhagen," *The Journal of the American Medical Association* 76(6): 381, 7 February 1920.
2. K. West, *Epidemiology of Diabetes and Its Vascular Lesions* (New York: Elsevier, 1978), p. 227.
3. R. Gubner, "Overweight and Health: Prognostic Realities and Therapeutic Possibilities," in *Obesity: Causes, Consequences, and Treatment,* ed. L. Lasagna (New York: Medcom Press, 1974).
4. " 'Quest for Immortality' Boosts Cost of Hospital Care," *The Arlington Journal,* 25 March 1982.
5. For one estimate, *see*: J. G. Chopra, A. L. Forbes, and J.-P. Habicht, "Protein in the U.S. Diet," *The Journal of the American Dietetic Association* 72: 253, March 1978.
6. *See* Chapter 8, "Various Other Degenerative Diseases."
7. Quoted in J. S. Peters, "Pritikin's Program for Vegetarians," *Vegetarian Times* 43: 21, January-February 1981.

6. Atherosclerosis

1. R. I. Levy and J. Moskowitz, "Cardiovascular Research: Decades of Progress, A Decade of Promise," *Science* 217: 121, July 9, 1982.
2. (a) R. L. Phillips, et al., "Coronary heart disease mortality among Seventh-Day Adventists with differing dietary habits: a preliminary report." *American Journal of Clinical Nutrition* 31: S-191, October 1978. Cited in J. A. Scharffenberg, Problems With Meat (Santa Barbara: Woodbridge Press, 1979), p. 24.
   (b) Stoy Proctor, "The Advantages of Vegetarianism: A Scientific Background." Speech at 27th World Vegetarian Congress, Catonsville, Maryland, July 31, 1984.
3. J. Brody, "New Research on the Vegetarian Diet," in *The New York Times,* October 12, 1983.

4. K. West, *Epidemiology of Diabetes and its Vascular Lesions* (New York: Elsevier, 1978), p. 227.

5. J. N. Leonard, J. L. Hofer, and N. Pritikin: *Live Longer Now* (New York: Charter Books, 1974), p. 46.

6. G. Kolata, "Cholesterol-Heart Disease Link Illuminated," *Science* 221: 1164, September 16, 1983.

7. (a) N. S. Scrimshaw and M. A. Guzman, "Diet and Atherosclerosis," *Laboratory Investigation* 18(5): 623, 1968.

   (b) J. P. Strong, D. A. Eggen, and R. E. Tracy, "The Geographic Pathology and Topography of Atherosclerosis and Risk Factors for Atherosclerotic Lesions," in *The Thrombotic Process in Atherogenesis,* ed. A. B. Chandler et al. Advances in Experimental Biology and Medicine, vol. 104, 1977.

8. P. Hausman, *Jack Sprat's Legacy* (New York: Richard Marek Publishers, 1981).

9. N. Pritikin and P. McGrady, *The Pritikin Program for Diet and Exercise* (New York: Bantam Books, 1980).

10. B. O'Brien, "Human plasma lipid responses to red meat, poultry, fish, and eggs," American Journal of Clinical Nutrition 33: 2573, 1980.

11. J. McDougall, *McDougall's Medicine* (Piscataway, New Jersey: New Century Publishers, 1985), pages 106-112.

12. M. Hardinge and F. State, "Nutritional Studies of Vegetarians. 2. Dietary and Serum Levels of Cholesterol," *The Journal of clinical Nutrition* 2(2): 83, March-April 1954.

13. Edward R. Gruberg and Stephen A. Raymond, *Beyond Cholesterol* (New York: St. Martin's Press, 1981).

14. B. Armstrong, H. Clarke, C. Martin, W. Ward, N. Norman, and J. Masarei, "Urinary Sodium and Blood Pressure in Vegetarians," *The American Journal of Clinical Nutrition* 32: 2472, December 1979.

15. J. Arehart-Treichel, "Eating Your Way Out of High Blood Pressure," *Science News* 123: 232, April 9, 1983.

16. Ibid.

17. (a) R. Gubner, "Overweight and Health," in *Obesity: Causes, Consequences, and Treatment,* L. Lasagna, ed. (New York: Medcom Press, 1974).

   (b) R. W. Stout, "Insulin and Atherosclerosis," in *Insulin and Metabolism,* ed. J. S. Bajaj (Amsterdam: Excerpta Medica New York, 1977).

18. See chapter 8.

19. G. Kolata, "New Puzzles Over Estrogen and Heart Disease," *Science* 220: 1137, June 10, 1983.

20. Ibid.

21. N. Pritikin and P. McGrady, op. cit. p. 72.

22. Ibid.

23. J. N. Leonard, J. L. Hofer, and N. Pritikin, op. cit., chapter 3.

24. E. A. Lew and L. Garfinkel, "Variations in Mortality by Weight Among 750,000 Men and Women," *Journal of Chronic Diseases* 32(8): 563, 1979.

7. Cancer

1. B. S. Reddy, L. A. Cohen, G. D. McCoy, P. Hill, J. H. Weisburger, and E. L. Wynder, "Nutrition and Its Relationship to Cancer," *Advances in Cancer Research* 32: 237, 1980.

2. National Research Council, *Diet, Nutrition, and Cancer* (Washington, D.C.: National Academy Press, 1982), pp. 1-14 through 1-16.

3. A. D. Upton, "Progress in the Prevention of Cancer," *Preventive Medicine* 7(4): 476, 1978.

4. B. S. Reddy, et al., op cit.

5. (a) R. Hur, *Food Reform: Our Desperate Need* (Austin, Texas: Heidelberg Publishers, 1975), chap. 1.

(b) E. Whelan, *Preventing Cancer* (New York: W. W. Norton & Co., 1978), chap. 2.

6. E. Whelan, op. cit., chap. 11.

7. S. J. Haught, *Has Dr. Max Gerson a True Cancer Cure?* (London Press, 1962, reprint ed., Canoga Park, California: Major Books, 1979).

8. Ibid., p. 92.

9. K. K. Carroll, "Experimental Evidence of Dietary Factors and Hormone-Dependent Cancers," *Cancer Research* 35: 3374, November 1975.

10. S. H. Waxler, "Obesity and Cancer Susceptibility in Mice," *The American Journal of Clinical Nutrition* 8: 760, September-October 1960.

11. (a) A. Tannenbaum and H. Silverstone, "Nutrition in Relation to Cancer," *Advances in Cancer Research* 1: 451, 1953.

(b) F. A. Lew and L. Garfinkel, "Variations in Mortality by Weight Among 750,000 Men and Women," *Journal of Chronic Diseases* 32(8): 563, 1979.

12. A. Tannenbaum and H. Silverstone, "The Genesis and Growth of Tumors. IV. Effects of Varying the Proportion of Protein (Casein) in the Diet." *Cancer Research* 9(3): 162, 1949.

13. M. H. Ross and G. Bras, "Tumor Incidence Patterns and Nutrition in the Rat," *The Journal of Nutrition* 87: 245, 1965.

14. A. Tannenbaum, "The Dependence of Tumor Formation on the Composition of the Calorie-Restricted Diet as Well as on the Degree of Restriction," *Cancer Research* 5(11): 616, 1945.

15. J. Stamler, "Elevated Cholesterol May Increase Lung Cancer Risk in Smokers," *Heart Research Letter* 14: 2, 1969, cited in N. Pritikin and P. McGrady, *The Pritikin Program for Diet and Exercise* (New York: Bantam Books, 1980), p. 385.

16. National Research Council, 1982, pp. 9-1, 9-2.

17. G. M. Williams, B. S. Reddy, and J. H. Weisburger, "The Role of Metabolic Epidemiology and Laboratory Studies in the Etiology of Colon Cancer," in *Advances in Medical Oncology, Research and Education,* vol. 3, *Epidemiology* (New York: Pergamon Press, 1979).

18. Ibid.

19. Ibid.

20. M. Nagao, M. Honda, Y. Seino, T. Yuhagi, and T. Sugimura, "Mutagenicities of Smoke Condensates and the Charred Surface of Fish and Meat," *Cancer Letters* 2: 221, 1977.

21. D. C. Topping and W. J. Visek, "Nitrogen Intake and Tumorigenesis in Rats Injected with 1,2-Dimethylhydrazine," *The Journal of Nutrition* 106: 1583, 1976.

22. J. H. Cummings, M. J. Hill, E. S. Bone, W. J. Branch, and D.J.A. Jenkins, "The Effect of Meat Protein and Dietary Fiber on Colonic Function and Metabolism. II. Bacterial Metabolites in Feces and Urine," *The American Journal of Clinical Nutrition* 32: 2094, October 1979.

23. (a) H. J. Freeman, G. A. Spiller, and Y. S. Kim. "A Double-Blind Study on the Effect of Purified Cellulose Dietary Fiber on 1,2-Dimethylhydrazine-induced Rat Colonic Tumors," *Cancer Research* 38: 2912, September 1978.

(b) D. Fleiszer, J. MacFarlane, D. Murray, and R. A. Brown, "Protective Effect of Dietary Fibre Against Chemically Induced Bowel Tumors in Rats," *The Lancet* 2: 552, 9 September 1978.

24. Y. Nishizuka, "Biological Influence of Fat Intake on Mammary Cancer and Mammary Tissue: Experimental Correlates," *Preventive Medicine* 7(2): 218, June 1978.

25. C. W. Welsch and H. Nagasawa, "Prolactin and Murine Mammary Tumorigenesis: A Review," *Cancer Research* 37: 951, April 1977.

26. Ibid.

27. (a) P. Hill, and E. Wynder, "Diet and Prolactin Release," *The Lancet* 2: 806, 9 October 1976.

(b) P. Hill, P. Chan, L. Cohan, E. Wynder, and K. Kuno, "Diet and Endocrine-Related Cancer," *Cancer* 39: 1820, 1977.

28. N. Breslow, C. W. Chan, G. Dhom, R. A. B. Drury, L. M. Franks, B. Gellei, Y. S. Lee, S. Lundberg, B. Sparke, N. H. Sternby, and H. Tulinius, "Latent Carcinoma of Prostate at Autopsy in Seven Areas," *International Journal of Cancer* 20: 680, 1977.

29. B. S. Reddy et al., op. cit.

30. B. Vorherr, *Breast Cancer* (Baltimore: Urban & Schwarzenberg, 1980).

31. B. Armstrong and P. Doll, "Environmental Factors and Cancer Incidence and Mortality in Different Countries, with Special Reference to Dietary Practices," *International Journal of Cancer* 15: 617, April 1975.

8. Various Other Degenerative Diseases

1. K. W. Heaton, "Food Intake Regulation and Fiber," in *Medical Aspects of Dietary Fiber*, ed. G. A. Spiller and R. M. Kay (New York: Plenum, 1980).

2. Ibid.

3. P. Björnthorp, "Carbohydrate and Lipid Metabolism in Human Obesity," in *The Regulation of the Adipose Tissue Mass*, ed. J. Vague, J. L. Boyer, and G. M. Addison (Amsterdam: Excerpta Medica New York, 1974).

4. R. Gubner, "Overweight and Health," in *Obesity: Causes, Consequences, and Treatment*, ed. L. Lasagna (Medcom Press: New York, 1974).

5. D. Rabinowitz, "Hormonal Profile and Forearm Metabolism in Human Obesity," *The American Journal of Clinical Nutrition* 21(12): 1438, December 1968.

6. J. Anderson, *Diabetes*, p. 87 (Arco Publishing: New York, 1982).

7. "Evaluation of Longevity Center 26-30 Day Inpatient Program—An Analysis of 893 Patients," Longevity Research Institute, P. O. Box 40570, Santa Barbara, CA 93103.

8. J. Peters, "Pritikin's Program for Vegetarians," *Vegetarian Times* 43:21, January-February 1981.

9. J. Mayer and J. Goldberg, "Nutrition" (syndicated column), *Washington Post*, 26 July 1981.

10. F. R. Ellis and V.E.M.E. Montegriffo, "Veganism, Clinical Findings and Investigations," *The American Journal of Clinical Nutrition* 23(3): 249, March 1970.

11. F. M. Sacks, W. P. Castellik, A. Donner, and F. H. Kass, "Plasma Lipids and Lipoproteins in Vegetarians and Controls," *The New England Journal of Medicine* 292(22): 1148, 29 May 1975. (Some of the "vegetarians" in this study ate fish, though only a minority.)

12. (a) F. R. Ellis and T.A.B. Sanders, "Angina and vegan diet," *The American Heart Journal* 93(6): 803, June 1977.

(b) M. Hardinge and F. State, "Nutritional studies of Vegetarians. 1. Nutritional, Physical, and Laboratory Studies," *The Journal of Clinical Nutrition* 2(2): 73, March-April 1954.

13. The original study was: W. Kempner, "Treatment of Kidney Disease and Hypertensive Vascular Disease with Rice Diet," *North Carolina Medical Journal* 5: 125, April 1944.

But *see also: The New England Journal of Medicine* 243(5): 177, 3 August 1950; 243(23): 899, 7 December 1950; and 245(10): 354, 6 September 1951.

14. G. K. Tokuhata, W. Miller, E. Digon, and T. Hartman, "Diabetes Mellitus: An Underestimated Public Health Problem," *Journal of Chronic Diseases* 28: 23, January 1975.

15. G. M. Reaven, "Insulin Resistance in the First Stages of Diabetes," in *Diabetes and Obesity,* ed. J. Vague and Ph. Vague (Amsterdam: Excerpta Medica New York, 1979).

16. (a) R. F. Ogilvie, "Sugar Tolerance in Obese Subjects. A Review of Sixty-Five Cases," *Quarterly Journal of Medicine* 4: 345, 1935.

   (b) *The Lancet* 1:537, 1927; cited in K. West, *Epidemiology of Diabetes and Its Vascular Lesions* (New York: Elsevier 1978), p. 233.

17. K. West, *Epidemiology of Diabetes and Its Vascular Lesions* (New York: Elsevier, 1978), p. 273.

18. J. W. Anderson and K. Ward, "High-Carbohydrate, High-Fiber Diets for Insulin Treated Men with Diabetes Mellitus," *The American Journal of Clinical Nutritiion* 32: 2312, November 1979.

19. (a) Ibid.

   (b) J. D. Brunzell, R. L. Lerner, W. R. Hazzard, D. Porte, and E. L. Bierman, "Improved Glucose Tolerance with High Carbohydrate Feeding in Mild Diabetes," *The New England Journal of Medicine* 284(10): 521, 11 March 1971.

   (c) K. West, op. cit., p. 15.

20. (a) N. E. Johnson, F. M. Alcantara, and H. Linkswiler, "Effect of Level of Protein Intake on Urinary and Fecal Calcium and Calcium Retention of Young Adult Males," *The Journal of Nutrition* 100: 1425, December 1970.

   (b) L. H. Allen, E. A. Oddoye, and S. Margen, "Protein-Induced Hypercalcuria: A Longer-Term Study," *The American Journal of Clinical Nutrition* 32: 741, April 1979.

21. F. R. Ellis, S. Holesh, and J. W. Ellis, "Incidence of Osteoporosis in Vegetarians and Omnivores," *The American Journal of Clinical Nutrition* 25: 555, June 1972.

22. W. F. Robertson, M. Peacock, and A. Hodgkinson, "Dietary Changes and the Incidence of Urinary Calculi in the UK Between 1958 and 1976," *Journal of Chronic Diseases* 32(6): 469, 1979.

23. J. McDougall, *McDougall's Medicine: A Challenging Second Opinion* (Piscataway, New Jersey: New Century Publishers, 1985), chapter 9.

24. K. Heaton, "Gallstones and Cholecystitis," in *Refined Carbohydrate Foods and Disease,* ed. D. P. Burkitt and H. C. Trowell (New York: Academic Press, 1978).

25. Ibid.

26. J. F. Fraumeni, "Cancers of the Pancreas and Biliary Tract: Epidemiological Considerations," *Cancer Research* 35: 3437, November 1975.

27. (a) A. P. Hall, P. E. Barry, T. R. Dawber, and P. M. McNamara, "Epidemiology of Gout and Hyperuricemia," *The American Journal of Medicine* 42: 27, January 1967.

   (b) D. Berkowitz, "Blood Lipid and Uric Acid Interrelationships," *The Journal of the American Medical Association* 190(9): 856, 30 November 1964.

28. A. P. Hall et al., op. cit.

29. P. Beighton, L. Solomon, and H. A. Valkenburg, "Rheumatoid Arthritis in a Rural South African Negro Population," *Annals of the Rheumatic Diseases* 34: 136, April 1975.

30. L. Solomon, P. Beighton, H. A. Valkenburg, G. Robin, and C. L. Soskolne, "Rheumatic Disorders in the South African Negro. Part I. Rheumatoid Arthritis and Ankylosing Spondylitis," *South African Medical Journal* 49: 1292, 26 July 1975.

31. A. B. Price, "Diverticular Disease (Pathology)," in *Fiber Deficiency and Colonic Disorders*, ed. R. W. Reilly and J. B. Kirsner (New York: Plenum, 1975).

32. N. S. Painter, "Fiber Deficiency and Diverticular Disease of the Colon," in R. W. Reilly and J. B. Kirsner, op. cit.

33. D. Burkitt, "Varicose Veins, Deep Vein Thrombosis and Haemorrhoids," in D. Burkitt and H. C. Trowell, eds., op. cit.

34. D. Burkitt, "Appendicitis," in D. P. Burkitt, and H. C. Trowell, eds., op. cit.

II. VEGETARIAN ECOLOGY

9. Environment and Food

1. (a) U.S. Department of Agriculture, *1980 Appraisal*, pt. I, p. 50.

   (b) "Land and Food: The Preservation of U. S. Farmland," American Land Forum Report/no. 1, Spring 1979 (Washington, D.C.: American Land Forum, 1979).

2. R. Neil Sampson, *Farmland or Wasteland: A Time to Choose* (Emmaus, Pennsylvania: Rodale Press, 1981), chap. 11.

3. James A. Schmid, "The Environmental Impact of Urbanization," in *Perspectives on Environment*, ed. I. R. Manners and M. W. Mikesell (Washington, D.C.: Association of American Geographers, 1974).

   See also:

   (a) *World Agricultural Economics and Rural Sociology Abstracts* 21, January-July 1979, nos. 75, 583, 589, and 599.

   (b) *World Agricultural Economics and Rural Sociology Abstracts* 22, January-July 1980, nos. 67 and 1952.

   (c) M. R. Biswas, "Environment and Food Production," in *Food, Climate, and Man*, ed. M. R. Biswas and A. K. Biswas (New York: John Wiley & Sons, 1979).

10. Land Use

1. (a) Plato, *Republic* 372-374. In E. Hamilton and H. Cairns, eds., *The Collected Dialogues of Plato*, Including the Letters. Bollingen Series LXXI (Princeton, New Jersey: Princeton University Press, 1971).

   (b) P. B. Shelley, *A Vindication of Natural Diet* (Darby, Pennsylvania: Folcroft, Library Editions, 1975).

   (c) M. Hindhede, "The Effect of Food Restriction During War on Mortality in Copenhagen," *The Journal of the American Medical Association* 74(6): 381, 7 February 1920.

2. Points elegantly made in P. Colinvaux, *Why Big Fierce Animals Are Rare* (Princeton, N.J.: Princeton University Press, 1978).

3. R. Neil Sampson, *Farmland or Wasteland: A Time to Choose* (Emmaus, Pennsylvania: Rodale Press, 1981), p. 222.

4. R. F. Brokken, C. W. O'Connor, and T. L. Nordblom, "Costs of Reducing Grain Feeding of Beef Cattle," USDA Agricultural Economics Report, cited in *World Agricultural Economics and Rural Sociology Abstracts* 23(4), no. 2808.

5. J. F. Karubian, "Polluted Groundwater: Estimating the Effects of Man's Activities," National Environmental Research Center (Las Vegas, Nevada, July 1974).

6. D. Pimentel, and M. Pimentel, *Food, Energy and Society* (New York: John Wiley & Sons, 1979), p. 61.

7. United Nations, Food and Agriculture Organization, *Production Yearbook,* vol. 29 (Rome: United Nations, 1975).

8. United Nations, Food and Agriculture Organization, *Provisional Indicative World Plan for Agricultural Development,* vol. 1 (Rome: United Nations, 1970).

9. Ibid.

10. U.S. Department of Agriculture, *Agricultural Statistics 1979* (Washington, D.C.: U.S. Government Printing Office, 1979), pp. 9, 10, 35, 36.

11. United Nations, Food and Agriculture Organization, *Provisional Indicative World Plan for Agricultural Development,* Summary and Main Conclusions (Rome: United Nations, 1970).

12. Based on data in G. Borgstrom, *Harvesting the Earth* (New York: Abelard-Schuman, 1973), p. 88.

11. Forests

1. J. G. Bene, H. W. Beall, and A. Cote, "Trees, Food, and People: Land Management in the Tropics," International Development Research Center (Ottawa, 1977).

2. K. Openshaw, "Wood Fuels the Developing World," *The New Scientist* 61(883): 271, 31 January 1974.

3. H. W. Anderson, M. D. Hoover, and K. G. Reinhard, *Forests and Water. Effects of Forest Management on Floods, Sedimentation, and Water Supply,* Pacific Southwest Forest and Range Experiment Station, USDA Forest Service General Technical Report PSW-18/1976.

4. (a) R. Pascoe (Reuter News Service), "Flooding Blamed on Deforestation," *The Washington Post,* 21 September 1981.

   (b) K. Openshaw, op. cit.

5. J. Kittridge, "The Influence of the Forest on the Weather and Other Environmental Factors," in *Forest Influences,* United Nations, Food and Agriculture Organization, FAO Forestry and Forest Products Studies no. 15 (Rome, 1962).

6. M. I. Budyko, O. A. Drozdov, and M. I. Yudin, "The Impact of Economic Activity on Climate," *Soviet Geography* 12(10): 666, December 1971.

7. C. Simon, "Soil and land biota give, not take, CO_2," *Science News* 124(11): 166, September 10, 1983.

8. H. W. Anderson et al., op. cit.

9. D. A. Tillman, *Wood as an Energy Resource* (New York: Academic Press, 1978).

10. W. M. Johnson, "What Has Been Happening in Land Use in America and What Are the Projections," *Journal of Animal Science* 45(6): 1469, December 1977.

11. U.S. Department of Agriculture, *1980 Appraisal,* pt. I, p. 50.

12. Robin Hur, "Land," unpublished manuscript, 1981.

13. J. Omang, "Report to President Warns About Overcrowded Earth," *Washington Post,* 25 July 1980.

14. N. Myers, *Conversion of Tropical Moist Forests* (Washington, D.C.: National Academy of Sciences, 1980), pp. 3-4.

15. Ibid., p. 44.

16. Ibid. chap. 3.

17. (a) O. C. Stewart, "Burning and Natural Vegetation in the United States," *The Geographical Review* 41: 317, 1951.

   (b) R. R. Humphrey, "The Desert Grassland, Past and Present," *Journal of Range Management* 6(3): 159, May 1953.

18. J. L. Cloudsley-Thompson, *Man and the Biology of the Arid Zones* (London: Edward Arnold, 1977).

19. O. C. Stewart, "Fire as the First Great Force Employed by Man," in *Man's Role in Changing the Face of the Earth*, ed. W. L. Thomas, Jr., with the collaboration of C. O. Sauer, M. Bates, and L. Mumford (Chicago: University of Chicago Press, 1956).

20. J. L. Cloudsley-Thompson, op. cit., 1977.

21. M. W. Mikesell, "The Deforestation of Mount Lebanon," *The Geographical Review* 59(1): 1 January 1969.

22. M. B. Rowton, "The Woodlands of Ancient Western Asia," *The Journal of Near Eastern Studies* 26(4): 261, October 1967.

23. D. A. Tillman, op. cit.

24. J. L. Cloudsley-Thompson, op. cit., 1977.

25. C. G. Bates and R. G. Pierce, "Forestation of the Sand Hills of Nebraska and Kansas," USDA Forest Service Bulletin 121, 3 February 1913.

26. Commonwealth of Pennsylvania, Department of Forestry, "Reforesting Pennsylvania's Waste Land. What and How to Plant," Bulletin no. 15 (Harrisburg, Pennsylvania, 1916).

27. A. G. Grachev, "Shelter Belt: Kamyshin to Stalingrad," Israel Program for Scientific Translations (Jerusalem: S. Monson, 1960).

28. R. C. Ghosh, *Handbook on Afforestation Techniques*, Controller of Publications, Delhi, India, October 1977.

12. Water

1. (a) U.S. Department of Agriculture, *Agricultural Statistics 1979* (Washington, D.C.: U.S. Government Printing Office, 1979.)

   (b) M. Falkenmark and G. Lindh, *Water for a Starving World* (Boulder, Colorado: Westview Press, 1976).

2. Ibid.

3. *See* Chapter 10, "Land Use."

4. *See* Chapter 10, "Land Use."

5. G. Borgstrom, *Harvesting the Earth* (New York: Abelard-Schuman, 1973), pp. 64-65.

6. G. F. White, "Resources and Needs: Assessment of the World Water Situation," in *Water Development and Management*, Proceedings of the United Nations Water Conference, Mar Del Plata, Argentina, March 1977 (Pergamon Press, 1978).

7. C. A. Hunt and R. M. Garrels, *Water: The Web of Life* (New York: W. W. Norton & Co., 1972).

8. R. E. Olson, *A Geography of Water* (Dubuque, Iowa: Wm. C. Brown Co., 1970).

9. J. Adler et al., "The Browning of America," *Newsweek* 97(8): 26, 23 February 1981.

10. (a) Ibid.

   (b) W. A. Le Poi and R. D. Lasewell, "Impact of Increasing Energy Costs on Irrigation and Agricultural Production," in *Conflicts and Issues in Water Quality and Use*, p. 239, cited in *World Agricultural Economics and Rural Sociology Abstracts* 20(2), no. 683, 1978.

11. J. Adler et al., op. cit.

12. C. J. Sale and M. E. Sale, *World Water and Environment* (Sidney, Australia: Shakespeare Head Press, 1967).

13. B. E. Lofgren, "Field Measurement of Aquifer-System Compaction, San Joaquin Valley, USA," in *Land Subsidence*, Proceedings of the Tokyo Symposium, Sep-

tember 1969, Studies and Reports in Hydrology no. 8, UNESCO/IASH (Belgium, 1970).

14. R. K. Gabrysch, "Land Surface Subsidence in the Houston-Galveston Region, Texas," in *Land Subsidence.*

15. R. O. Whyte, "Evolution of Land Use in South-Western Asia," in *A History of Land Use in Arid Regions,* ed. L. D. Stamp, UNESCO, 1961.

16. R. E. Olson, op. cit.

17. *See* e.g.: D. K. Fuhriman and J. R. Barton, "Ground Water Pollution in Arizona, California, Nevada, and Utah" (Washington, D.C.: U.S. Government Printing Office, December 1971).

18. Ibid.

19. U.S. Department of Agriculture, *1980 Appraisal,* pt. I, p. 199.

20. Calculated on the basis of:
    (a) BOD of slaughterhouses: H. R. Jones, *Pollution Control in Meat, Poultry and Seafood Processing* (Park Ridge, New Jersey: Noyes Data Corporation, 1974).
    (b) BOD of humans: M. Owens, "Chemical and Pesticide Pollution," in *Water Pollution as a World Problem* (London: Europa Publications, 1971).
    (c) Relationship of BOD of human and livestock wastes: R. E. Loehr, *Pollution Implications of Animal Wastes—A Forward Oriented Review,* Office of Research and Monitoring, U.S.E.P.A., Washington, D.C. 20460. (July 1968; reprinted June 1973).

21. M. Owens, op. cit., and R. C. Loehr, op. cit.

22. R. C. Loehr, op. cit.

23. Ibid.

24. A. V. Rasnik and J. M. Rademacher, "Animal Waste Runoff—A Major Water Quality Challenge," in *2nd Compendium of Animal Waste Management,* Missouri Basin Region (Kansas City, Missouri, June 1969), U.S. Department of the Interior, Federal Water Pollution Control Administration.

25. J. R. Miner and T. L. Willrich, "Livestock Operations and Field-Spread Manure as Sources of Pollutants," in *Agricultural Practices and Water Quality,* Proceedings of a Conference Concerning the Role of Agriculture in Clean Water, November 1969, Iowa State University (Ames, Iowa, November 1970); reproduced by National Technical Information Service.

26. (a) A. V. Rasnik and J. M. Rademacher, op. cit.
    (b) D. K. Fuhriman and J. R. Barton, op. cit.

27. K. Szesztay, "The Hydrosphere and the Human Environment," in *Results of Research on Representative and Experimental Basins,* vol. 2, Proceedings of the Wellington Symposium, December 1970, Studies and Reports in Hydrology, no. 12, UNESCO, 1972, p. 455.

28. M. I. L'vovich, *World Water Resources and Their Future,* English trans. ed. by R. L. Nace (American Geophysical Union, 1979).

29. P. Gwynne and M. J. Kubic, "Israel: Good to the Last Drop," *Newsweek* 97(8): 35, 23 February 1981.

13. Energy

1. D. Pimentel, L. E. Hurd, A. C. Bellotti, M. J. Forster, I. M. Oka, O. D. Sholes, and R. J. Whitman, "Food Production and the Energy Crisis," *Science* 182: 443, 1973. Found in *Food: Politics, Economics, Nutrition, and Research,* ed. P. H. Abelson (American Association for the Advancement of Science, 1975).

2. (a) C. W. Cook, "Use of Rangelands for Future Meat Production," *Journal of Animal Science* 45(6): 1476, December 1977.

   (b) D. Pimentel and M. Pimentel, *Food, Energy and Society* (New York: John Wiley & Sons, 1979), chap. 9.

3. (a) J. S. Steinhart and C. E. Steinhart, "Energy Use in the U.S. Food System," *Science* 185: 482, 1974. Found in P. H. Abelson, op. cit.

   (b) D. Pimentel and M. Pimentel, op. cit., p. 137.

   (c) R. Hur, "The Energy Cost of the Agri-Food System," unpublished manuscript, 1981.

   These three sources contributed the 12%, 16.5% and 20% figures respectively.

4. D. Pimentel, and M. Pimentel, op. cit. p. 8.

5. *See* Chap. 10, note 11.

6. *See* Chap. 11, "Forests."

7. C. Bowden, "The Impact of Energy Development on Water Resources in Arid Lands," Literature and Annotated Bibliography, Arid Lands Resource Information Paper no. 6, University of Arizona, Office of Arid Lands Studies, Tucson, Arizona 85721.

8. Ibid.

9. D. Pimentel, E. C. Terhune, R. Dyson-Hudson, S. Rochereau, R. Samis, E. A. Smith, D. Denman, D. Reifschneider, and M. Shepard, "Land Degradation: Effects on Food and Energy Resources," *Science* 194: 149, 8 October 1976.

14. Soil Erosion

1. V. A. Kovda, "Soil Reclamation and Food Production," in *Food, Climate, and Man*, ed. M. R. Biswas and A. K. Biswas (New York: John Wiley & Sons, 1979).

2. N. Hudson, *Soil Conservation* (London: B. T. Batsford, 1971).

3. D. Pimentel et al., "Land Degradation: Effects on Food and Energy Resources," *Science* 194: 149, 8 October 1976.

4. (a) R. Neil Sampson, "The Ethical Dimension of Farmland Protection," in *Farmland, Food and the Future*. ed. M. A. Schnepf (Ankeny, Iowa: Soil Conservation Society of America, 1979).

   (b) R. Neil Sampson, *Farmland or Wasteland: A Time to Choose* (Emmaus, Pennsylvania: Rodale Press, 1981), p. 124.

   (c) R. M. Smith and W. L. Stamey, "Determining the Range of Tolerable Erosion," *Soil Science* 100(6): 414, December 1965.

5. (a) D. Pimentel, et al., op. cit., 1976.

   (b) M. R. Biswas, "environment and Food Production," in *Food, Climate and Man*, ed. M. R. Biswas and A. K. Biswas (New York: John Wiley & Sons, 1979).

6. U. S. Department of Agriculture, *1980 Appraisal*, pt. I, Review Draft, pp. 3-46. For some reason this chart is not included in the final draft of the *1980 Appraisal*.

7. D. Pimentel, et al., op. cit.

8. Ibid.

9. (a) A. Warren and J. K. Maizels, "Ecological Change and Desertification," in *Desertification: Its Causes and Consequences*, compiled and edited by the Secretariat of the United Nations Conference on Desertification, Nairobi, Kenya, 29 August to 9 September 1977 (Elmsford, New York: Pergamon Press, 1977).

   (b) G. Novikoff, "Traditional Grazing Practices and Their Adaptation to Modern Conditions in Tunisia and the Sahelian Countries," in *Can Desert Encroachment Be Stopped? A Study with Emphasis on Africa*, ed. A. Rapp, H.

N. Le Jouerou, and B. Lundholm (Swedish Natural Science Research Council, 1976).

(c) B. Lundholm, "Domestic Animals in Arid Ecosystems," in *Can Desert Encroachment Be Stopped?*

10. (a) N. Hudson, op. cit.

(b) J. O. Klemmedsen, "Physical Effects of Herbivores on Arid Semiarid Rangeland Ecosystems," in *The Impact of Herbivores on Arid and Semiarid Rangelands,* Proceedings of the 2nd United States/Australia Rangeland Panel, Adelaide, 1972 (Perth, Western Australia: Australian Rangeland Society, 1977).

11. N. Hudson, op. cit.

12. E. H. Morris, "Archaeological Studies of the La Plata District, Southwestern Colorado and Northwestern New Mexico," quoted in H. H. Chapman, "Modern Overgrazing of Livestock as the Direct Cause of Ruin of Southwestern Agriculture," *Journal of Forestry* 46(12): 929, December 1948.

13. W. Sinclair, "Block Warns of Crisis in Soil Erosion," *The Washington Post,* 29 October 1981.

14. D. Pimentel et al., op. cit.

15. Agriculture and History

1. V. A. Kovda, "Soil Reclamation and Food Production," in *Food, Climate, and Man,* ed. M. R. Biswas and A. K. Biswas (New York: John Wiley & Sons, 1979).

2. (a) J. Schechter, "Desertification Processes and the Search for Solutions," *Interdisciplinary Research Reviews* 2(1): 36, March 1977.

(b) R. N. Sampson, *Farmland Or Wasteland: A Time to Choose* (Emmaus, Pennsylvania: Rodale Press, 1981), pp. 142-146.

3. L. I. Glynn, "The Archeological Evidence for the Activities of Early African Hominids," in *Early Hominids of Africa,* ed. C. J. Jolly (London: Gerald Duckworth & Co., 1978).

4. (a) O. C. Stewart, "Burning and Natural Vegetation in the United States," *Geographical Review* 41: 317, 1951.

(b) R. R. Humphrey, "The Desert Grassland, Past and Present," *Journal of Range Management* 6(3): 159, May 1953.

5. O. C. Stewart, "Fire as the First Great Force Employed by Man," in *Man's Role in Changing the Face of the Earth,* ed. W. L. Thomas, C. O. Sauer, M. Bates, and L. Mumford (Chicago: University of Chicago Press, 1956).

6. Ibid.

7. Antoon De Vos, *Africa, The Devastated Continent? Man's Impact on the Ecology of Africa,* Monographiae Biologicae, vol. 26 (The Hague: Dr. W. Junk b. v., publishers, 1975).

8. M. N. Cohen, *The Food Crisis in Prehistory* (New Haven and London: Yale University Press, 1977).

9. O. C. Stewart, op. cit.

10. B. Bender, *Farming in Prehistory. From Hunter-Gatherer to Food-Producer* (London: John Baker, 1975).

11. M. N. Cohen, op. cit. This is the source of much of the information in the succeeding three paragraphs.

12. D. Pimentel and M. Pimentel, *Food, Energy and Society* (New York: John Wiley & Sons, 1979), p. 31.

13. E. Isaac, *Geography of Domestication* (Englewood Cliffs, N.J.: Prentice-Hall, 1970).

14. K. V. Flannery, "Origins and Ecological Effects of Early Near Eastern Domestication," in *The Domestication and Exploitation of Plants and Animals*, ed. P. J. Ucko and G. W. Dimbleby (London: Gerald Duckworth & Co., 1969).

15. A comprehensive bibliography can be found in P. Paylore, *Desertification*. University of Arizona, Office of Arid Lands Studies (Tucson, 1976).

16. *See* this chapter, note 2.

17. (a) H.B.S. Cooke, "Pleistocene Mammal Faunas of Africa, with Particular Reference to Southern Africa," in *African Ecology and Human Evolution*, ed. F. C. Howell and F. Bourliere (Chicago: Aldine Publishing Company, 1963).

    (b) E. M. van Z. Bakker, "Paleobotanical Studies," *South African Journal of Science* 59: 332, 1963.

    (c) J. L. Cloudsley-Thompson, "Recent Expansion of the Sahara," *International Journal of Environmental Studies* 2(1): 35, June 1971.

18. R. O. Whyte, "Evolution of Land Use in South-Western Asia," in *A History of Land Use in Arid Regions*, ed. L. D. stamp, UNESCO, 1961.

19. W. C. Lowdermilk, "Man-Made Deserts," *Pacific Affairs* 8(4): 409, 1935.

20. (a) W. W. Kellogg and S. H. Schneider, "Climate, Desertification, and Human Activities," in *Desertification: Environmental Degradation in and around Arid Lands*, ed. M. H. Glantz (Boulder, Colorado: Westview Press, 1977).

    (b) J. L. Cloudsley-Thompson, *Man and the Biology of Arid Zones* (London: Edward Arnold, 1977).

    (c) W. C. Lowdermilk, op. cit.

    (d) I. B. Kake, "Where Are the Rains of Yesteryear?" *Ceres* 10(2): 29, March-April 1977.

21. A. S. Goudie, "The Concept of Post-Glacial Progressive Dessication," Oxford University, School of Geography Research Papers, no. 4, December 1972.

22. K. W. Butzer, "Accelerated Soil Erosion: A Problem of Man-Land Relationships," in *Perspectives on Environment*, ed. I. R. Manners and M. W. Mikesell (Washington, D.C.: Association of American Geographers, 1974).

23. J. L. Cloudsley-Thompson, op. cit., 1971.

24. J. Schechter, op. cit.

25. R. A. Bryson and D. A. Baerreis, "Possibilities of Major Climatic Modification and Their Implications. Northwest India, A Case for Study," *Bulletin of the American Meteorological Society* 48(3): 136, March 1967.

26. W. C. Lowdermilk, op. cit.

27. S. C. Raychoudhry, *Social, Cultural and Economic History of India (Ancient Times)* Delhi: Surjeet Publications, 1978).

28. (a) R. C. Dutt, *A History of Civilization in Ancient India*, vol. 1. (Calcutta: Thacker, Spink & Co., 1889), pp. 64-65.

    (b) R. R. Mitra, *Beef in Ancient Iindia* (Calcutta: Tarun Sengupta, 1967).

29. R. C. Dutt, op. cit., vol. 2, pp. 104-105.

30. (a) B. G. Gokhale, *Asoka Maurya* (New York: Twayne Publishers, Inc., 1966).

    (b) R. Thapar, *Asoka and the Decline of the Mauryas* (New York: Oxford University Press, 1961).

31. M. Lal, "Cow Cult in India," in *Cow-Slaughter: Horns of a Dilemma*, ed. A. B. Shah (Bombay: Lalvani Publishing House, 1967).

32. (a) M. W. Mikesell, "The Deforestation of Mount Lebanon," *Geographical Review* 59(1): 1, January 1969.

    (b) E. C. Semple, *The Geography of the Mediterranean Region. Its Relation to Ancient History* (New York: AMS Press, 1971; reprinted from the 1931 edition).

33. E. C. Semple, op. cit.

34. Ibid.

35. G. E. Fussell, *Farming Technique from Prehistoric to Modern Times* (Edinburgh and London: Pergamon Press, 1965).

    36. (a) F. M. Heichelheim, "Effects of Classical Antiquity on the Land," in *Man's Role in Changing the Face of the Earth.*

       (b) K. W. Butzer, op. cit.

37. F. M. Heichelheim, op. cit.

38. R. O. Whyte, op. cit.

39. K. W. Butzer, "Climatic Change in Arid Regions Since the Pliocene," in *A History of Land Use in Arid Regions.*

40. F. M. Heichelheim, op. cit.

41. Ibid.

42. E. C. Semple, op. cit.

43. K. W. Butzer, in *Perspectives on Environment.*

44. R. B. Held and M. Clawson, *Soil Conservation in Perspective* (Baltimore: Johns Hopkins Press, 1965), pp. 61-63.

45. Ibid.

    46. (a) *See* Chapter 14, "Soil Erosion."

       (b) R. N. Sampson, *Farmland or Wasteland: A Time to Choose* (Emmaus, Pennsylvania: Rodale Press, 1981).

16. Social and Political Implications

1. A. Pietila, "Deforestation is turning Ethiopia into a desert," Baltimore Sun, 23 December, 1984.

2. H. L. Tebicke, "Sustainable agriculture: an Ethiopian view," *Bulletin of the Atomic Scientists* 41(8): 39, September 1985.

3. T. Stauffer, "Water: the reason Israel can't give up the West Bank," *Arlington Journal,* 27 January 1982 (originally printed in the *Christian Science Monitor*).

III. VEGETARIAN ETHICS

17. Ethics, Animals and Reality

    1. (a) United Nations, Food and Agriculture Organization, *Production Yearbook,* vol. 29 (Rome: United Nations 1975), p. 239.

       (b) U.S. Department of Agriculture, *Agricultural Statistics 1979* (Washington, D.C.: U.S. Government Printing Office, 1979), p. 403.

2. Peter Singer, *Animal Liberation* (New York: Avon Books, 1975), chap. 3.

3. For example:

      (a) R. Harrison, *Animal Machines* (London: Stuart, 1964).

      (b) J. Mason and P. Singer, *Animal Factories* (New York: Crown Publishers, 1980).

4. P. Singer, op. cit., p. 151.

5. P. Singer, *The Expanding Circle* (New York: Farrar, Straus & Giroux, 1981), chap. 2.

6. D. Hume, *Enquiries Concerning the Human Understanding and Concerning the Principles of Morals* (Oxford: Clarendon Press, 1972), pp. 190-191.

7. T. Aquinas, *Summa Theologica,* Question 65, Article 3, cited in *Animal Rights and Human Obligations,* ed. T. Regan and P. Singer (Englewood Cliffs, N.J.: Prentice-Hall, Inc., 1976), pp. 119-121.

8. J. Bentham, *The Principles of Morals and Legislation*, chap. XVII, Sect. 1; cited in T. Regan and P. Singer, op. cit., pp. 129-130.

9. D. R. Griffin, *The Question of Animal Awareness* (Los Altos, California: William Kaufmann, 1981).

18. Hinduism, Buddhism and Jainism

1. M. M. J. Marasinghe, *Gods in Early Buddhism*, Vidyalankara Campus, University of Sri Lanka (Ceylon, 1974).

2. R. C. Dutt, *A History of Civilization in Ancient India*, vol. 2 (Calcutta: Thacker, Spink, & Co., 1889), pp. 104-105.

3. H. G. Rawlinson, *Intercourse Between India and the Western World* (New York: Octagon Books, 1971), pp. 155-160.

4. R. Thapar, *Asoka and the Decline of the Mauryas* (New York: Oxford University Press, 1961).

5. B. G. Gokhale, *Asoka Maurya* (New York: Twayne Publishers, 1966).

6. Ibid.

7. M. Lal, "Cow Cult in India," in *Cow-Slaughter: Horns of a Dilemma*, ed. A. B. Shah (Bombay: Lalvani Publishing House, 1967).

8. Ibid.

9. J. L. Kipling, *Beast and Man in India* (Lahore, Pakistan: Al-Biruni, 1891; reprinted 1978), p. 6.

10. Ibid., pp. 90-91.

11. Holmes Welch, *The Practice of Chinese Buddhism* (Cambridge, Massachusetts: Harvard University Press, 1967), p. 112.

12. H. C. Warren, trans., *Buddhism in Translations* (New York: Atheneum, 1969), p. 303.

13. Mahavagga VI, 31.14, in *Vinaya Texts*, pt. II. trans. T. W. R. Davids and H. Oldenberg, Sacred Books of the East, vol. XVII (Oxford: Clarendon Press, 1910).

14. Mahavagga VI, 23, in *Vinaya Texts*, pt. II.

15. W. L. King, *In the Hope of Nibbana* (La Salle, Illinois: Open Court Publishing Co., 1964).

16. H. Welch, op. cit.

17. Ibid., p. 112.

18. Ibid., pp. 365-366.

19. K. L. Reichelt, *Truth and Tradition in Chinese Buddhism* (Shanghai, China: The Commercial Press Limited, 1927), p. 91.

20. Y. Tamura and W. P. Woodard, *Living Buddhism in Japan*, A report of interviews with ten Japanese Buddhist leaders (Tokyo: Kashiwaya Insatsu Sho, 1960).

21. H. C. Warren, op. cit., p. 301.

22. A. L. Basham, "Basic Doctrines of Jainism," in *Sources of Indian Tradition*, compiled by W. T. de Bary, S. Hay, R. Weiler, and A. Yarrow (New York: Columbia University Press, 1958).

23. Jagmanderlal Jaini, *Outlines of Jainism* (New York: Cambridge University Press, 1916).

24. Padmanabh S. Jaini, *The Jaina Path of Purification* (Berkeley: University of California Press, 1979).

25. Ibid.

26. H. C. Warren, op. cit., p. 70.

19. The Jewish Tradition

All biblical quotations in this chapter are from *The New English Bible with the Apocrypha* (Oxford University Press and Cambridge University Press, 1970). All talmudic quotations are from the Babylonian Talmud (London: Soncino Press 1948).

1. J. J. Berman, *Shehitah* (New York: Bloch Publishing, 1941).
2. J. Hurewitz, "The Care of Animals in Jewish Life and Lore," in *The Jewish Library*, vol. 1, ed. L. Jung (London: Soncino Press, 1968).
3. Ibid.
4. N. J. cohen, *The Concept of Tsa'ar Ba'ale Hayyim (Kindness and the Prevention of Cruelty to Animals). Its Bases and Development in Biblical, Midrashic and Talmudic Literature*, Catholic University of America, Washington, D. C., October 1953, typescript of a dissertation in the Library of Congress.
5. R. K. Yerkes, *Sacrifice in Greek and Roman Religions and Early Judaism* (New York: Charles Scribner's Sons, 1952), p. 147.
6. Rabbi Joseph Rosenfeld, "The Religious Justification for Vegetarianism," in *Tree of Life*, ed. P. L. Pick (Cranbury, New Jersey: A. S. Barnes and Company, 1977).
7. J. J. Berman, op. cit., 1941.
8. N. N. Glatzer, *The Writings of Josephus* (New York: Meridian Books, 1960).
9. Joe Green, "The Jewish Vegetarian Tradition," Johannesburg, South Africa, October 1969, typed manuscript (2000 copies made). I am indebted to Ellen Murphy of the Library of Congress for making this available to me.
10. Ibid.
11. Ibid.
12. Ibid.
13. Ibid.

20. Christianity

1. G. N. Drinkwater, *Food in the Early Church* (London: St. Alban Press, 1956), p. 14.
2. Ibid.
3. Carl Skriver, *Die vergessenen Anfänge der Schöpfung und des Christentums* (Bad Bellingen, Germany: Order of the Nazoreans, 1977), Section II, Part 3. (English translation, *The Forgotten Beginnings of Creation and Christianity*, now in manuscript.)
4. Clement of Alexandria, On Sacrifices, Book VII. Cited in J. Todd Ferrier, *On Behalf of the Creatures* (London: The Order of the Cross, 1983), p. 19.
5. M. R. James, trans., *The Apocryphal New Testament* (Oxford: Clarendon Press, 1975), p. 10.
6. Drinkwater, op. cit., p. 3.
7. Hans-Joachim Schoeps, *Jewish Christianity: Factional Disputes in the Early Church*, trans. D. R. A. Hare (Philadelphia: Fortress Press, 1969), p. 120.
8. C. A. Skriver, op. cit., II, 3.
9. Ernest Renan, *The Life of Jesus* (New York: Doubleday Dolphin Books, n.d.), p. 173, 169.
10. C. Skriver, op. cit., II, 3.
11. C. Skriver, op. cit., II, 5.
12. H.-J. Schoeps, op. cit., p. 11.
13. Ibid.
14. C. Skriver, op. cit., II, 5.
15. H.-J. Schoeps, op. cit., pp. 99-101.
16. C. Skriver, op. cit., II, 7.

17. Cited in C. Skriver, op. cit., II, 7.
18. C. Skriver, op. cit., II, 7.
19. C. Skriver, op. cit., II, 4.
20. C. Skriver, op. cit., II, 7.
21. C. Skriver, op. cit., III, 1.
22. H.-J. Schoeps, p. 92 ff.
23. Cited in C. Skriver, op. cit., III, 1.
24. C. Skriver, op. cit., III, 1.
25. Ibid.
26. Ibid.
27. Ibid.
28. Ibid.

21. Plato and Ancient Philosophy

All Platonic quotations in this chapter are from *The Collected Dialogues of Plato*, including the Letters, ed. E. Hamilton and H. Cairns, Bollingen Series LXXI (New Jersey: Princeton University Press, Princeton, 1971).
    1. (a) Plutarch, "Of Eating of Flesh," in *Plutarch's Morals*, vol. 5, corrected and revised by William W. Goodwin (Boston: Little, Brown & Co., 1871).
      (b) Ovid, *Metamorphoses*, bk. XV (Bloomington: Indiana University Press, 1973).
      (c) Diogenes Laertius, "Pythagoras," in *Lives of the Philosophers*, trans. and ed. A. R. Caponigri (Chicago: Henry Regnery Co., 1969).
      (d) Hobart Huson, *Pythagoras: The Hyperborean Apollo*, typed manuscript in the Library of Congress, 1966.
      (e) P. Gorman, *Pythagoras: A Life* (London: Routledge & Kegan Paul, 1979).
    2. P. Gorman, op. cit.
    3. Diogenes Laertius, op. cit.
    4. (a) Diogenes Laertius, op. cit.
      (b) H. S. Long, *A Study of the Doctrine of Metempsychosis in Greece from Pythagoras to Plato* (Princeton, New Jersey: J. H. Furst, 1948).
    5. C. J. De Vogel, *Pythagoras and Early Pythagoreanism* (Assen, Netherlands: Royal Van Gorcum, 1966).
    6. Empedocles; *Fragments of Empedocles*, trans. W. L. Leonard (Open Court Publishing Company, 1908).
    7. H. Huson, op. cit.
    8. *Great Dialogues of Plato*, trans, W.H.D. Rouse, ed. E. H. Warmington and P. G. Rouse (New York: New American Library, 1956), p. 169.
    9. (a) A. Cameron, *The Pythagorean Background of the Theory of Recollection* (Menasha, Wisconsin: George Banta Publishing Co., 1938).
      (b) C. J. De Vogel, op. cit.
      (c) P. Gorman, op. cit.
      (d) Plato, *Meno* 81, *Phaedo* 75, 92, and numerous others besides.
    10. C. J. Gianakaris, *Plutarch* (New York: Twayne Publishers, 1970), p. 105.
    11. In *Plutarch's Morals*, vol. 5.
    12. In *Plutarch's Morals*, vol. 5.
    13. In *Plutarch's Morals*, vol. 1.
    14. Porphyry, "On the Life of Plotinus and the Arrangement of His Work," in Plotinus, *The Ethical Treatises*, trans. Stephen Mackenna (London: Philip Lee Warner, 1917).

15. Porphyry, "On Abstinence from Animal Food," in *Select Works of Porphyry,* trans. Thomas Taylor (London: Thomas Rodd, 1823).

16. D. R. Griffin, *The Question of Animal Awareness* (Los Altos: William Kaufmann, 1981).

22. Modern Philosophy

1. Richard McKeon, ed., *Introduction to Aristotle* (New York: The Modern Library, 1947).

2. R. Descartes, "Animals Are Machines," in *Animal Rights and Human Obligations,* ed. T. Regan and P. Singer (Englewood, New Jersey: Prentice-Hall, 1976).

3. (a) Spinoza, *Ethics,* II, prop. 57, cited in F. Copleston, *A History of Philosophy,* vol. 4 (New York: Doubleday & Co., 1963).

   (b) Spinoza, *Ethics,* IV, appendix, C. 27, cited in A. Schopenhauer, *The World as Will and Representation,* vol. 2 (New York: Dover Publications, 1958), p. 645.

4. Leibniz, *Theodicy,* 250, cited in F. Copleston, op. cit., vol. 4, p. 331.

5. F. Copleston, op. cit., vol. 4, p. 315.

6. John Locke, *Thoughts on Education* (1690), cited in H. Williams, *The Ethics of Diet* (London, 1883), chap. 16.

7. David Hume, *A Treatise of Human Nature* (Oxford: Clarendon Press, 1968), p. 176.

8. David Hume, *Enquiries Concerning the Human Understanding and Concerning the Principles of Morals* (Oxford: Clarendon Press, 1972), p. 180.

9. Ibid., p. 191.

10. *See* Chapter 17, "Ethics, Animals and Reality."

11. Jeremy Bentham, *The Principles of Morals and legislation,* chap. XVII, sect. 1, cited in T. Regan and P. Singer, op. cit., pp. 129-130.

12. Cited in P. Singer, *Animal Liberation* (New York: Avon Books, 1975), pp. 218-219.

13. I. Kant, *Lectures on Ethics* (New York: Harper & Row, 1975), pp. 239-241, cited in T. Regan and P. Singer, op. cit., p. 122.

14. I. Kant, *Groundwork of the Metaphysics of Morals* (New York: Harper Torchbooks, 1964), p. 101.

15. I. Kant, *Critique of Pure Reason,* B131 (New York: St. Martin's Press, 1929).

16. A. Schopenhauer, op. cit., I, p. 372, footnote.

17. The Fundamentals of Marxist-Leninist Philosophy (Moscow: Progress Publishers, 1974), p. 116.

18. Frederick Engels, *Dialectics of Nature* (Moscow, 1972), p. 174, cited in *The Fundamentals of Marxist-Leninist Philosophy,* pp. 117-118.

19. *Animal Liberation,* p. 163.

20. Peter Singer, *Practical Ethics* (New York: Cambridge University Press, 1979), chap. 5.

21. Ibid., p. 32.

22. *Seward's Anecdotes II,* 171, cited in J. Ritson, *An Essay on Abstinence from Animal Food, As a Moral Duty* (London: Richard Phillips, 1802).

23. A. C. Fraser, *Life and Letters of George Berkeley* (Oxford: Clarendon Press, 1876), pp. 213, 216.

24. (a) J.Y.T. Greig, ed., *The Letters of David Hume,* I (Oxford: Clarendon Press, 1932), pp. 112, 159-160, and 369.

   (b) E. C. Mossner, *The Life of David Hume* (Oxford: Clarendon Press, 1970).